To ∩

with

this helps a little

The Discovery of the Dingle Diamond

summer 2010

Also by the same author:

A Different View - A Geometry of the Black Mountains (2002)

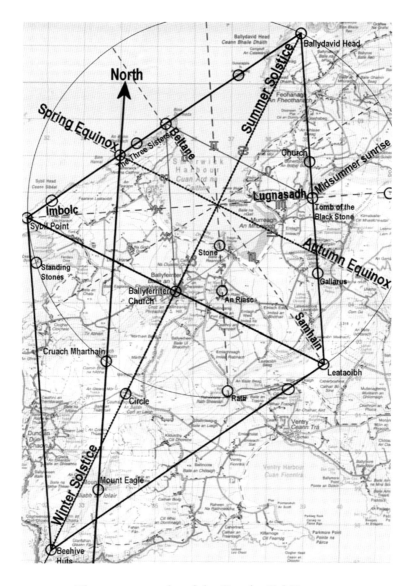

The great temple of the Tuatha Dé Danaan
West Kerry, Ireland

The Discovery of

The Dingle Diamond

C. P. R. May

Banton Press

The Discovery of the Dingle Diamond
C.P.R. May

Copyright © C.P.R. May
2006

Maps reproduced by courtesy of Ordinance Survey Ireland
Permit No. 7797
© Ordinance Survey Ireland & Government of Ireland

ISBN: 185652 178 8
ISBN(13): 978 185652 178 9

The Banton Press
Isle of Arran, Scotland
www.bantonpress.co.uk

Acknowledgements

There have been a great many people who have helped in the creation of this book and I would like to offer my heartfelt thanks to them. Especially to: Mark Brown, my publisher, for his constant unconditional support and encouragement, Ursula Tramski, who has been a steady companion throughout the process of writing and Trisha Howley for editing help beyond the call of duty. Lastly I would like to say thank you to all the folks in Dingle who have made this book possible.

This book is dedicated to the spirit of the past that touches everyone who lives in or visits the magical place called the Dingle Peninsula.

Contents

Contents

Introduction

The book you hold in your hand is a quest - a journey of discovery into the first stirrings of the human spirit. Some may call this an ancient form of magic, others see in it as an awesome symmetry of natural forces played out against the backdrop of an immense universe upon which the mote of dust that is the blue pearl of our planet spins endlessly; an incubator for the reason of existence.

Looking out from my window on those days when the sky is clear and blue I can see the dappled flanks of the range of mountains that isolate the Peninsula of Dingle from the mainland of Ireland; an imposing wall of ancient rocks dwarfing the dwellings resting on their sides.

From a sacred grotto dedicated to Mary, Mother of Jesus, it is possible to ascend, via a path marked with a series of wooden crosses and bleak standing stones, to reach the summit of the greatest of these hills, Brandon Mountain, the second highest peak in all of Ireland. The trail of crosses delineate an ancient pilgrimage route that was sacred before the word of Christ was heard, and the mountaintop is crowned with ancient ruins; half buried forms in the heather clad slopes that have been witness to the many changes in faith from which are fashioned the stories, told and re-told over generations, that define our history.

Here, 'on the top of the world', was built a shrine to the power of the earth and a retreat from humankind. The generations who have sought its sanctuary have done so for no other reason than a desire to fathom the deep mystery of existence. Certainly they have declared that the world is too busy to hear the voices that they knew would speak in the immeasurable solitude that haunts this place. Perhaps they too were touched by the ancient magic that lives on in this isolated part of Europe. Perhaps their thoughts, as they gazed at the vast panorama beneath their feet, were guided by a history of myth and spirituality that stretches far back into a half-forgotten past, populated by the ghosts of gods and dark demons of the soul.

It is this spirit of the past, an unbroken thread that sings in the wind and sparkles in the air, that has guided the thoughts and discoveries that lie in this book. A spectre of a time when humans still lived their lives in harmony with the currents of seasonal change; still alive and vital it whispers of our real heritage, subtly creeping into the present, into the uncharted subconscious and into the dreams of those who live or visit these shores; a bond as strong as time and one that is touched with every visit to the ancient monuments that clutter the Kingdom of Kerry.

These legacies left in the landscape hint to us in our quest for understanding. From the enigmatic upright stones to the eerie early Christian churches there lies in every sacred site the promise of a revelation. A promise that has spawned a million words, from the poetic to the scientific, each author adding their charismatic nuance to the mystery, and like the crosses marking the Brandon pilgrimage, in time they assemble to create a staircase upon which we can ascend.

The folklore and mythology of Ireland is a remarkable and precious seam, and none is so productive as this particular piece of West Kerry. In quarrying its secrets a tale has revealed itself. It evokes the same atmosphere of gnosis that bound the mystics who sought answers in the mountains, it leads from myth to archaeological site and back to myth, deeper and further into the past, until it abruptly coalesces as an insight into our genesis as spiritual beings. I do nothing more than tie this nosegay of history with the syntax of reason, for it is a heritage that belongs to each and every one of us. Perhaps, by reaching an understanding with our past we can create an empathy with our present, and in this way begin to heal the rift that has alienated us from the entity that we call home, our planet earth.

Chapter One
The Dingle Diamond

"There are more things in heaven and earth, Horatio, than are dreamt of in your philosophy."
Shakespeare, Hamlet, act I, scene 5

Standing just off the north-western shore of the European continent lies the small country of Ireland. Its location engenders an impression of isolation, as if it were detached from the events and circumstances that have shaped Europe. It is a conception that is deceiving, for even the most cursory glance into its history shows that Ireland has consistently been an eminent contender in the European saga. From the earliest Celts to the formation of America, Irish people and their culture have strongly influenced civilisation. The arts have similarly been impacted, for a myriad of famous Irish voices have transfigured world literature, theological debate and mythology.

If you were to travel across Ireland from east to west, following in the footsteps of countless invaders and refugees, you would eventually stand on Europe's most westerly point, the Dingle Peninsula. Its sharp promontory of hills are flanked on either side by the sea and at its back stands a range of mountains. The rocky shoreline of coves, cliffs and beaches thrusts out like a spearhead pointing across the Atlantic. Arguably, it is here that the epicentre of Ireland's ancient culture originated. (Diagram 1.1)

On wild days, when the west wind hurls the rain against the windows and cloud obliterates the hills, you could be forgiven for thinking the land is not wholly part of this world. It is a feeling with which generations of mystics, druids and monks have empathised; all of whom left monuments and myths as a testament to their beliefs. This area has one of the most concentrated assemblages of ancient structures in the

Diagram 1.1
The wild Atlantic coast has provided the inspiration for many
stories and legends.

world; tombs, temples, standing stones and early churches litter the
countryside.

To these shores came exiles from Stone Age Europe, invaders from
Spain, shamans from Norway, spiritualists from Egypt: here they settled. Monks from the Dark Ages walked the same sandy shores as
magical druids from the mythical age of the faerie folk. What were they
seeking, these pilgrims and mystics? What were they looking for as
they eked out their lives on the barren sea rocks of Skellig Michael or
laboured to erect the megalithic stones that pin-prick the hills? Were
they demented seekers of solitude, or men and women who had found
something; something precious and human amid the confusing welter
of religions and gods?

On this charismatic peninsula seven thousand years of history and
legend fuse seamlessly together. The layers of myth, left like high-
water marks on the beaches, tell of their triumphs and tragedies. But

there is more to these tales than mere history, for from them emerges a common theme, one that is implicitly bound with the hills and coast. It is a theme that answers a yearning in the soul of humans; the story of a hidden secret, an arcane knowledge passed down through the generations and vigilantly guarded as a treasure of incalculable worth. It is the same tantalising, deeply hidden heart that resides like a diamond at the core of every faerie story, religious epic and ancient legend that has ever been recited. Related here, between the sea and the hills, the theme is not veiled in the impenetrable symbolism that falls like a cloak around so many fables; instead, remarkably pragmatic and as clear as the mountain streams, it shines forth, accessible to all with eyes to see and ears to hear. (Diagram 1.2)

It was to this place that I came one springtime. I had arrived to research a strange discovery, a temple of extraordinary antiquity that spread across the hills, shaped by sacred places and legend. Together with a friend who lived on the peninsula I had stumbled across its remains and it had captivated my imagination. For months, before I made the decision to move to Ireland, we had scrutinised maps and pored over myths and we had identified the builders. From their legends,

Diagram 1.2
A standing stone marks an ancient site above Smerwick Harbour.

embedded in the geometrical form of their temple, a curious story emerged, a story that had a definite origin, for it was rooted in the first spiritual awakening.

As the epic unravelled it revealed an ancient conflict between humans and the forces of the spirit world, centuries of struggle between The Dark and The Light, a struggle that is still being played out today. What shocked us was not the tale of the struggle, common to nearly every religion and myth, but the fact that it contained the answer to one of the greatest questions in philosophy, perhaps the greatest question that there is: what is the nature of God? Its message is as relevant today as it was to the past - and once I had read it I knew that I would never look at the world in the same way again. Suddenly we were no longer dealing with an archaeological investigation, instead we were confronted by a frightening exposure of our spirituality and a key that could unlock the potential of the human soul. At first we were fearful of its reality, but as we checked and cross-referenced the material the facts fell into place until we were left looking across the aeons with a clarity that abruptly brought the realm of the spiritual into the world of the scientific.

But every story has a beginning, and this one starts with the discovery of a temple in West Kerry. Later, we were to name it 'The Dingle Diamond' but for now there was only one simple myth and a line drawn on the landscape, a leyline.

It has long been suspected that the ancient sacred sites were not scattered randomly, many authors[1] guessed that there might be some hidden order to them. But any serious attempt to systematically chart and record the patterns had to wait until the 1930s when Alfred Watkins set about publishing alignments of the sacred sites that he had found on the Welsh Borders. Upon finding that these 'straight tracks' could cover many miles and that a great many of the sites had 'ley' names[2] he called them 'leylines'.[3] Although the established scientific community was slow to recognise his ideas, his efforts caused a wave of interest in 'ley' hunting and there is now a general acceptance of his theories. The Collins Concise English Dictionary commemorates him by defining a ley as 'a line joining two prominent points in the landscape, thought to be a prehistoric track'. The prominent points referred to are generally sacred sites. Some, such as churches and wells, are easy to recognise as their traditions and rituals are still remembered and performed. Others, like the megaliths, stone circles and woodland glades have sunk into obscurity, though they carry a haunted air about them as if generations of veneration have imbued them with meaning. Although the histories of many of the lines have been all but lost to us they are dimly remembered in the folklore or place names associated with them. Recently, archaeologists have started to map some of these alignments, often correlating them to celestial events, but more popularly they are attributed to the movement of the earth's electromagnetic energies.

Our investigations centred on one of these leylines. We spent most of one night discussing and measuring a definite alignment of mountain peaks, an alignment that was accurate within a tenth of a degree to true north[4]. We had a leyline, and on an unusually bright February morning we set off to see it for ourselves; climbing one of the area's more prominent landmarks - Cruach Mhárthain.[5] The summit emerges abruptly from the surrounding hills and its pyramidal shape has been a reference point for many lost tourists. Locally it is known as 'Pointy Mountain'. From its summit we could see all of the hilltops that we had identified the night before and, holding a map in the shelter of a rock, we traced the fine line that linked them. It emanated from the rounded bulk of Mount Eagle to the south, through the point of 'Pointy Mountain' right under our feet and off to Binn Hanrai, the most western of three hills that stand on the northern Atlantic shore. Back at home we re-checked our measurements and carefully drew the north/south line on the ordinance survey map. (Diagram 1.3)

We stared at the leyline and wondered to what use it could have been put. True north is a helpful guide for travellers, but we had no way of knowing whether or not the leyline was utilised for such things.

I had been reading a collection of Irish myths recorded during a brief 'Celtic revival' in the eighteenth century by the author Jonathon Swift and the historian Winslow. Amongst the tales of ghosts and faeries was one that seemed to me to be far older than the rest. The legend tells us of the earth goddess Garbh Orgh (the Rough Giant) who lived amongst the hills. An impression of the age of this story comes with the description of the 'giants' chariot which was drawn by Irish elk - a species that has been extinct for eight thousand years. When she hunted she took with her a pack of seventy hounds, each named after a bird. She drank deer's milk and dined on eagles' breasts. Something, and the legend

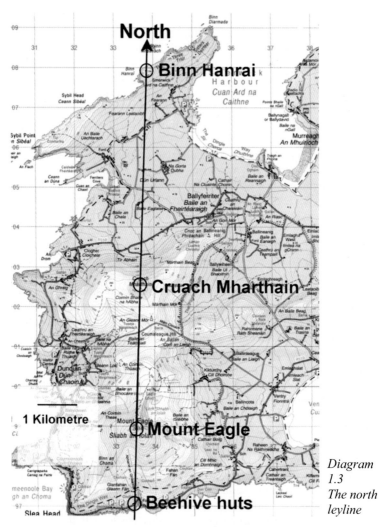

Diagram
1.3
*The north
leyline*

was not clear as to what, upset her reign and she hid herself in the landscape. But before she retired into the hills, 'in the season', as the legend
carefully notes, 'of the heather bloom', she constructed three great

cairns to mark her resting-place. It was this brief Irish legend that was to give us the answers to the riddle of the leyline.

Many myths are cryptic and this one seemed as puzzling as any, but something about the three cairns had caught my eye. It could be that these cairns actually existed and there was possibly a landscape reference in this legend. After all, the line we had traced from the top of 'Pointy Mountain' passed north through one of three hills. Sitting by the stove as the evening sky darkened we saw the connection between the myth and the map.

Binn Hanrai, as the hill on the northern end of the leyline is called by the ordinance survey, is one of the Triúr Deirféar, The Three Sisters. In mythologies world-wide the three sisters are part of the symbolism of the Goddess. They are said to weave the web of fate, and as if to confirm this link the next hill is called after their loom. On the seaward side of these dramatic hills is sheer cliff and they march in rank along the coast forming a progression leading towards a protruding headland of cliffs called Sybil Point. Here was an unexpected term, and a search of the place names in Ireland did not bring to light any other location with a similar name. The Sybil, or Cybele as she was known, was an oracular goddess from the early classical period in the Mediterranean. We looked on the map: the pencil line crossed The Three Sisters, left the land at Sybil Point and grazed a rock known as The Mother and The Crow, whose strange geology juts out of the sea like an Egyptian temple, before progressing south-west to the island of Inishtooskert. This island has a strange profile; from the land it looks exactly as if it were a giant body resting on the sea and it is colloquially called 'The Sleeping Giant'; a fitting monument in the western seas to the resting place of Garbh Orgh.

When we extended our line to the north-east it crossed an ancient tor on Ballydavid Head: the ley was complete. The line left the tor, crossed the neck of Smerwick Harbour, ran over The Three Sisters, Sybil Head and Sybil Point and on through an odd needle-like pillar on the neck of 'The Sleeping Giant', with unerring precision.

We had discovered a technique that breathed life into the old legends. Secreted within the tale of Garbh Orgh was the information that had led us to this important alignment. All the crucial parts of the myth were represented: the giant, the Goddess, the eagles and the three cairns that signified her resting place. (Diagram 1.4) There was another small

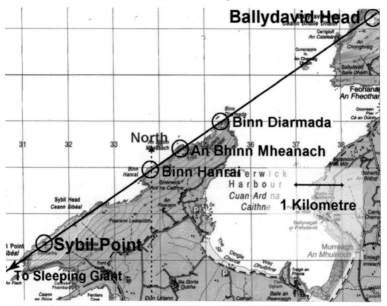

Diagram 1.4
The Three Sisters and Sybil Head make up the leyline of Garbh Orgh,
The Sleeping Giant.

clue in the story of Garbh Orgh, one that would become clearer. She
was linked to the midsummer season of the heather and thus was a
goddess of the midsummer.

Three sisters, the oracular Sibyl Head, a rock called The Mother and
a sleeping giant who is a goddess: it was a very female relationship. I
was beginning to see why this peninsula has been called 'the place of
the Goddess'. There was another female location nearby that we had
been told of, a women's burial place, perhaps the site of the ancient
priestesses' temple on Leataoibh Hill.[6] Here, on the southern flank of
the hill, stands an ancient megalith, its bare stones once covered with
layers of turf and clay. In ancient mythology the Sibyl herself was a
priestess of the Earth Goddess, much like Garbh Orgh, and such priestesses are part of an oracular heritage.

The Dingle Diamond

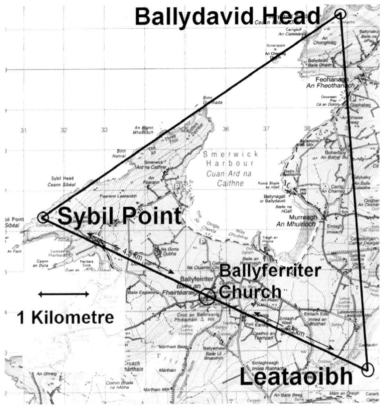

Diagram 1.5
The triangle of leylines showing Ballyferriter Church in the centre of the base line.

The map showed us that the association was more than mythology-cal. A line drawn from the megalith met our original leyline at Sibyl Point. To our complete surprise the angle formed by the two lines was precisely the sixty degrees of an equilateral triangle, an angle that was universally associated with the Goddess. It did not take long before we had uncovered the rest of the triangle. From Leataoibh to the monument on Ballydavid Head another leyline completes the trinity and a precise equilateral triangle lay across the Kerry hills. With a sense of

9

incredulity we noted that the church in the little village of Ballyferriter fell precisely at the midpoint of the base of this triangle. (Diagram 1.5)

Saint Vincent's Church in Ballyferriter is relatively new; it was built as part of the great Gothic revival that spread across Ireland in the time of the famines of the nineteenth century. Notwithstanding the poverty of the people the programme saw the construction of several hundred new churches and cathedrals. Architects steeped in the Gothic tradition often designed the churches, and there is more than an echo of the grace of the cathedrals of the Middle Ages in their projects.

The significance of the church at Ballyferriter was hinted at by its proximity to a place called the 'altar of the sun', and one sunny day, whilst I stood in the shade of the church, I picked out the shape of the altar on the hill above. According to local tradition it had been a place where the solstice dawn was welcomed; the sun and the church.... Briefly I noted places that had this connection: Chartres Cathedral, the Newgrange passage tomb, the Pyramids, Stonehenge.... the list was long and international, each having a definite alignment or relationship to the sun's position at a specific time of the year. But I could see nothing in this church that made such a connection. I sighed and looked up. Above me, on the west wall of the church was a seven-sided mosaic of the Madonna and Child. It looked as if it were meant to have been a 'rose' window but it had been blocked in, or perhaps it was never completed. The golden background of the scene and the halo declared this to be Christ, the sun king, light of the world. (Diagram 1.6)

Diagram 1.6
Seven-sided mosaic of
the Madonna and
Child in the west wall
of Ballyferriter
Church.

The Dingle Diamond

Abruptly, it occurred to me that whoever had built the church proba-bly knew about the triangle of the Goddess, and they may have left other intimations hidden in the architecture. I walked once around the church, looking for any other clues, and then stepped into the gloom of the interior.

Our earlier research into the church had failed to discover why it had been built in the exact centre of the leyline, although we had thought that pre-Christian people might have used the site. The most obvious sources, such as the priests of Ballyferriter or the local archaeologists, said that they were sure that no ancient site existed before the church and since we could find no reference to any ancient monuments we concluded that it was coincidence that had placed it there.

At this point one of many such serendipitous happenings that ac-companied our research occurred. We met Seán Mac Síthigh. Seán is a local man who had just returned to the Kerry after completing a doctor-ate researching old Irish place names on the Dingle Peninsula, and his specialist knowledge was to prove invaluable to our research.

When we met him under the shadow of Sibyl Head he was able to tell us the correct name of the field in which the church had been built. Reputedly there had been a large flat boulder on the site and the field had been called 'gort na scláta', the 'field of the slab'. The neatly cropped lawn of the churchyard held no traces of the slab though we thought that the church may have been built on this very stone. The mystery regarding the position of the church in the Triangle was solved. The site had probably been in use since Neolithic times.

The church was cold and dark. I could make out the inside of the blocked in window; there was no mosaic on this side, just plain plaster. I wandered outside and counted the sides again: seven. There was a solar connection here. It is particularly difficult to construct a regular heptagon and very few churches have seven-sided masonry for this very reason. Whoever had commissioned the blocked window had a rationale for their extra expense. Since a week has seven days, a frame of seven sides is, symbolically, a calendar reference for rituals connected with the seasons and hence of a solar deity. The gold of the 'Madonna window' hinted also at a connection with the Goddess and the sun.

My tour of the inside of the church lasted the remainder of the after-noon; with a sketchbook and pencil I jotted down notes about he apparent allusions to the year or the sun and their associations with the God-dess. In her more arcane aspect, Mary, Mother of Jesus, represents the Christian face of the old pagan Goddess, and it seemed to me to be this side of her that permeated the church.

I stood facing the altar. Directly in front of me the stained glass window of the apse, facing the rising sun, is in the shape of the three pillars of the Qabala, the Hebrew Tree of Life. A scene from Saint Bridget's 'Vision of Mary' occupies the central pillar; a fitting por-trayal of an Irish saint and an allusion to her powerful pagan predeces-sor, the ancient Goddess Bride.[7] To her right a beardless apostle, ready to record the word of God, carries his quill and book. He stands above a chalice, representing not only the cup of the blood of Christ, the Holy Grail, but also of the Celtic 'cauldron of knowledge'. Coiled above the cup is a serpent, the self-same beast that led Eve to the Tree of Knowl-edge. The window to the left of the altar shows the builder, probably Saint Joseph, holding a set square, his bearded face turned towards the mystery of Bridget's Vision. Both the set square and the design of the *fleur-de-lis* beneath his feet are Masonic references.[8] The window is not aligned with the more traditional east/west church plans, as the church seems to have been constructed a few degrees out of true, to face Bran-don Mountain.

Of the many characters portrayed in the rest of the stained-glass of the church's windows two stood out as being of particular relevance to the locale. The first of these faces the entrance and is Brendan the Navigator holding a boat.[9]

Brendan was born in 377 AD and was an ambitious seafarer. From a small creek, that now bears his name, not far from Ballyferriter, he launched his search for the 'heavenly islands' and his many exceptional adventures are recounted in the medieval book *Navigatio*.[10] A more factual description credits him with the discovery of America.[11]

Saint Brendan is the Christianised version of an ancient mythologi-cal seafarer, Bran of the fabled Tuatha Dé Danaan, the faerie folk of Irish myth. Both Brandon and Bran are recorded as being offspring of the great solar god Lugh, another of the Tuatha Dé Danaan. This guided me to the second potent image in the church, that of St Michael (the Christian form of a solar deity such as Lugh) as he thrusts the spear of the sun into the mouth of the earth serpent. This spear is pro-fessed to represent the sun at midsummer. Saint Michael and his oddly peaceful-looking serpent make up the last of the church's twelve windows.[12] (Diagram 1.7)

By now my notebook was full of solar references: Brendan and Bridget; a window with the solar god's seven sides; a field of slabs

Diagram 1.7 Ballyferriter church, stained-glass: Saint Brandon on the south wall with his boat, Saint Michael standing on the Dragon on the north wall.

below the 'altar of the sun'; Michael, the solar god's champion and the elusive thread of the Tuatha Dé Danaan running throughout. All this is dedicated to Mary the Goddess, linked with the acquiring of occult knowledge and oriented on the sun. The evidence amounted to an unequivocal message telling us that this was the heart of a temple dedicated to a solar god and the Goddess, and that these deities belonged to the time of the Tuatha Dé Danaan.

These characters were pagans and have little to do with a Christian patriarchal society, so just what were they doing hidden away in a nineteenth-century Catholic Church?

To discover more we tracked down Dingle's senior ecclesiastical figure, Monsignor Pádraig Ó Fiannachta. The Monsignor was a professor of Celtic studies at the National University of Ireland for thirty-four years. His work of translating the Bible from the original Greek and Hebrew into Irish, and his translations of several volumes of Irish poetry, led to the granting of the honorary title of 'Monsignor' by the Pope.

During the three-hour interview the Monsignor warned us that much of what was recorded was simply the propaganda of the victors to justify their atrocities. Nevertheless, he said that the stories 'seem to show that wells and lakes are considered holy places and are dedicated to gods or often the Goddess.' He went on to tell us that 'the battle of Magh Tuireadh is the first time the 'gods of light' are told of. Here, they fight the 'forces of darkness'. It was not until 200 BC that the Celts arrived to marvel at the ancient stone monuments that they found in Ireland. When they found these they attributed them to their own gods. The language itself shows that it goes back to a time before the Indo-Europeans. The inclusion of words that do not appear in any other form in other languages show that this is the case.

He also suggests that 'some places, areas, lines and directions exude potency of some sort' and concluded the interview by saying a little about the motives of the Tuatha Dé Danaan. 'The Tuatha Dé Danaan were trying to follow the earth and its seasonal changes. This showed they knew about the same religion and methods from many other lands where this was observed.'

The hints that the Monsignor gave lent their weight to the cryptic symbolism we had found in the church and the many references to the Goddess in the landscape. The Tuatha Dé Danaan had the beliefs and the mythology that fitted with the facts and they seemed to be likely candidates as the builders of this geo-temple.

Our research into the imagery displayed in the church exposed a hidden theme based upon the Goddess of the Earth. It knitted the seemingly disparate symbolism into a cohesive narrative, and the key was their relationship to the sun. The dragon that Saint Michael slays represents the telluric forces of the Earth and his spear is historically associated with the sun. Saint Brendan the Navigator links the Christian church to the Celtic god Bran and, through their common ancestry, to the great pagan sun god Lugh – who incidentally also possessed a magical spear of light. The Celtic Bridget was an Earth Goddess who was the guardian responsible for the sun's winter reincarnation. Further to this, it seemed to us, that these Christian saints had been carefully chosen, for their Celtic equivalents, they were all of the Tuatha Dé Danaan, the children of the Earth Goddess, and referred to in legend as 'the Gods of Light'.

We found that the same theme held true for the legends associated with the surrounding hills. The 'Rough Giant' was a Goddess who retired into the earth in the season of the heather; in mythology the heather is sacred to midsummer as it flowers at this time. Even the association of the Sybil with the near-by headland commemorates this motif; the Sybil's priestesses are called *Melissae*, or honeybees, another midsummer symbol. The Monsignor had indicated that there was a connection between the Tuatha Dé Danaan and seasonal changes: we had discovered which season this was. The symbolism used in the church nestled just as cleverly into the mythology of the landscape as the stone and mortar of the building did into the geometry of the traingle.

The compass readings that we had taken as we stood by the front of the Church indicated that it faced a little off the traditional east-west axis, and, as if to draw our attention to the fact, it overlooked Brandon Mountain. It was this evidence that allowed us to understand why the allegories of the Earth and the Sun abounded in the church and the country around it.

During the summer of that first exciting year in Dingle the connection between Brandon Mountain and the midsummer sun literally arose from the tradition of the land. I was told that every summer, at the end of July, the local Church conducted a eccentric festival on the side of the mountain to celebrate the sun. Called Lughnasa, after the Celtic sun god Lugh (though it is celebrated in honour of his mother) it consisted of a pilgrimage, often involving hundreds of people, that culminated at the cross on the summit of Brandon Mountain. This ancient festival goes back to a time well before Christianity, as is witnessed in an obscure ritual which was part of the traditional ceremony in which the participants would bury a carved stone head in the near-by hills. Until a few years ago there used to be such a stone head in a ruined church at foot of the mountain. It dated from pre-Christian times; but unfortunately it was stolen in 1996. Even today the Lughnasa festival is still popular and is often led by a priest. Strangely, for the mountain is over nine hundred metres high, there have been substantial stone buildings on its very pinnacle since the early Bronze Age. Christian times have seen stone altars and even churches raised there, a strong verification of the sacred importance of the mountain.

We had discovered legends that told us of a perplexing relationship between a god of the sun and the Goddess of the earth. The god was linked to the mountain and the midsummer sun; the Goddess lay in the topography of the land. The mythology came together in the church where her serpent-like symbol wrapped its coils around the grail of the blood of Christ.

What was the sun god doing on Midsummer's Day? And why was the church the centre of these events?

During a particularly long conversation that lasted deep into the night we realised that the church was not only at the centre of the mythology, it was also physically in the middle of the triangle's base line, and for a reason. All that was needed was to connect the myths to the map - and so the ordinance survey map was taken out. Three hours later the answer was clear.

At dawn, on the midsummer solstice, the first rays of the sun appear from behind the holy well on the top of Lugh's mountain as if it were gathering a spear of radiant light. In a flash all the ingredients of the myth, the solar hero and the Goddess of the Earth, the references to the sun and midsummer come together in a single beam of sunlight, piercing the veil of the triangle and centring precisely on the Church at Ballyferriter. It forms a temporary line of light in harmony with the geometry of the triangle; a perfect merging of the triangle and the co-ordinates of the solstice dawn.

However, there are some things that we will probably never fully understand: the methods the ancients used to achieve the wonders that they created being one of the most impenetrable mysteries. The builders of the triangle not only had to find the alignments, but had to take precise measurements over a long period of time in order to place the sacred sites, especially the Field of the Slab and the Altar of the Sun, in such a way as to ensure that that the temple worked. All this for one brief, solitary instant once a year. The significance of this event must have been huge, but it was not the only place that the builders had expended a massive effort to ensure the marriage of a solar event with the Earth.

The summer solstice episode in Kerry is repeated, albeit for the winter solstice, at the Neolithic temple of Newgrange, the most prominent of the Dé Danaan's works, and the Heel Stone of that most famous of ancient monuments, Stonehenge, serves the same purpose. In fact, there are hundreds of megalithic monuments across Ireland and the British Isles which are aligned to capture the moment of the solstice. The phenomenon is not restricted to the Stone Age: in historical times the symbolism was used in sacred architecture. For example, three thousand years after the last Neolithic monument was built, the French cathedral of Chartres allows a single beam of midsummer sunlight to enter the dark interior of the building. It falls precisely on a marked stone situated above the ancient pagan cave of the Black Virgin, upon which the whole edifice is constructed. Two themes are consistent in all such monuments; the solar event represented by the sun god and the acceptance into the earth personified by the Goddess. A sacred marriage ceremony takes place and at this moment the earth is fertilised.

In Kerry, the triangle displayed on a huge scale the philosophy of the northern European tribes of the Neolithic. The path of the midsummer sun forms a temporary leyline, it exists only for a few minutes. The definition of a leyline as a path or straight track between two points is true only for this brief time. Because of this unorthodox aspect I have termed the straight path of the sun as a solar ley. (Diagram 1.8)

Where the solar ley meets the side of the triangle it enters a defined geometrical space. At this location, once a year, there is a symbolic meeting of the sun and the earth. This crucial spot forms the last point of a small triangle that nestles into the larger one. With reference to the 1:50,000 scale map I was able to see that two of the corners of the

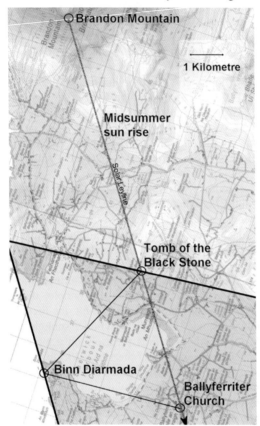

Diagram 1.8
The solar ley defines
the position of the
Tomb of the Black
Stone.

smaller triangle were marked by significant features. The first being Binn Diarmada, or Dermot's Hill - one of the Three Sisters, and the solar connection can be seen in the myths surrounding the site. Dermot, who had eloped with the beautiful Gráinne, wife of the high king Fionn Mac Cumhaill, was on the run from the king's wrath. On this hill the two lovers consummate their relationship and with the help of the sun god, Lugh, make good their escape when a band of 'sea pirates' try to capture them.

The lower point of this internal triangle of the sun is occupied by the church of Ballyferriter. But, to our immense frustration, on the third corner, which is the most important part of this smaller triangle, being where the solar ley enters the main Triangle, there was nothing. The map and the archaeological guides drew a blank.

The disappointment was not just over the lack of a tangible marker, it was also a failure of faith. The discoveries that we had made seemed very real to me and I felt the missing point as a mortal blow to the story. With this in mind, and unable to rest a moment longer, we dug my friend's car out of the mud that a week of rain had turned into a quagmire and drove through the deepening storm to An Charraig, just below the place where the sun met the earth. It wasn't an especially inspiring walk, past the dripping fuchsia bushes and out onto the fields above.

In front of us was a small rectangular block of stone about the height of a table, and on it were the remains of a small fire that had blackened the stone. I poked amongst the wet charcoal - whoever had lit the fire had placed small pieces of red rock in it; a queer enough place to have a fire, but this was not the only time that we had come across hints that some of the older customs were still being secretly observed by the local population.

A track led up the hill and at the top was a small mound. I felt my pulse quicken. A standing stone marked the mound, and dug into one side, facing The Three Sisters, was a square hole. A large white quartz boulder had been placed in the entrance. It appeared to be a tomb.

A stone-sided tunnel led into the hillside and, though the passage was full of rubble, a lintel of roughly hewn stone and the walled stone slabs of the tunnel could be clearly seen. Around us a series of standing stones marked the perimeter of the courtyard, and a peculiar structure of large stones lay just to the north of the mound.

We had discovered the third marker.

At this exact spot the first rays of the midsummer sun and the geometry of the triangle meet, and here, despite everything, was a megalithic monument. (Diagram 1.9) All the archaeologists and experts on the landscape assured us that we were mistaken, and it was not until my friend took some of them to see the site that they rather reluctantly agreed that it was indeed a tomb.[13]

The correct classification of the tomb is difficult, but such places are collectively called 'courtyard tombs' because of the enclosed space by the entrance. There is little evidence to show that these sites were ever

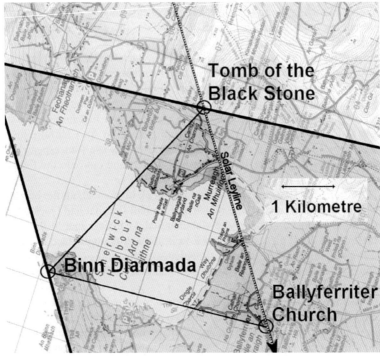

Diagram 1.9
The Tomb of the Black Stone is one corner of a smaller internal trian-
gle, illuminated by the midsummer solar leyline.

used as actual tombs, certainly not as we understand them today. They
were, however, used for important spiritual rituals. This sacred place
acted in the same way as the 'light-box' at the temple of Newgrange,
which functions as a threshold over which the Solstice sun has to cross
before penetrating the interior of the temple.

One more connection appeared regarding the theme of the Goddess
and the sun. The tomb was situated in a field that bore the name An
Clochan Dubh, The Black Stone. Such a stone is associated with the
oracular priestesses of the Sybil, the name born by the western point of
the triangle. There was a connection here, and our first task was to
discover why the unusual name 'Sybil' had been given to the hill. The

story of Sybil Point was not difficult to find as it has been told in many of the guidebooks that describe the area.

As the story is told, Sybil Lynch was born to a well known family in Galway in the 1650s. When she came of age she met a young country lad from Kerry and, in an echo of Dermot and Gráinne's tragic tale, she ran away with him to hide in their castle near Ballyferriter. Sybil Lynch caused quite a stir and an army was sent to get her back, but unfortunately before they could reach her she was tragically drowned as she hid in a cave by the sea.

The claim that the headland was named after this unlucky maiden is unlikely to be true as it carried the name 'Sybil' well before her time. It was also called the 'Altar of the Fire', and until relatively recently the *Beltane* fire, which was lit to celebrate the coming of spring, was built here. The *Beltane* festival was significant in that it commemorated a sacred marriage between the Goddess and her consort the sun king.

The rocks that thrust out of the wild Atlantic just below the sea-cliffs of Sybil Point have names that are even older. One is called the 'mother and the crow' and another 'the hunter'. The crow is a totem-bird of the solar king, lover of Cybele; in Rome he was known as Attis, in Ireland he was Bran. There can be little doubt that this locale has had a long association with the Mother Goddess and her solar champion, probably dating back to the time of the people who constructed the first megaliths.

The Sybil has an equally distinguished and unusual history. She was always associated with a black stone, and her name, which derives from her early title Cybele, means cubic - a reference to the stone's shape. There are many historical citations purporting to be about her stone and it has appeared in many places and in many guises, but the stories are not mythical. One such reference is the Ka' aba or the 'black stone of Mecca' and it is the focus of anger for millions of Muslims as they make their annual pilgrimage to the 'Holy Land'. The Ka'aba is indeed cubic and was probably a meteorite.[14] The stone of Fal, which the Tuatha Dé Danaan brought to Ireland, is also said to have been black. The cubic hieroglyph, that describes the Sibyl' name, was the first written reference to her and the same text goes on to tell us that she was the Mother Goddess, whose priestesses forecast the future and told of the past.

The most comprehensive description of this powerful deity comes from the Roman historian Lactantius who wrote about her in 260 BC. He stated that, though she had her home in Pharagua, her priestesses were established all over the world. Lactantius listed ten oracular priestesses of the Sibillia living in Italy and stated that they lived in cubic temples carved out of the living rock in which they housed the source of their power, a black stone that was said to have fallen from heaven.

These Cumea Sibillia had a unique relationship with the Roman State. In the spring of 217 BC Rome was threatened by Hannibal's advancing armies. The Romans were at a loss and many had already emigrated, anticipating the coming slaughter. The priestesses of the Sibillia met with the Roman government and told them that if they brought the Cybele herself and her black stone from Asia and honoured her in Rome as the Romans' chief deity then Rome would be saved. The Romans, acting promptly on her advice, sent a special expedition to Turkey to bring her and the black stone back to Rome. Once she was safely in Latin territory they built a temple for her on the Capitoline Hill in the very heart of Rome. For the next 300 years her creed dominated Roman politics and religious orders.[15] A great fire in AD 83 destroyed her sanctuary and although her recorded prophesies, along with the black stone, were said to have been saved from the flames, they then mysteriously disappeared. (Diagram 1.10)

The most famous of the orders of the Sybil were housed in the hills of Piano Grande in Umbria, Italy. Their expertise in prophecy was such that even in more recent times the Vatican has acknowledged them. Several tombs of the various incumbent Sibillia can be found in the cathedral in the centre of Sienna where they are still held in high honour by the Catholic Church.

Despite the rough way that history has treated her, several versions of her writings have survived. The most famous of these, the *Sibylline Prophecies,* is still a source for controversial historical debate amongst historians. There is a general consensus that books III, V and VI of these prophecies were originally written by the Sybil herself. In these chapters she declares herself to be the daughter-in-law of Noah[16] and the daughter of the Earth Goddess. Suddenly we find that the story of the black stone leads us to a direct historical reference to the Sybil and Ireland.

Diagram 1.10 The Roman Cybele holding a drum and riding a chariot pulled by lions.

There are several ancient Irish histories recorded by the Christian missions to Ireland, which describe, in some detail, the various tribes that have landed on Ireland's shores. The first recorded group of immigrants were fifty women and three men. They were led by a woman whose title was Cessair, 'keeper of the knowledge'. The Irish Annals describe her as being the granddaughter of Noah and the daughter of the earth. This Cessair is none other than Cybele. We can be left in little doubt that her creed was established in Ireland and that she founded a basis for the links between the Mother Goddess and the sun that seem to be the theme for later religious and spiritual projects. This connection is investigated in later chapters.

Our method of combining the mythology and the geometry not only led to the archaeology but also uncovered a great deal about the history.

Returning home after our mission to the 'tomb of the black stone' I put more coal onto the fire and sat back to read the story of Lugh. Like all sun heroes he wielded a spear (magical spears are quite common in mythology). Lugh's spear was a national treasure and could obliterate his enemies. Such a weapon pierced the side of Jesus, and every

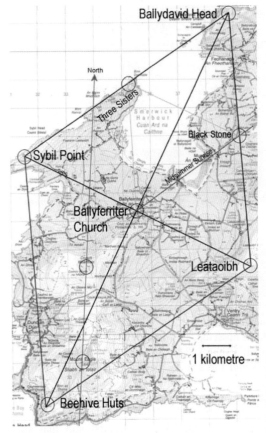

Diagram 1.11
The Dingle Diamond,
a geometric temple
aligned to the midsum-
mer sunrise.

dragon-slaying saint is equipped with one. The dragon, an ancient metaphor for the earth energy (or lines of *chi* as the Chinese record) is pierced by it. Here the spear points downwards through the dragon and into the earth. If this was translated as geometrical iconography then what was below this shaft of sunlight and where did it point? The ordinance survey map names the western tip of the peninsula as Slea Head.

Slea is an Irish word for spear. As if by some divine providence the tip of the landfall at Slea Head forms a perfect inverted triangle, a mirror image of the original one. When mated, the two triangles form the shape of a lozenge or diamond. This icon was once the pictogram for the Sybil herself and was used as such for many thousands of years. Here it was, depicted in pencil on the landscape of the peninsula. A diamond. The Dingle Diamond. (Diagram 1.11)

To travel down to the point of the spear of Lugh at the southern tip of the Diamond is to pass through some of the most beautiful scenery in the world. On rounding the corner that marks the head of the point the chain of islands called The Blaskets comes into view, stretching out into the western ocean. On the very corner there is a large white statue of the crucifixion of Christ, and around him, looking up adoringly, are the Three Marys. This almost exact Christian, and therefore relatively modern, embodiment of the three fates, or three sisters, reflects the three hills of the Goddess. The north pointing line from the hills of the Three Sisters, after passing through 'pointy mountain' and Mount Eagle, exits the land at this place.

A strange collection of stone monuments mark the precise southern tip of the Diamond. Many of these are beehive huts, though others are solid columns of dressed and carefully arranged stone that give all the appearances of a ritual complex. There has never been any archaeological investigation of these monuments and historians and archaeologists can only suggest that the stone structures were a by-product of the farmers clearing the fields. The evidence is against them as there are no other examples of these 'clearance piles' in other parts of the peninsula. Nor are the many beehive huts explained, the care taken in their construction would suggest a ritual usage, not one connected with farming. White lichen has grown over their surface and, in the light of the setting sun, they take on an eerie glow that adds to their enigmatic appeal.

I bought more tracing paper and a new 1:50,000 scale map of the peninsula and redrew the Dingle Diamond. It was perfect. The geometry of the leylines worked out precisely and now incorporated the solar ley of the midsummer sunrise.

Midsummer is the turning of the year, when, at its height, the summer begins to slowly wane. It was as if the Diamond were a womb that in a moment of orgiastic climax was fertilised by the sun's energy, bringing new life to the land and fulfilling an age-old ritual.

The Dingle Diamond contained a great many more revelations; however, at this point there was one question that needed an answer. If it had been the Neolithic inhabitants of Ireland who had built the Diamond then who were they?

The Monsignor had mentioned the Tuatha Dé Danaan (and Lugh was certainly one of the more famous of their tribe) as candidates for the erection of the stones. Perhaps it was these magical people, half-godlike beings, who had created the Diamond. What was their history and, more precisely, why had they come to Ireland?

I retired to my study and began to search for references to the Tuatha Dé Danaan, the faerie folk of Irish mythology.

Diagram 1.12
The Church in the village of Ballyferriter

Chapter Two
Tuatha Dé Danaan

"May the road rise to meet you, may the wind always be at your back…"
An Irish blessing.

T he dawn that day was a long time in arriving. A gloominess of
fog and cloud lay over the bleak shores of the Fifth Province.[1]
Smoke in thick dreads wreathed the beaches and the sound of war came
from the Hill of the Kings.[2] Here the Tuatha Dé Danaan had beached
their vessels, and here too they had set flame to them before establishing camp. But the 'men of bags',[3] who held the land around, saw nothing of their activities for the mists concealed even the *Beltane* fires of
that miasmal day. In the village of the Horse King[4] there was little in
the way of festivities. A council had been called, and to the Grey
Ridge[5] had been summoned chieftains from all the nearby provinces
who were discussing the news from the scouts. It was not at all clear as
to what had occurred, and the unnatural mists had confused the reports.
It seemed that an army had flown on the high air to land on the Hill of
Kings.[4] Whether they were diabolic demons or a black cloaked assault
of men was not known. Having been plagued by nightmares and beset
with a sense of foreboding, the mood of the king was not helped by the
druids' interpretation of an invasion. To settle the matter, for good or
ill, a champion was chosen to investigate. So it was that Sreng, a
mighty man of arms, took up his two thick-handled spears and red-
brown shield and with the advice and hopes of the clan, set out for the
Hill of Kings.

Before he had been travelling for two days he had the feeling he was
being watched, and on the twilight of the second day a tall fair-haired
stranger hailed him, a stark silhouette against the dark mass of cloud
behind him. There was wonder then, for Sreng had never seen such
armaments. He held a gracefully tapered spear, its sharp point towards

the ground, and he rested against a two-toned shield that glinted in the last of the evening's sun. It was in Sreng's native tongue that the stranger had spoken and Sreng had answered with a question, so it was not long before the two champions sat down together. The stranger introduced himself as Bres of the Tuatha Dé Danaan and asked if he could see the sturdy spear that Sreng carried. He wanted to know if all the Fir Bolg had such weapons. Sreng told him that the name of the weapon was *Craísech*. The razor-sharp edges of the spear, sharpened on both sides though not at the point, was used to sever the opponent. No armour or shield would survive such a crushing blow, Sreng explained, especially with the full weight of the spear behind the impact. They exchanged their weapons so that they might take them back with them and each side could see the weapons that the other used. Then the warriors sat at their ease, each feeling a growing respect for the other, and Bres outlined his people's terms. His conditions were precise: one half of Ireland to be given in peace and if that was not gifted there would be nothing for it but war.

It was in friendship that the two parted the next morning. Sreng was impressed with the spear and its almost magical flight from his hand. When he returned it was with a small deer over his shoulder, and that caught with ease by the edge of the oakwood. As he stood in front of the gathered assembly of druids, kings and sages he urged peace, for, as he reasoned, a war with people who were so better equipped could only end in loss. But the High King disagreed, pointing out that such a powerful enemy would take not only half the land, but the whole land. Bres, whose journey back was shorter, showed the heavy spear to his council of elders and told of the muscular, sturdy black-haired man he had met. There was, he thought, going to be a fight, for these people were proud and well versed in war-craft.

So it was that the two tribes met, the new challenging the old, and in this way the history of the land was to enter another age.[6]

Much of what we know about the pre-Christian peoples of Ireland comes from a series of early Christian and medieval books, the principal one being *Lebor Gabála Érenn*, The Book of Invasions. Originally a collection of manuscripts painstakingly inscribed by monks of the seventh century as they recorded an oral tradition[7] embracing five thousand years of history, its pages archived the arrivals and struggles of six

The Tuatha Dé Danaan

different invaders as they landed on the green shores of Ireland, giving us a unique glimpse into a dark age of our history. These earlier debutants had travelled far in their search for a new home and they brought with them snatches of myth and lore from Persia to Norway, all faithfully documented by the surprisingly impartial monks. The legends contain references to many other lands and weaving in and out of them are regular references to foreign royal families such as those of Egypt,[8] Spain, Rome and Greece.

To remember the vast scope of these stories must have been an almost impossible task were it not that the shamans and druids who memorised them did so in the most methodical way. They did this by wrapping the histories of many peoples around a common theme. On to this structure they appended the gods and battles, inventions and philosophies, as well as the music and poetry, creating a single story with many levels of understanding contained within it. In this way they created the language of myth. "Its meaning is the true learning of sages."[9] It is a surprisingly accurate method of transferring information, with negligible change in the stories being evident even over long stretches of time. This manner of remembering the past died a gradual death with the advent of the written word. As the new fashion for writing superseded the idea that "when people have the help of text they let their memories rust",[10] it was the Christian mission that helped to dust off the past. There has always been a strong but misunderstood link between the Western Isles and the Christian Church. The Vatican records, for instance, show that the first Bishop of Rome, installed by St. Paul in 58 AD, was one Prince Linus of Britain, the son of Caractacus the Pendragon. Just why there should be this 'special relationship' becomes clear when the story of the Tuatha Dé Danaan is re-told.

The Christian religion came early to Ireland and its first missionaries were spiritual explorers, people who were not underwritten by a state or army. Indeed they were often lonely esoterics seeking something more than the official dogma of Constantine. They found an empathy with the spiritual beliefs of the people living in Ireland at that time, which they incorporated into their creed forming a gnostic, Celtic version of Christianity. Almost as soon as they arrived the monks began a difficult and momentous task: to record the tales of pagan Ireland. They were searching for something, something that induced them to override the typical antipathy of their religion towards unbelievers. Whatever

29

they were questing for frequently brought them into a close relationship with individuals who held a 'heathen' philosophy and so delivered them into the realm of the heretic. St. Patrick, one of the first apostles of Christianity in Ireland, came into conflict with the established church in doing so. He was fully aware of his dilemma, for he asked his two guardian angels if it was the will of the 'king of heaven and earth' that he should be listening to the tales. They answered with one voice. "Dear holy cleric," they said, "these old warriors tell you no more than a third of their stories because their memories are faulty. Have these stories written down on poets' tablets in refined language, so that the hearing of them will provide entertainment for the lords and commons of later times."[11] Patrick then turned to the old Irish warrior, Cailte, who stood by the fire. Cailte was the last surviving member of Fionn Mac Cumhaill's legendary war band. "May victory and blessing be yours, Cailte, for you have lightened both our spirits and our minds. Tell us another of these glorious stories... even though our religious life is being disrupted and our prayers neglected."[12]

The care taken to make these records as accurate as possible is unrivalled in the work of Christian missions, as can be seen from the scribes' notes. *The Book of Leinster*, a source of many epic Irish tales, contains a postscript, written in Irish, to the legend of the *Tain*: "A blessing on everyone who will memorise the *Tain* faithfully in this form, and not put any other form on it."

The thirty years that Patrick spent on his mission in the fifth century also saw the final collapse of the Roman Empire. The rapid and dramatic changes were unprecedented and most of Europe fell into chaos. As it did so, Ireland, under the sway of Patrick's Christian brethren, achieved stability. A comparative renaissance of freedom and intellect flourished in the stone abbeys and mountain cells. The trade in slaves was ended, intertribal wars became less frequent and small towns grew up around the new abbeys. The steady decline that had been the fate of Ireland was reversed. These centres of learning and religion were the earliest universities and became the nucleus of culture and trade. Wealth and wisdom flowed through them and they expanded into the first significant population centres in Ireland.

This great work of recording was a co-ordinated and organised undertaking, necessitating hundreds of scribes. In monasteries and abbeys across Ireland a veritable industry was generated. Columcille,[13] who succeeded Patrick, founded forty-one of these universities where, in austere cells, monks committed heresies that would have resulted in burning at the stake if they had been undertaken in Rome. The outcome was a corpus of ancient literature that is a unique testament to Celtic lore. So vast was this work that, even today, only a small proportion of these writings have been translated.

Early Christian Ireland became a receptacle for the knowledge of Europe. The fall of Rome had seen wholesale destruction of books and learning that engulfed the continent. As the great libraries burnt and the places of wisdom were ransacked for their wealth, it was to the safety of the monasteries of Ireland that scribes and historians, visionaries and men of learning came. Greek texts, Egyptian tomes, classical myth and Celtic lore filled the shelves of its libraries. Bede, born at the height of this renaissance in 673 AD, and author of the *History of the English Church and People*, comments:

"Many of the nobles of the English nation and lesser men also had set out thither, forsaking their native island either for the grace of sacred learning or a more austere life. All these the Irish willingly received, and saw to it to supply them with food, day by day without cost, and books for their studies, and teaching, free of charge."

It was not only English scholars who availed themselves of this generosity; many of Europe's elite came to study in Ireland and at this time the Irish minuscule script that adorns the illustrated codices of many mediaeval books was developed. It was so successful that it was adopted as the common script of the Middle Ages, and Irish copies of holy works are still treasured in churches from Kiev to Rome. With the arrival of these scholars came also books. Not since the heady days of the great Egyptian university and library at Alexandria, had so much wisdom and history been gathered in one place. Indeed many of the books rescued from the sackings and fires of the third and fourth centuries after Christ ended up in Irish cloisters. (Diagram 2.1)

The Christian Church is generally not known for its great anthropological works. From the Celtic offensive in the early part of the millennium to the mediaeval conquistadors of Spain, the Roman Catholic Church has not hesitated to burn books, persecute the native pagan believers and to generally conduct a campaign of eradication in the name of faith. Why would Christian missionaries and scholars risk the wrath of the Vatican to record the events of pagans in a small country

*Diagram 2.1
The incredible love
and attention lav-
ished by the monks
in creating the
Celtic Christian
books is evident in
their beauty.*

like Ireland? The answer lies in the nature of the myths they came to record and for this we have to look to the unique testimony of the Christian writers, taking us back to the origins of the Tuatha Dé Danaan. (Diagram 2.2)

The archaeological record shows that Ireland's first inhabitants appeared around nine thousand years ago and in comparison with their continental cousins they lived very simple lives, hunting and fishing on the margins of the island.[14]

The earliest histories tell of a series of landings by tribes led by a woman called Cessair, also known as Banbha.[15] The word *cessair* appears to be derived from the Gothic *eddas* and is a title, not a name. *Cessair*, or *kvasir*, means 'wise one' and a *kvasir* was a 'guardian of the magic cauldron'. This cauldron is the container of the spirit holding the sum of human erudition and was guarded, in Celtic mythology, by

*Diagram 2.2
Cernunnos, the Lord of the Animals. From continental Europe.
When the Church failed to ruth-
lessly eradicate this faith they
turned instead to ideology. Cernunnos was used by the Church as the
traditional model for Satan, a
measure of the extent of his power
and its threat to the mediaeval
Christian Church. He holds a gold
torc in one hand and a serpent in
the other, symbolic of the marriage
between a god and a goddess.*

Ceridwen, the 'wise one of the white crow'. It is symbolic of the power of the earth, harnessed and incorporated into the structure of a peaceful matrilineal society.[16]

Cessair, it is reported, came to Ireland with fifty women and three men. Her later title was Sybil, the Oracle and as we have seen, she was the daughter of Bioth, supposed by the Christian monks to be a grandson of Noah. The appearance of such an internationally famous deity at the roots of Irish culture is a hint of the significance of Ireland in the religious affairs of the continent. A modern equivalent, perhaps, were if the Vatican 'upped-sticks' and moved wholesale to Ireland. Bioth (another name for 'the world') appealed to his father, Noah, asking for space for himself and his daughter on the Ark, but he was refused. Cessair knew that this would be the case and was told in a vision to consult a certain idol, probably one of the black stones.. The advice received was for them to forsake the God of Noah, make their own ship and put to sea to escape the coming deluge.

However, the story conceals an event in pre-history that mirrors the fictional dialogue with Noah. In this way, the story of the Flood and the story of escape from a catastrophe that enveloped the known world become one and the same. Put plainly, the story of the invasions recounts that the 'guardian of the sum of human knowledge' consults her mother, the earth Goddess, and is given advice as to where to go to avoid a coming cataclysm. No doubt she took with her a great deal of the living traditions of the time. Her last resting place is reputed to be a substantial cairn of piled limestone boulders on the prominent hill of Knockmaa to the north of Galway.

There is little doubt that when the Tuatha Dé Danaan arrived in Ireland they knew that it was previously the home of the Goddess, for they were her people. They probably saw in Ireland a fertile ground into which they could transplant their traditions and beliefs. There is also little doubt that they were aware that a people who were not friendly to the ways of the Goddess had already subjugated Ireland, namely the tribes of the Fir Bolg.

The roots of the Fir Bolg were very different to those of the shamanic warriors of the Goddess. They stemmed from a tribe who have been called the 'sons of Nemed'. Nemed, or Neimheadh,[17] was said to be of the royal line of Agnoman, a Greek name for the rulers of a loose confederation of tribes known later as the Scythians.[18] This reference places them clearly as part of the peoples who conquered and dominated the central European civilisations. No longer are we looking at an ancient people fleeing the wrath of unsettled times; instead, a picture emerges of an elite class of warrior peoples who were the rulers and royal families of a new world order.

Around 4200 BC a change in the archaeological record dates the arrivals of the tribes of Nemed and the Fir Bolg. This was marked in Ireland by a dramatic alteration in the pollen record charting a sudden decline in woodland. Evidence of pollens preserved in lakes, mud and bogs reveal that woodland was cleared for farming. This was due not only to a shift in European weather patterns but also to the appearance of full-blown agriculture as practised in central Europe.[19] This, and the artefacts that they left behind, allow us to compare the beliefs and life-styles of those who dwelt here with those of peoples from Europe, and to come to some conclusions about their origins.[20]

A mark of the success of these farmers is their rapid spread. In little more than five hundred years they had changed the natural environment of Ireland. Forest clearing and road building were not their only industries, they also built large numbers of fortifications and erected megaliths of different types across the land. In doing this they were converting, or perhaps upgrading, the already ancient sacred sites of their predecessors by replacing wood with imperishable stone.[21]

Their history is inconsistent with the preceding peoples of Ireland; the fact that this patriarchal dynasty had in its retinue warriors skilled in the art of battle shows us that this was not only a tribe looking for a place to settle, but that it was looking for a land to conquer and rule. Ireland provided this.

On reaching Ireland, Nemed and his people had to fight long and hard with the indigenous Fomorians. The Fomorians, or 'people of the sea', appear throughout Irish history as the native inhabitants. Of all the peoples of Irish myth the Fomorians are the most interesting. Like chameleons they change their form and nature with each age, seemingly representing the spirits of the land or of the peoples who inhabit it. The metamorphosis that the Fomorians experience can be utilised as a measure of the sociological organisation of a particular period. A society often measures its strength against that of its enemies.

Cessair, the 'daughter of the earth', like the Fomorians appears in many guises throughout Ireland's history and she takes on a different mien in each epoch. In many respects her spirit becomes the prize of these long struggles between the heroes and the incumbents.

Meanwhile, Nemed managed to establish the first cities of stone in the shape of his royal forts.[22] His rule was short-lived and after his death his sons were obliged to fight for the kingdom again. The resultant slaughter saw all but thirty of Nemed's followers dead. Some returned to Greece where they were enslaved and some, under Fergus Red-Side, one of Nemed's sons, moved to Scotland or Alba, where they successfully established themselves.

Those enslaved in Greece were purported to have been put to work carrying earth in leather bags. From this they have been given one of their names: Fir Bolg, the 'people of the bags'. This royal family split into three factions and escaped from their masters in Greece, returning to Ireland. They landed in three different places and are known, respectively, as Fir Bolg (after the bags of leather), Fir Domnann (after the pits that they had dug during their captivity) and Gaileoin, a fierce warrior people whose name comes from the multitude of their javelins.

We are told, in The Book of Invasions, that they made one successful incursion into Ireland under a high king. Their reign was cursory and bloody, as the lore of Ireland records. A struggle for power amongst the chieftains saw five serious battles in the ten years that they are supposed to have held power. Despite the poverty of their history, a single great change in the history of Ireland can be associated with the Fir Bolg. It was a change that bore the characteristic hallmark of a people who follow a male god, for the Fir Bolg are credited with the bringing of law to Ireland. In the course of their struggles, they established the first High King and, left to themselves, their reign might have continued. But the histories of Ireland are unanimously clear on this point: the Fir Bolg were not left to themselves and the massed ranks of javelins were challenged by the arrival of a superior force. They faced, after only a short period of time in Ireland, the coming of another tribe, the Tuatha Dé Danaan.

Whilst the 'men of Dea' were building their stronghold, three of their queens, the 'Three Sisters of War' (Badh, the crow goddess, Macha, the red-haired and Morrigu, the mare goddess)[23] crossed to Teamhair where the Fir Bolg were preparing for the conflict. The journey through the exposed lands of their enemy was dangerous and difficult but they contrived to arrive unseen. Gathering in a yew glade they sent forth their enchantments. First, a cloud of mist and darkness fell over the house of the High King and all within were filled with terror but when they sought to find the source of this confusion, a shower of fire sent them running for cover and all their energies were spent in dousing the flames. This was followed by a fall of blood in thick droplets until the entire village was spattered in red. For three days the Fir Bolg endured these curses. At the end of this time the Horse King summoned his most powerful druids, Cesarn, Gnáthach and Ingnathach.[24] Together, these men broke through the witching and dispelled it but the effort exhausted them. The Fir Bolg knew by this that they had to force a parley and sue for terms or else they would be defeated, even before the first blow was struck in anger. Eleven battalions of the Fir Bolg marched. Rank on rank of brave warriors lined the glen and they beat their shields and roared their challenge to the Tuatha Dé Danaan, for these were not men to be cowed by the sorcery of the Goddess, but the bravest of the brave and most able to stand a fight.

Nuada, the High King of the Dé Danaan, sent Brigit and several more of his poets to speak with the men of the Fir Bolg. In eloquent terms they asked again for a chance for peace, pointing out that the Dé Danaan had no place to go and that the land was as wide as it was vast. 'One half we will have in peace and will war no more,' they said. But again, in his pride, the Horse King would have none of it. So the messengers asked when he would have battle with them. The king knew that he could not immediately engage the superior weapons of his enemy — he was shrewd enough to realise this folly. Stepping forward flanked by his druids, he requested a delay for he needed space to put the arms and armour in order and to construct weapons such as those used by the Dé Danaan and he slyly suggested that the men of the Goddess might want time to build spears such as his own men used. Brigit knew that the weapons she held were far better in the art of war than the heavy cudgels of the Fir Bolg, but she knew as well that there would be no honour in the slaughter of such a poorly armed opponent. She wanted peace but, failing that, a decisive victory in fair conditions would be the only way to decide the rule of Ireland. The emissaries of the Dé Danaan accepted a delay and the date for the battle for Ireland was set for midsummer, a quarter year from their arrival on Ireland's shores.[25]

On the summer solstice eleven battalions of the Fir Bolg stood ready, each warrior holding a long sharp spear. Against them were arrayed the smaller force of the Dé Danaan, their blue cloaks and black shields lined in mesmerising battle order, a tightly disciplined force of seasoned warriors against a horde of native fighters. In the tradition of the day, twenty-seven hurlers from the Dé Danaan stepped up and were faced by twenty-seven hurlers from the Fir Bolg. The rest of the armies stood back. But the men of the Goddess were beaten and every one of them was killed. Then from amongst the corpses in front of each wall of shields a messenger rode forth, emissaries charged with determining the terms of the battle. It was decided that they would fight every day, but that an equal number of warriors from each side would face each other. The Horse King was not well pleased with this bargain as his men out-numbered the Dé Danaan. So it was that the conflict was engaged, a huge spectacle that went on for four days. But on the fourth day the experience and tactics of the 'men of Dea' secured victory and the Fir Bolg were driven back. Together with one-hundred and fifty men, their king was slaughtered on a long strand near Sligo that still carries his name, Traigh Eothaile. At last, tired and weary, three hundred of the Fir Bolg were left, led by Sreng. Nuada, weary of the killings, proffered peace and to sweeten their loss gave them a choice of any one of the five provinces of Ireland that they would have. Sreng chose Connacht and there he and his people lived, and their descendants after them, for it was a fair land and a generous gift from a victor who could have taken all.[26]

The Tuatha Dé Danaan are perhaps the most enigmatic and elusive of Ireland's peoples. As we know, the name means the 'folk of the goddess Dana', a reference to the triple-goddess of old European tradition, and stems from the villages and townships of Neolithic times on the river Danube. The dates suggested by the archaeology and the mythology for the arrival of the 'folk of the Goddess' would seem to be around 3000 BC. If this is so, then these tribes are strong candidates for the building of the megalithic tombs, cromlechs, dolmens, circles, passage graves and henges that are characteristic of the people of these times. Their mythological history is equally interesting and shines a light on why they came, searching for a home, to Ireland's shores. (Diagram 2.3)

*Diagram 2.3
Looking out from
inside a Neolithic
place of worship
at Carrowkeel.
The massive stone
lintels frame the
passage to the
light.*

According to Keating's *History of Ireland*,[27] they originally came from a region of Greece called Achaea where they became learned in the magical arts. Around 3000 BC this area of the Peloponnese on the Mediterranean Sea was still a flourishing part of the Mycenaean Empire. Based on the island of Crete and protected by the waters of the Aegean, it was a refuge for an old lifestyle that no longer existed on the mainland of Europe. Here, the Goddess was the chief deity and the belief system was in opposition to the patriarchal and warlike societies of the male gods who dominated European culture. This last bastion continued the traditions of the Goddess for two thousand years, maintaining a constant struggle against an enemy that sought not only to conquer but also to overturn their religion. They succeeded remarkably well in holding at bay the armies of the new city-states until an earthquake and volcano destroyed the heart of their world.

Whilst in Achaea, the Tuatha Dé Danaan are reported to have helped the Mycenaeans repel an invasion from Syria, which at this time was part of the Mesopotamian empire. The Syrian army represented the forces of a male god intent on subduing and assimilating the last vestiges of the peoples of the Goddess.

This was no ordinary struggle. The armies of the new city-states met with fierce and organised resistance from this dedicated band of shamanic warriors. These precursors of the warrior priests of King Arthur (on which the Knights Templar were modelled) were the best of the Mycenaean warriors. Learned in magic and steeped in ancient lore and tradition, they were backed by the full power of the Goddess. It is not surprising that magic was the theme of the battle. Every evening, we are told, the Dé Danaan were able to resurrect their dead so that their soldiers could fight again. However in a legend that evokes shades of vampires, the Syrians combated this ability by driving a stake of the 'quicken-tree' into every dead body.[28] By this ruse the Mesopotamians were able to win the day and the Tuatha Dé Danaan fled, not stopping until they came to the country of Lochlonn in the land of Dancia, which is said to be in Denmark.[29] Later retellings of the story say that here they built the four famous cities: Filias, Gorias, Finias and Murias, in each of which lived a powerful sage who taught the citizens the arts and sciences.

From this powerful base they emigrated to Scotland where they stayed for seven years at Dobhar and Iardobhar by the River Dobhain in Argyll, before moving to the north of Ireland.

That they were the direct descendants of a matriarchal goddess-worshipping people, complete with the beliefs and culture of those peaceful agriculturists, can be seen in the gods and goddesses after whom they were named. Their triple-goddess, Dana, had three daughters:[30] Banba, the goddess of wisdom who married Mac Cuill, the hazel god; Fótla, the summer goddess of the corn, married to Mac Ceacht, the god of the plough; and Ériu, the spring consort of Mac Gréine, the sun god.[32]

It seems that the people who built and used the Dingle Diamond were refugees from a titanic clash of cultures. On one side was the Goddess and the traditions and beliefs of a matriarchal society; on the other was an aggressive, warlike people whose armies overran Europe and established the first empires in the name of a male god. It was small wonder that the Tuatha Dé Danaan built a temple that had so many references to the Goddess in it. Here was the very soil that Cessair the Sybil, the mighty mother goddess herself, 'daughter of the earth', had blessed. What is more interesting is that the Diamond seemed to be attempting to take this male sun god and, in some way, unite him in harmony with Mother Earth. It almost seems as if they were trying to heal a rift in the spiritual world. Why would such a people attempt to heal a division like this? This is especially relevant, since they had just defeated the patriarchal tribes of the Fir Bolg and had established their rule over Ireland, which was, after all, far from the events unfolding in Europe. If it were possible to find an answer to this question, it might be possible to discover the purpose of the temple of the Dingle Diamond and see just how it worked in practice.

Chapter Three
Mother

"The crane must aye, Take nine steps 'ere shee flir."
Polwart, Flying with Montgomery (1605)

The Tuatha Dé Danaan are remembered in mythology as being magicians. In Ireland it is often said that every skilled man that had music and did enchantments secretly was of the Tuatha Dé Danaan. Their reputation for practising magic and the arts, as well as for being a very intelligent, often cunning people, is ubiquitous across Ireland, as are references to their embodiment of a culture that emanated from the worship of the Goddess. Of all the ancient manuscripts that refer to them, it is from Keating's history that we learn the most. As has been mentioned, he wrote in the seventeenth century and includes in his sources over one hundred books that have since been lost or destroyed.[1] Keating tells us: 'The People of Dana spent some time in Macedonia', where they are reported to have been in the service of the Mycenae, a clan that, like the more famous Minoans,[2] were matriarchal goddess worshippers. It is quite likely that the Dé Danaan did become mercenaries of a kind, but this would have been after an event that compelled them to flee from their homelands. The distinctive appearance of their monuments — megaliths, graves and dolmens — leaves us with an indelible record of their presence. In the valleys of central, northern and eventually western Europe, these monuments are a calling card, a stone trail that leads back to their origin. The stones, pots and books are not the only clues to the complex migrations of these people: it is in their name that we find the origins of their tribe. Dana, the principal goddess of the Tuatha Dé Danaan, is the deity associated with the River Danube, a massive river that runs across southern Europe providing navigation and trade links between the Black Sea and the south of Germany. This region is an intense and complex focus for a rich archaeology that has only relatively recently been tapped. Neolithic settlements such as Lepenski Vir on the Danube, with its monumental stone carvings, are still providing fresh insights into the habitats and lifestyle that formed the basis for the culture of the Tuatha Dé Danaan.

The conflict that the Tuatha Dé Danaan were engaged in was the last vestige of an ancient and wider war between a matriarchal people of the Goddess and a patriarchal people led by a god. It was a struggle that had been ongoing for nearly one thousand years and it resulted in the displacement of hundreds of thousands of people. Evidence from the archaeological sites of this period is consistent throughout Europe and shows that a remarkable change in lifestyle and living conditions occurred for the population around six-thousand years ago. Although signifying an abrupt end to a widespread and established culture and its replacement by an alien one, it was not something that happened overnight. Sweeping out of the east from the plains of Siberia, this movement encroached upon the mountains of Europe like a wave. It reached across the Urals and penetrated into the heart-lands of the home of the Dé Danaan. Anthropologists call the invaders Proto-Indo-Europeans. When they arrived in Europe they found an indigenous people who grew crops, lived in settled and large communities and had a well developed culture and art. What they also found was that these people were relatively peaceful and not at all skilled in the methods of warfare, a matter that they took great advantage of. But this position was quickly reversed, for the warring ways of the Proto-Indo-Europeans were a lesson that these people of the Goddess learned surprisingly quickly.

For the greater part of the twentieth century, this period of history (called the Neolithic or New Stone Age) was considered the dark hour before the dawn of civilisation, inhabited only by wandering cannibals and skin-clad hunters.[3] It took the determined work of the archaeologist Marija Gimbutas, and the more liberal ethos of the 1960s, to bring the facts to light. In overturning this 'based on ignorance' theory, she has transformed our understanding of this vital part of human evolution and she did this using a radical new method of analysis: archaeomythology. She coined the term 'Old Europe' for this vast and richly cultured civilisation.

In museums around the world there are drawers, cabinets and boxes full of neatly labelled and dated pieces of history, all but the most spectacular unnoticed or forgotten. To the orthodox scientist it seems as if these dusty artefacts are all that has been bequeathed to us, for the voices of the vibrant societies that produced them have long been silent. A great many are inexplicable. Archaeologists can sometimes hazard a guess at techniques used in their construction, even going so far as to try and understand their uses, but unless the relationship between the object and the society is understood the artefacts remain a mystery. They create the walls of a labyrinth that can only be navigated with the key of interpretation. Unfortunately, this has often been subject to the political or religious opinions of the time, creating a false view of history which clouds our attempts to find the truth.

As a result, most archaeologists have no definitive reconstruction of past societies beyond the scientific analysis of physical remains. This materialistic view of anthropology has recently been challenged by the advent of the relatively new science of archaeomythology. With this tool we can trace the echo of ancient cultures in the myths that have been passed down to us. This approach to the past leads to a more precise exposition of their world, and one that is independent of the particular philosophy of the inquirer.

Archaeomythology was first applied in 1876 when Heinrich Schliemann used Homer's poem as a guide to discover the fabled city of Troy. Until this time, the city and the epic poem had been regarded as mythical. Schliemann was ridiculed when he suggested that mythology could be as real a source of archaeological understanding as any artefact. It was his stubborn refusal to give up his beliefs that resulted not only in finding the city but also in uncovering the Mycenaean civilisation and, with it, an understanding of the growth of early Greek culture. This put archaeomythology on the road to more general acceptance[4] and nowadays many students of history rely on it to inform their research.[5]

However, the fight for recognition of our ancestors' ability to record their own lives is far from won. There are still many archaeologists and anthropologists who will not entertain archaeomythology, yet the results have spoken for themselves, for it is by using this theory that the awareness of ancient history can become a science: by analysing the peoples of Old Europe in this light, we can piece together their story.

From our modern viewpoint, it would seem that the peoples of Old Europe made a sudden appearance in the archaeological record. Their artefacts and buildings first appear around ten thousand years ago. This semblance of an arrival from nowhere is misleading as it simply marks the start of a period of settled communities. An established agricultural society has the time and space to create objects that would, quite simply, be too cumbersome to be carried by nomadic peoples. These objects survived the passing of the years in a way that the few possessions of a people who regularly moved large distances could not. The sophisticated style and decoration of these earliest remains, together with an evidently fully developed mythology, allows us to infer that the majority of their culture was inherited from their nomadic past.

The development in the technology of clay firing that accompanied this settled existence preserves a great source of imperishable items, cultural and sacred as well as utilitarian. Expressions in stone also provide an unchanging record of their activities. Probably Old Europe's best documented, but paradoxically least understood, contribution to our world was the building of large stone monuments, a testament to the deeply spiritual times in which its people lived. What is less well known is that they left behind other sacred sites. Some were huge terraformed constructions, others only a glade by a river. All had one thing in common: they linked the earth to the divine, creating the bedrock upon which is built our present day spiritual heritage. Whenever we attend a religious service or read a fairy-story, glimmers of these roots colour every word. It is a hidden vein of wisdom rarely revealed, a chimera of truths through which the energies of the universe cascade into human cultural manifestation, touching and teasing our minds with its latent message. To comprehend how deeply these roots go, we have to understand the people who created the monuments and shaped the myths that surrounded them.

The longevity of some of these archaeological sites humbles our concept of antiquity. Nestling between the mountain barriers of the Transylvanian Alps and the Balkans are vast numbers of mounds, or 'tells'. Each tell is composed of the year-on-year layering of the debris of ordinary life. These extraordinary ancient dwelling places show a continuous development over four thousand years. This is not uncommon in this region: there are many examples of similar periods of habitation.[6] From them it is possible to reconstruct a detailed picture of their world.

Amongst the exquisitely glazed vases recovered from such tells, and from other archaeological sites, are a large number of figurines. Animals, anthropomorphic and natural, are represented but by far the most common are humanoid, thirty thousand of which have emerged from the small proportion of tells that have been excavated. Moreover, only a very small percentage of these are male figures, the majority being female. Coming from all regions and periods, their shapes fall into well-defined categories most of which are not in the least naturalistic. In this remarkable collection of figurines we can begin to see why the legacy of the Goddess was the root of the culture of the builders of the Dingle Diamond, for it is in the goddess figurines that the basis for the legends of the 'people of the Goddess' are laid.

If the design and symbolism of the goddess figurines that have been unearthed are grouped according to their similarities, three basic types emerge. These are the representations of the triple-goddess, the single most important deity of this ancient world, a direct descendent from the first time that her form was ever carved.

Two of these types of female figurines have no face. This is important because the Goddess represents a concept. She was born out of a need to transfer an ideology from the living into the spiritual realm. To represent a face would be to entrap the deity not just as human but also as a physical object, and this she was not. It was not the stone or clay of the artefact that was deified but the concept that lay behind it, the concept that was born in the realm of the human mind. Its power is such that it remains anonymous and for this reason the Goddess appears veiled in ancient myth. This hidden mystery is still represented in our present society, for nuns (the modern priestesses of the Goddess) take the veil when they accept their vocation.

The most common of these faceless forms is a figurine with massively exaggerated buttocks. Her head is usually represented as a plain pillar, though sometimes this is in the form of a phallus, often with markings on top.[7] This is an expression of sexuality, an effigy of the divinity in which the miracle of conception is embodied. Inside her body she takes the male axiom and combines it with the female. But she is not the representative of birth, this being an act of manifestation. With her, all things have yet to be and all possibilities exist. (Diagram 3.1)

This long-necked and rounded sexual portrayal of the Goddess is later represented as the consort of the Hero, who through fighting a

Diagram 3.1
The Lespugue figurine
from Haute-Garonne in
France. Dating from
22,000 years ago and
carved from mammoth
ivory she stands just 14cm
tall.

common enemy gains her love. From this symbolism comes the oldest of love stories dating back in written form to the early Mesopotamian epics. The Goddess takes the old rituals into her body in the form of an egg, the representation of the vanquished 'serpent' of the old year and the symbol of spring and renewal. In taking the mystery of the rites of spring into herself, she becomes imbued with the power of creation which is allied with the force of the Warrior to create the wellspring of human potential. So strong was this part of our spirituality that across the world it is still remembered in the form of the Easter egg.

The bonding of the Goddess and the Warrior, in a tryst of love, is symbolised by the bull. In many cultures, including the Celtic, the bull represents the spring and our ancestors invested in the Goddess the newly liberated power of the earth in springtime. She arises from the earth to review the world, a familiar theme from classical Greek myth, and because of this she is found, in many depictions, half buried or being pulled from the ground.[8]

In every culture her form is a celebration of all that engenders life. Where she walks, flowers appear. In her young form she is the crescent moon and her colour is red, the colour of love and passion. Her mysteries are amongst the most profound in the mythical world, for she holds the key to the hidden secrets of nature.

The second type of figurine is pregnant, shown by her exaggerated breasts and belly. Her head is always either blank or covered in a veil, inferring that she does have features but that these are hidden from our sight. This hidden characteristic is quintessential to her mystery for she presides over the woman's secret, the act of childbirth. This feat of transforming the hidden forces of the earth, giving birth to the manifest, is not confined to the physical world but extends into the realm of ideas. She is responsible for bringing ideas from the realm of the mind into the physical. She turns thoughts into actions and ideas into creations. Because of this, she is imbued with the greatest of the triple-divinity's powers, control or authority over the Warrior, and it is she that represents the physical manifestation of his force. As such, a lion or leopard, as a symbol of power, often accompanies her. Paradoxically, to her is given the protection of the home and the hearth. Perhaps it was the Warrior that originally gave this protection. Like Demeter, her symbols are the ear of corn and freshly baked bread, an identification of her role within settled society. Hers is the full harvest moon and her colour is the gold of the field of ripe corn. Her form is found at archaeological sites from as early as thirty thousand BC, usually escorted by her lion warrior. In cultures from the Celtic to the Egyptian, the lion is the symbol of the summer and its solstice. (Diagram 3.2)

The third type of figurine is different in many ways from the other two forms described. She almost always has a triangle inscribed over her womb, the badge of her office as the greatest and most powerful of the trinity, one of the most enduring symbols of Old Europe. It appears on their pottery, incised on stone monuments, and on the clay tablets that preserve the earliest scripts.[9] She is the receptacle of the wisdom of sacred words recorded far in the past and the secrets and magic of the oldest knowledge are carried in her legends, speaking to our

Diagram 3.2
The Willendorf figurine
from Austria is about
24,000 years old and is
carved from limestone.
She is 11 cm tall.

unconscious. As such, she represents the mysteries of the other world, the unseen, and she presides over the dead. Her function was also to oversee all forms of worship and her image can be seen moulded into the roofs and walls of her temples. (Diagram 3.3) She alone has been given a face and although often stylised or minimalist, it is always the same. Huge eyes stare out at us separated by a long nose with no forehead and only a small chin. Her features are carefully exaggerated out of any proportion that could be called human, in marked contrast to other figurines from the Neolithic. This continuity of her expression hints that she was modelled on a real physical archetype. Perhaps her image had been passed down the generations in a direct line, faithful to the original model. So striking is this 'old woman of wisdom' that archaeologists such as Marija Gimbutas declare that it must be a representation of a mask. Masks are used in ritual when the person or being takes on the powers and the persona of another. This was the mask of a being who had precisely defined facial features, features that would make a massive impression on the human psyche. Her large eyes, long nose, sloping forehead and weak chin reach out from the past to touch a part of us that subconsciously remembers her form. Even today her features emotionally affect people.[10] From Europe to Japan her image

Diagram 3.3
Figurine from Mal'ta in
Siberia, dating from around
18,000 years ago, she is
carved from mammoth ivory

appears the same, recalling, perhaps, a racial memory of a time when this deity walked the earth.

Her realm is deep in the womb of the earth and the sacred shrines of the people of the Palaeolithic or Old Stone Age. From her all wisdom is drawn and she represents a twenty-thousand-year continuum. Her symbol appears adorning the walls of megalithic monuments such as Newgrange in Ireland. She is a provider and teacher and also the gateway into another realm. The mysteries of music and civilisation, law and justice always accompany her. The serpent, symbol of the earth force, reveals her presence and it is this emblem that represents the passing of the year.

The three aspects of the Goddess present us with three faces. From the Three Muses of Greek myth to the Three Marys who accompanied Christ, the triple-goddess is an archetype that has accompanied our passage through time. Her three aspects represent the journey through life and each of her forms has been, or will become, the others. In this sense there is no division between the three: they are all one. The young virgin has yet to be; she has no eyes, for the future has not yet come to pass and all things are possible within her. The old wise one has already been; her bright eyes can see her past life, which is still the future for her younger forms. Only the pregnant goddess exists in the here and now; with her blindfold firmly in place, she does not easily reveal what is already determined. Future, present and past become locked together in this single mythology.

The resourceful way that this matriarchal philosophy unifies so many divergent facets of our human condition was achieved by creating a duality between the parts and the whole. Although each of the representations of the Goddess is unique, together they portray a dynamic view of a single being and this is the symbolic meaning of the triangle. As the first geometrical shape that can be constructed inside a circle, the triangle has transcended the extinction of Old European society and appears, today, in its role as a representation of the Trinity.

The triangle is also an emblem of her capacity as the moon goddess with the three aspects of the Virgin, the Mother and the Wise Woman represented by the young crescent moon, the pregnant full moon and the disappearance of the old moon. The most familiar personification of the phases of the moon today is in the symbol of the Virgin Mary, deity of the spring, who is often accompanied by the crescent moon.

In these figurines, made by the direct ancestors of the Tuatha Dé Danaan, we have our first glimpse of the nature of the triangles in the Dingle Diamond and, perhaps, it is also a seasonal representation of the triple-goddess. If this is the case, then from their society we can glean an understanding of the roots of the Irish culture and the nature of the Irish monuments that they built.

The minimalist naturalism of the figurines is a mark of a well-developed belief system. At its root it has a universally understood iconography. A similar symbol familiar to people today is the Cross. If we try to categorise this symbol in isolation from the culture that surrounds it, we have little chance of discovering its meaning. The same is true of the figurines of Old Europe. It is only when we compare other figurines exhibiting similar features that we can find, from their relative positions in buildings, shrines or graves, what they stood for. We find that many of the large-buttocked 'egg' figurines have spirals and chevrons inscribed on their bodies and are found buried in sacred groves and temples. The pregnant form is often found by the hearth or buried under a dwelling where she protected the family. The old wise goddess has been unearthed in her thousands in tombs and graves, showing her role as a portal to the other world and a means of transformation. These forms were common across Old Europe from different periods and were familiar enough to be reduced to the abstract.

The figurines form a symbolic link covering fifteen hundred miles and twenty thousand years of diverse peoples crossing cultural and geographical boundaries, using a form of shorthand that would have been recognisable to anyone of their day and remaining essentially unchanged over this time. The society that prospered under her triple-face was equally strange to our modern eyes, for it was not patriarchal but matriarchal. The implications of adopting such a seemingly inconsequential viewpoint are immense. Like a barometer it informs the reasons for, and the nuances of, every cultural action. Nothing in society is left unchanged and it seems to transform the mundane into an impossible ideological atmosphere, forcing investigators to doubt their findings, preferring instead to try and impose a 'primitive-savage' interpretation on what was a remarkable collection of peoples.

In the remains of the ancient small city of Catal Huyuk, a characteristic Old European city in Anatolia, the skeleton of an old woman was unearthed beneath the floor of one of the largest and most impressive shrines. She was draped with jewellery made of shells and buried with the care that would have been accorded to a revered ancestor. This tradition of burying the matriarch of the family under the floor of the dwelling is found in many parts of Old Europe. It points to the establishment of the family as a community of females, the line being passed down from mother to daughter.[11] The Hamangia cemetery on the Black Sea coast contains many hundreds of burials, of which some three-hundred and fifty graves have been excavated. Often these graves are self-contained units with up to thirty skeletons in each. The work done on blood groups of individuals buried here shows that adult females and children who were buried together were related, whilst the males were not.[12]

The dwellings, especially in towns and small cities, were clustered around a large central building with its shrine. The many clay models of temples and shrines found as burial goods (an enduring testament to the gentle rites that were performed) attest to the importance of the shrine and its association with women. One such model temple from Zarkou in Thessaly, dated around 5000 BC, shows an open altar surrounded by nine female figurines.[13] The mother-daughter relationship and the significance of women in temple and religious activities, along with the large number of figurines that have been recovered, is the most direct evidence that these societies were matrilineal.[14]

Among all the evidence for a matrilineal society, nothing has ever been discovered to support the belief that these societies were hierarchical. None of the graves excavated bears any resemblance to the later rich burials of chiefs or kings. There is no evidence that one part of the society was more favoured than any other. Indeed the houses in their towns are remarkably uniform.[15]

What stands out amongst the grave artefacts recovered is the care and attention that was paid to the dead person's contribution to society. Many women are found buried with ornaments, symbols not of wealth but of respect for a loved relation. The copper and gold of these decorations is the first evidence of a technology for the extraction of metals and it is significant that they were employed in the observance of the spiritual life. Both men and women have been found buried with tools for wood-working, clay decoration and weaving, pointing to tasks that society considered important. There is no direct evidence for weapons or the materials of war. Despite this, archaeologists have argued that these tools could have been used for military purposes but it would take a great deal of imagination to see these remains as the burials of soldiers. There is no record of rank or privilege, or evidence of the spoils of war that are common to all later military burials.

This leaves us faced with an important question, one that is especially poignant in today's world: how did this stable and long-lived society organise itself in such a way that war and conquest, as well as the unequal distribution of wealth, were unknown? This is no small curiosity in the history of our existence as the size and longevity of this civilisation dwarfs any other, including our own. It is the standard by which we can judge our own development and, in this light, the last five thousand years of slaughter, greed and war become the anomaly. To decipher this riddle we must examine the great rule that governed the actions of the people who built this civilisation: the role of the Goddess in the cycle of the year. (Diagram 3.4)

The circle of life stares out at us from a thousand ancient stones. From old manuscripts and clay tablets it serves to remind us of another way of looking at time, an alternative to the linear concept of a beginning and an end. For thousands of years this was the hub from which humanity had measured the rhythm of life and like the pulse of the earth itself, it has been the heartbeat of our evolution. The circle has another dimension, one of synthesis of the movements of the cosmos and the seasonal changes on the earth. This ability to 'draw down the heavens' was explored by the many peoples who lived within its circumference and is the main characteristic of the many monuments they left behind.

The evidence clearly shows us that these peoples were united by the paradigm of a non-linear time frame. This belief still lingers in the lore of many tribal societies such as the African Bushmen and Inuit tribal shamans. It appears in the oldest of Celtic and Nordic legends and in Native American myth. Amongst the Basque people of the Pyrenees it is still part of a living tradition. The wisdom of the stories presents a universal panorama of a time when everyday reality was created by the circle of life turning in the consciousness of people. In these legends it is often referred to as the 'earth dream'.

In the diverse lifestyles of these widespread and loosely related peoples, we meet our first exotic concept. The cultures of many older civilisations are relatively homogeneous; for example, Egypt was

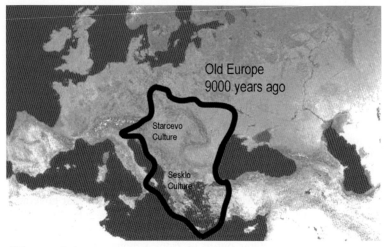

Diagram 3.4
The Starcevo and the Sesklo, the two major cultures at the heart of Old Europe.

united not only by a communal belief system but also by a style or canon of culture.[16] Paradoxically, during the long existence of Old Europe there are examples of many contemporary cultures living close to each other, exhibiting different artistic styles yet all displaying a nearly identical spiritual ideology. Perhaps cultural identity and individuality had become a celebrated objective to be encouraged. Maybe we are seeing for the first time that humans did not fear difference nor feel the need to make 'unlike' peoples conform. It may be that the 'norm' that we hold so dear in our own era did not exist for the peoples of Old Europe.[17]

The symbol of the Goddess, the triangle, originated many thousands of years before the peoples of Old Europe settled to pursue an agricultural way of life.[18] The symbol occurred later in such diverse cultures as the Irish Celts and the ancient Greeks. Even today, the triangle appears in our folklore and is a common analogy in our religious texts. (Diagram 3.5)

In Old Europe we see this potent symbol representing the real power of the feminine, occurring most often as the pubic triangle decorating the womb of the figurines. The very heart and soul of a woman's divinity is revealed in this, for the triangle represents not only the womb but also the power of birth, death and re-birth.

Today, we are encouraged to view this gift as little more than the use of the body of a woman as an incubator. The miracle of life has been removed from the womb and reduced to the role of dividing cells and chemical reactions. A woman is no longer considered to be the source of this power, a role inherited by the male God for whom the woman is just an instrument. Women have been disinherited from every function they once performed and this makes it hard for us to see the simple truth that was evident in Old European society.

If we can cast off for a little while this great alienation that has become accepted in our time, we can begin to glimpse the real power behind it. To the people of Old Europe it appeared, through the miracle of childbirth, that a woman does not die: her own flesh and blood walks the earth, she is as immortal as the turning seasons.

The male has a different gift. Nothing of him appears to live on. He is to die and in dying, it seems he ceases to exist. In order to share in this immortality a male has to be reborn in the womb of a woman, so the deity, although female, is in fact the source of both sexes. This observation is complicated by the role of the male, who through sexual union gives the female the power to reproduce. It is the male who carries the spirit that initiates the process. The same principle applies to the Great Goddess and the cycle of the seasons.

Every aspect of Neolithic life was mirrored in the turning of the year, so we see in the first calendar the form of the triangle as placed over the womb of the Goddess. Their year was divided into three seasons, spring, summer and winter, with each corner representing a part of the cycle. The two upper points cover the ovaries and represent spring, the young goddess symbolising conception, while summer is represented by the pregnant mother celebrating the mysteries of birth. Lastly, closest to the vagina, the third point represents the portal into the physical world uniting the two mysteries. Both conception and birth occur through this passage and the Great Goddess presides over this.

The male plays a vital role in this calendar. This is shown by the symbolism of his lover, the young goddess, who is often depicted with a parallelogram on her chest. This shape is made up of two equilateral triangles and represents the coming together of the male and female,

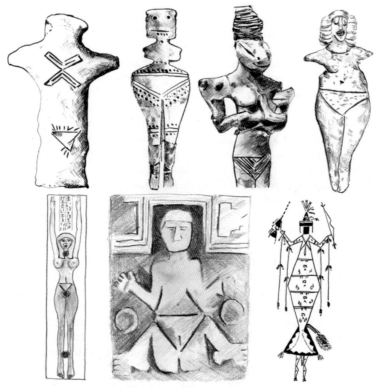

Diagram 3.5
The pubic triangle as a universal symbol of the Goddess.
From top left: 5500 BC, East Balkan; 5000 BC, Central Europe;
4000 BC, Babylon; 1500 BC, Iran; 525 BC, Egypt;
Circa 1000 AD, Ecuador; Historical, Native American.
Art work Ursula Tramski.

the point of conception. A male has, as his first experience of the feminine, his mother, followed by his lover who replaces the mother figure. The mother of his children follows and lastly, before he goes on his uniquely male journey into the other world, he sees the wisdom of the feminine in the old woman that has created his future womb.

In this way, the twin triangles, or lozenge, complete the calendar of the turning year and introduce the correct placement of the male principle into the year of the Goddess. We can now begin to fathom the language and meaning of the symbols of the Neolithic and hence, of the Dingle Diamond. The representation of the male part of the year is traditionally the eagle and in many calendars it categorises winter, symbolically the time of birth of the male child. The child, born in a cave in the mountains, grows to be the Hero-Warrior of legends, many of which were old before the earliest glimmer of civilisation. It is through him that the Goddess liberates herself and society. The four cardinal points mark out the equinoxes and solstices, and the triangle and the lozenge weave around each other as the earth and the seasons weave around the movement of the planets and the stars.

The sacred geometries mapped out in the circles and henges of the people of the Goddess in Old Europe are there to precisely bring together the solar and heavenly dance with that of the earth. It is more than doubtful that the popular explanation of these geometries as being a method of tracking time is entirely true. In the myths of the Goddess are clues that point towards something fundamental to human society, clues that suggest that something greater than mere time-keeping was being explored. In any case, not one of the myths refers to a method of keeping time or even of using such a large timepiece. However, the associations with the symbols and sections of the year is an almost universal phenomenon and has been faithfully preserved, occurring in every corpus of myth including that of the Christian Church.

The holistic way in which these beliefs of the Old Europeans, and of the Upper Palaeolithic peoples before them, weave together the Warrior and the Goddess aligns closely with the natural world and displays an understanding of the earth in terms of geometry. To the peoples of Old Europe, these figures created the circle of the year around which humans dance. They divided the circle into regions of significance: spring, summer and autumn all mark points on its circumference. Thus we see an emerging sacred geometry. It is this geometry that is embedded in the Dingle Diamond, its points representing the seasonal changes in the cycle of life.

Since the triple-goddess represents aspects of the moon, the earth and the seasons, this sacred geometry reveals the part played by the heavens incorporated, bringing together the male role of the sun and the female role of the earth.

The three goddesses form, within the circle, an equilateral triangle. When the male god, with the narrative of the underworld of winter, is included, the geometry becomes the four points of a square or a diamond, the hieroglyphic icon of the Goddess and, incidentally, the main glyph used to name the Sybil. The round temples and circular sacred areas built in their hundreds by the peoples of Old Europe, as well as the henges and stone circles, all celebrate this sacred geometry. There can be little doubt that the triangles and diamond shape of the Dingle Diamond is a direct descendent of this tradition

Such theories were thoroughly explored by the peoples of Old Europe as an inherent function of their belief in the Goddess. Perhaps more than anything it is this spiritual aspect of the earth that is a passport to understanding the monuments they left behind. In the simple harmony of their form, they point to powers that affect our minds and souls and in this they draw down the power of the heavens into the womb of the earth. The Dingle Diamond, like many other monuments, graphically portrays this action. The midsummer light is drawn down into the earth and is used as a source of power to replenish and renew the land and the people.

As above, so below. This sacred and arcane formula of a later age was, to the peoples of Old Europe, a natural understanding of the world order. By belonging to the one dream, the earth dream, the world and all that was in it was created and maintained. The Goddess was all things material: the clay of the earth that rose and shaped itself, becoming pregnant with life, the spirit-imbued egg from which all things were born. Throughout this, the animating principle is the instigator that incites the earth's potency flowing through the land and through each one of us. Between the material and the spirit swims all of creation.[19]

Through the lens of this perception, the peoples of Old Europe saw in themselves that which they considered their special gift as humans. This was the harmony of mind, body and spirit through which they interpreted and shaped the earth energy itself. There is an echo of these teachings in Eastern martial arts and meditative practices, and the Buddhist philosophies are the direct inheritors of this knowledge. The balance of these forces was echoed in the geometrical ratios of the feminine triangle and the masculine cross, and it was this balance that gave humanity a choice of paths to follow. It was a conscious and informed choice: they could create and they could destroy.

Seven thousand years ago among the woods and mountains of central Europe, the people of the Goddess started to put these ideas into physical form by building large circular enclosures. These were surrounded by a bank and ditch and were often of considerable size. Called 'roundels', the structures were built on carefully selected land that was in some way considered sacred.

The alignment of posts or stones as key markers in their construction points to their use in an astronomical context, and the relationships between groups of roundels, standings stones and sacred hilltops tells us that the earth itself was being measured. This moulding and transformation of the earth to mark and celebrate geometrical patterns is a universal phenomenon. From the ancient civilisations of South America to the dragon lines of China and Japan and the stone alignments of Europe, people have felt the need to mark a perceived 'force' within the earth, linking it to celestial events. In Africa and the Middle East, in North America and Siberia, the story is the same. The building of churches, temples and mosques on the same holy sites creates a link through the centuries, bringing the purpose of the past into the life of today.

The four cardinal directions were marked out on the circle of life as the four quarters of the year. At the north, south, east and west were the gates that bore the appropriate symbol for that part of the year. Wooden posts or standing stones marked the divisions of the circle into other patterns or pointed out alignments to other roundels and sacred sites. Each locale had its place in creating the pattern of a ritual landscape that criss-crossed the land. Hills, mountaintops and other prominent features played an important part in the alignment patterns and the sacred life of the peoples of Old Europe. Hills were often transformed, their tops flattened and ritual objects and animal bones have been found at these terra-formed sites.[20]

A great deal of effort must have been spent on their construction. Archaeologists maintain that millions of man-hours went into their building. Silbury Hill in England is estimated to have taken eighteen million man-hours to build over a period of one hundred and fifty years.

The Neolithic builders also made wooden henges similar to roundels but instead of a ditch there would be a ring of wooden posts, sometimes many metres tall. These wooden henges were common in Britain and long after the abandonment of the roundels of Europe and the retreat from the rituals connected with the earth, British builders continued to update and modify their henges.[21]

Despite repeated attempts by archaeologists to explain these sites as military forts, living places or burial grounds, there is little or no evidence that their use was anything other than ceremonial; indeed we find a great deal of evidence pointing to their use in ritual activity connected with certain times of the year.[22] For instance, at Dolauer Heide, an enclosure in Germany, a votive pit produced symbols of the Goddess' rule over death and re-birth. Hourglass-shaped clay drums decorated with triangles and vases with round owl-like eyes were found mixed with white chalk balls representing the egg.

The discovery of the temple of the Dingle Diamond showed that the sacred ground on which the roundels were built did not have to conform to a circle. As long as the places of power marked on the earth corresponded to the four cardinal points of the solar year and included the three sides of the lunar year, then the temple would function as if the circle of the year had been drawn around these markers. This allowed the builders to cover large areas. It is as if these sacred places were the telescopes of their day, the size of the 'lens' increasing the power of the temple.

The mystery of death and rebirth, the existence of love and beauty, even the manifestation of spring were central to the life of the peoples of Old Europe in ways that we can only dimly perceive in today's world of alienation from nature.

These aspects were unified to create a synthesis of world and spirit that was celebrated in the sacred enclosures. Both are mysteries that come from, or exist in, a realm other than the physical. It was this linking of geometry (literally, 'the measurement of the earth') to the world of the spirit that gave a definite form to the rituals of the Neolithic peoples.

Something had opened a portal in the human mind. Across its threshold had entered a new concept, that of the Goddess. This had allowed humans to envisage another existence, allowing a break with a way of life that was tied to the material realms, merging with the rhythms of the physical world. Through its eyes they had come to believe in another world that became just as real, a world that had no physical existence, the world of the concept.

Mother

The elaboration of the themes of the Goddess uncovered in the tells of Europe and the Middle East show that these people were seeking to determine the boundaries of this new world and the human being's place within the limits of this conceptualisation.

These explorations laid the basis for the myths and archetypes that are part of our psyche today. Through this process new forms of expression of the link between the mortal and the spiritual were explored, a bridge between the corporeal world and the world of the concept. Language and mathematics merged with shamanic practices and art, and the result was a practical and spiritual understanding of the earth and a way to harness the unleashed potential of the concept.

For the thousands of years that Old Europe existed there were no laws and no religious institutions. There was no need for our ancestors to feel flawed in respect to each other or subdued by the forces of the cosmos. Instead, people explored those aspects of the heavens and life on earth that were non-physical, finding ways to incorporate them into their daily lives so as to enhance and beautify the earth dream. This created a world of the spiritual without the incursion of worship or religion, and most importantly it allowed individuals to make such choices of their own free will. These societies grew and evolved in a natural and gentle way, making, over the succession of aeons, a paradise of the world.

The way that the roundels and other sacred sites fitted in with the cyclical nature of the seasons and the movements of the celestial bodies, especially the sun, drew the newly awakened power of human potential into a binding tryst with the earth dream and guided its actions. The success of this social system was so great that its achievements became the cornerstone of all later culture. The evidence points to this civilisation as being the root of the complex and holistic understanding of the way the world works. Acupuncture, *feng shui*, the Taoist philosophy of life and an understanding of death and re-birth look likely to have their roots here. It is also likely that these first 'civilisers' established agriculture, pottery and writing across most of their world, spreading into the Americas and Africa. It is not unexpected to find that they had a very old tradition of sea-faring. Unsurprisingly, many people have argued that these later so-called 'high' civilisations must have had their origins in the distant past. From the lost boat people to the fabled continent of Atlantis, alternative thinkers and the modern interpreters of archaeological history have searched in vain for evidence of such a 'high' culture. The many books describing the search for this lost world are quite correct; there was a great and noble civilisation that pre-existed all others, yet this was no mighty walled city, peopled by experts in war and technology; instead, we find a society that was peaceful and un-dramatic.

Then, about six thousand years ago, in an echo of the myths of the destruction of Atlantis, a cataclysm occured. The world of the Goddess was destroyed and the rule of the God, the rule of the sword and the king, descended upon Old Europe. The twist drew a veil over the origins of our spirituality. The nightmare years had begun.

The Dingle Diamond, built by the fabled Tuatha Dé Danaan, can be seen as a 'temple of light'. In an exact geometrical ratio, the science of the day drew down the sun (the male aspect) into the story of the triple-goddess. It is part of an unbroken tradition that goes deep into the history of a time when humans were matriarchal, peaceful and curious. The cardinal points of the compass and the sacred places of the earth had a profound meaning, one that is perhaps lost to us today. But the Goddess and the geometrical forms of her temples have not always been a part of our world. She came into being at a particular point in history and along with her the strangely powerful male force appeared in our minds. The respect and concern with which these ancient peoples treated their rituals and holy circles tells us that the forces that they were invoking were powerful and perhaps dangerous. To the citizens of Old Europe, who practised these techniques, it was of the greatest importance that they were kept alive. Their peaceful, almost idyllic society seems to have rested on such foundations. If we can discover the origins of the triple-goddess we could, perhaps, find out why this was so and how it affected their culture. The question of the origins of the Goddess seems to bear directly on our patriarchal and violent world of today, and perhaps through the link in the temple of the Dingle Diamond we can rediscover, in the message and the technique they used, an answer to our own problems.

Two pertinent questions arise from the mystery of Old Europe: who was the curiously featured 'old woman' of the triple- goddess and when did she originate?

Chapter Four
Goddess

"There are forces out there of which even we have no knowledge."
Queen Elizabeth II

The Goddess nestles in the kernel of the mystery of the Dingle Diamond in just the same way as her church appears at the physical centre of its geometry. Her names are recorded in the hills, her rituals in the myths and as the seasons change, so facets of her story emerge in the landscape, a pageant of history held briefly in the spotlight of the sun. We can follow the development of this paradigm back across time and, as we have seen, her people can be traced back to the valleys of central Europe. It is a culture that has a long heritage. A remarkable set of cave drawings from fourteen thousand years ago attest to the existence of the Goddess at Cogul in Spain. Here, nine female forms representing the three aspects of the Goddess dance around a naked male figure. Twenty-two thousand years ago, as far away as Ma'lta in Siberia, her three forms were carved from ivory. Twenty-six thousand years ago she was modelled from clay in the Czech Republic. Thirty thousand years ago she was carved in stone in France. Yet this heritage marks only the flowering of human culture, the first shoots of which made their appearance many aeons before. The key of the Goddess opens a portal that leads us back behind this dazzling period of advancement on a direct trail of recovered artefacts, deep into a silent past. She accompanies us further than the figurines and sites prized by the archaeologists, for through the lens of her cognisance we can begin to see the origins of a remarkable incident in human history: the occurrence of consciousness and the creation of art.

Few people ever question the validity of art or even stop to wonder why it is that, in a world where market forces and profitability rule every nuance, it has been given a value and importance that far exceeds its apparent usefulness or productivity. In more cosmic terms, art is an extremely interesting phenomenon; it can change the very fabric of our universe, rearranging and aligning matter to make new creations where none existed before. Whatever we can imagine can be described and even created. Art is a channel that expresses the unseen world of ideas, allowing them to manifest in the material world. Language, music, religion and science, all stem from this unseen irrational landscape and all cause effect and change in the physical world. And so we prefer a certain colour on our walls, or spend hours contemplating the arrangement of paint on a canvas, or read meaning into dots and lines of ink on a piece of dried plant, or any of a myriad of strange activities that confirm art as integral to every single action we take. It is doubtful whether human culture could even exist without its light, for it is the matrix on which all our social interactions and institutions are based. Yet there was a time in our history when there was no art, no paintings to grace any walls, no sculpture to rest in sacred shrines, no symbols to read and no music created.

It was the longest of times, this time before art. Tens of thousands of generations came and went without any obvious sign of innovation. Then around forty thousand years ago it ended, and it did so with the suddenness of a breaking wave. The relics and artefacts that survive from this time are a testament to the swiftness of the change and are tangible enough. Individually they would seem to be insignificant objects — the appearance of a few carved stones, scratches on mammoth tusks or red ochre in deep caverns. Nevertheless, art's singular occurrence suddenly and radically transformed every facet of human existence. However, despite the importance of this episode we know almost nothing about the events that provoked its appearance. Conventional understanding, in the form of the received history of human beings, collates a catalogue of novel 'finds' associated with this period highlighting the dramatic technological achievements of the epoch, but it is silent when pressed for an explanation as to why, or how, this one peculiar expression, that more than anything else delineates a human being, came to be. Just to lift the skirts of this collection of facts and explanations reveals a mass of contradictions, unanswered questions and mysteries, all of which serve to show that the legitimate story has yet to be told.[1]

Our history is a riddle of serendipity and in deciphering it we hold a key that can unlock our understanding of what we have become. The almost obsessional focus on understanding and manipulating the material universe that is the hallmark of today's world can obscure this key, for it is hidden not in the mechanisms of the atom but in the workings of the mind. Nevertheless, the material side of archaeology is an essential ingredient in creating a picture of the past. Towards this end humanity has recently made huge strides, especially in recovering and cataloguing the artefacts our ancestors left behind. But they are not the only source of information. We also have the written form of the thoughts of people who lived thousands of years ago. Once written down they became permanent bridges to our era, opening up a treasure-trove of knowledge. A few of these manuscripts have been translated and are accessible but many are still waiting, like a secret code, to be cracked. The span of these bridges is short. The earliest of these snapshots appear only five thousand years ago. We would have to reach back twice as far as this to touch the first settled communities that gave rise to many of the oldest myths we have today. Fortunately it is possible to see beyond this 'barrier' for though some of these ancient writings are factual accounts and give us only a cameo of the society that created them, others are myth and legend, embodying a far more ancient oral tradition. A myth is not just a simple story. It contains a great deal of symbolism, symbolism that has not changed since the first act of art appeared and it can retain its meaning and its potent effects on our minds over many thousands of years. Myth, however, is a very difficult language to decode for it depends upon understanding and interpreting the symbolism used. Even when linguists have successfully deciphered an ancient script they do not always comprehend the meaning of the stories, especially references to gods, spirits or creatures that are other than human.

One problem with this process of decoding myth arises as a result of the dogma that governs our present day view of the past. It is commonly held, in the orthodox scientific community, that history leads like an arrow towards the evolution of an ever more sophisticated humanity at the apex of which we now stand, a view that has hindered our vision for it lends credence to the erroneous idea that the ancients were, at best, naively fanciful and incompetent chroniclers, often invalidating their work; the gods and mythological creatures that appear in the old

65

stories are often derided as wishful creations of an unscientific mind. It is a rigidly human-centric way of looking at our development. Such a paradigm of evolution, from the savage to the sophisticate, creates an artificial ladder of cultural development and implacably refutes any reference in myth and legend to other intelligent beings that could have been rivals in our story. It appears that this tide is now beginning to turn. Very recent discoveries have produced scientific evidence that shows that the earliest societies and cultures were not created by human beings alone. For the first time, this presents a basis for a new understanding of the meaning of the language of myth. It provides a cipher with which we can reinterpret the stories, and the results are a revelation. Evolution has produced other conscious entities in the world, entities that for the vast majority of our existence shared and shaped our reality, and these beings left an indelible footprint within the stories and legends that make up our present collective body of myth.

We were neither the first nor the only thinking beings to have walked the face of this planet.

One of these non-human conscious beings is so new to science that it has only just been given a name — Homo florensis — but it seems to have been isolated and had little global impact on the human race. The other non-human relation was more widely distributed and its interaction with humans had far more profound implications. Only in the last century or so have we become aware of this early 'brother' of ours, and only in the last twenty years have we recognised this species as our equal. We have come to realise that some one hundred thousand years ago, spirit and culture flourished in a world inhabited not only by the mammoth and the sabre-toothed tiger but also by our cousins, a people like us, yet not like us. We have come to call these people Homo neanderthal.[2]

It has been the work of science and linguistics, of mythology and of those who still practice the old traditions that has allowed us to open the door on this past and like a child, stare mesmerised through the crack. (Diagram 4.1)

Researchers tell us that it is solely from artefacts, the stone tools and carved bones, that they can glean any idea of the form that the lives of these ancestors of ours took, and they can deduce a surprising amount of data from these bare bones. For example, stone tools can be examined at high magnification for scratches and cuts; the type of wear on a

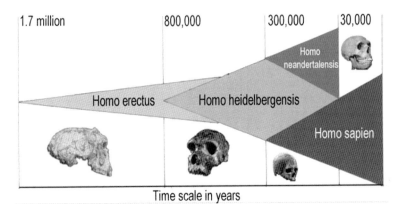

1.7 million | 800,000 | 300,000 | 30,000

Homo
neandertalensis

Homo erectus | Homo heidelbergensis

Homo sapien

Time scale in years

Diagram 4.1
Homo neanderthal and Homo sapiens evolved together from a common
parent.

tool can be analysed to find out what it was used for; cutting edges can
be matched to cuts on bones and can give us a precise picture of the
methods of hunting and food preparation. If the results of such archaeological processes are matched with an analysis of molecular residue left
on these stones, we can even tell what they were last used for. These
modern archaeological methods have allowed ever more complex questions to be asked and the answers are often unexpected, leading to further revelations. Archaeologists find that by far the most common use
for sharp-edged stones was to work and shape wood, but what was
actually made and the techniques that were used are a matter of conjecture.

Throughout the vast epoch that was the Palaeolithic or Early Stone
Age, whether made by neanderthal or sapiens in Africa or in Europe,
these stone tools were very similar and, enigmatically, were made to a
pattern that rarely changed, a sort of universal toolkit found at nearly
every Palaeolithic site that has ever been uncovered. Such monotonous
assemblages of slightly varied, flaked and shaped stones glory in the
name 'Mousterian' after the French valley in which they were first
discovered.[3] Despite the widely diverse communities that existed and
the huge geographical range involved, not one stone tool from this
period breaks with this tradition. (Diagram 4.2)

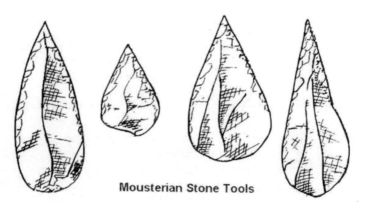

Mousterian Stone Tools

Diagram 4.2
The stone toolkit of the Palaeolithic was common across the globe.

Only when we step outside of the field of archaeology can we make more sense of these Mousterian tools. For example, when they are compared to the stones of a more recent stone-tool-using society — the Aborigines of Australia, for example — we find that though the majority of edged stones are similarly simple tools, the craftsman used them with complex techniques to craft sophisticated objects. Without such comparisons it would be all too easy to fall into the trap of thinking that simple stone tools were a product of a simple society. Even so, nothing in this arsenal of archaeological science can tell us anything about the beliefs or worldview of the people who used the Mousterian tools, and only little about their society and its structure.

This is the paradox of archaeological remains: we can find out a lot about the practical side of human existence but little about the society. The further back in time we go, the fewer the remains and, moreover, these scarce finds become more degraded and harder to interpret. The idea that we are actually dealing with human beings as complex and as involved as ourselves disappears, and we tend to look back across the gulf of time and see only a primitive, somehow lesser, human being.

We cannot put the jigsaw together if we rely exclusively on physical evidence, so we draw upon characteristics of modern human societies to infer some of the basic behaviours of our forebears. It is likely that we sat around communal fires and told stories whilst our elders sat in huts and constructed beliefs. From these beliefs and stories evolved the archetypes of our present myths, which are still told or recorded today by different cultures.

As the archaeological evidence fades, the mythological grows. Kings become gods and armies take over worlds, mountains move and floods cover the face of the earth. Each story has a kernel of truth but the embellishments give us a differing view to that of the physical re-mains. This is where comparative science comes into its own, the sci-ence of archaeomythology, the balance of myth and archaeology.

Myths build up like pearls layer on layer and have always been re-told in the light of a new age. Long after the original meanings of the actions in the tale have been forgotten, the stories remain. The myth, or legend, is to be ignored at our peril for it is an aspect of the reconstruct-tion which allows us at last to see the tribal life that surrounded the stones and, even though we cannot see any further back than the origins of the artefacts themselves, it is here that the creation myths of our world originate.

The first clues to a people with whom we can feel a sense of identity start appearing around forty thousand years ago. The change in the archaeological record is staggering: among the cleavers and hand-axes of the Mousterian era there appears a plethora of new implements; furthermore, these have fashions and styles of diverse geographical influence that contrast dramatically with the monotonous regularity of the previous one hundred and fifty thousand years of stone tools. Along with these new tools appear the first true art forms: statues, figurines, cave art and symbolic icons. It is almost as if a creative genius had been liberated in the psyche of Homo sapiens. Neanderthals did not share in this wonder; not only do they fail to make the changes but they disappear from the archaeological record entirely. Within a relatively short space of evolutionary time they become extinct.

The extinguishing of Homo neanderthal is one of the most mystery-ous and emotional episodes in Palaeolithic history and it was a process that led to the emergence of a recognisable human culture from which evolved the framework of human civilisation. About thirty thousand years ago, the end of the opening movement of human history had come about. The world had changed. It was a moment of crisis in history and the stage was reset to bring Homo sapiens into the limelight as the single most important actor: the whole of our very human history was ready to unfold. The story touches us at a most basic level. Not only did Homo sapiens share habitats and cultures with the neanderthals but, also, there is the possibility that they were complicit in their demise. Whatever happened to the neanderthals is a subject that has a great deal to say about our humanity. Was our first act as inheritors of the earth the destruction of the only other intelligent non-human peoples that have ever existed?

For one hundred and ten thousand years, Homo neanderthal and Homo sapiens had been living, if not tooth by jowl, certainly next door to each other. They had shared the same tools, the same environments, the same hunting and gathering methods of existence and yet had remained essentially unchanged in themselves. Recent analysis of DNA from neanderthal and human bones has shown that the populations did not seem to mix or interbreed with each other. Yet the neanderthals must have been a constant part of human society and they would have played a large part in the development of our consciousness, their presence influencing our own legends and mythologies.

Perhaps amongst the first manuscripts there is a dim echo of the neanderthals' presence. These writings originate in the first townships, whose traditions lead directly back to an earlier form of society, and it is probable that the myths and legends of their citizens would still contain the lore of these nomadic predecessors. The myths of hunter-gatherer societies have been shown to be amongst the most stable and enduring of all human societies and such an echo would be connected to the neanderthals by a thread of twenty thousand years of hunter-gatherer continuity.

In such a script recovered from the ancient Sumerian civilisation of five thousand years ago are disturbing references to another form of being, called the 'Martu' by the Sumerians. A part of this legend purports to be from an even more ancient epoch. Within the clay tablets, this older legend is incorporated into a story of a wedding between one of the Martu and a Sumerian maiden.[4] If we can accept that the Sumerian scribes were faithfully recording an old legend, then we can interpret the myth in the light of a time when neanderthals walked amongst us. The Sumerian description may well be one of the few portraits of the neanderthals that we have.

'Now listen, their hands are ruinous, their features are those of monkeys. They are the ones who eat that which the Goddess has forbidden and they do not show her any respect. They never cease in roaming the land and are an anathema to the sacred places. Their ideas are confusing and they cause a great agitation in the mind. They are clothed only in animal skins and live in tents, exposed to the wind and rain. They can not properly recite the holy rituals. They live in the mountains and ignore the places of the Goddess and know not how to worship her. They dig for truffles in the foothills and eat raw flesh. When they die it is not given to them to cross to the land of the dead. The Goddess gave them colossal limbs so that no one could threaten them and she invested them with an authority that accompanies them like a shield. Endowed with fearsomeness like a raging lion, like a rampant bull they can subdue all their rivals.'[5]

There is a sense of hostility in this brief text: it is almost a warning clarifying certain dangerous characteristics of the Martu. It describes a fearsome powerful being, one that can affect the human mind, and it is described as being in a position of immediate authority over humans. Mixed with this are pictures of a very primitive existence, closely in tune with nature. Modern archaeology has shown that the neanderthals were intelligent beings: shell beads, animal skulls and red ochre pigment surrounded their elaborate burials; magnificent houses they inhabited were crafted from wood, stone and bone; they looked after their sick and injured and used a large variety of medicinal herbs. All of this must have had a cultural influence on our forebears and it is quite possible that, as the Sumerian description points out, the neanderthals were in some way 'in authority' over us. Perhaps they were our teachers.

Just why our ancestors recorded such detail can be understood if we compare the attributes of neanderthals and humans. The size of the neanderthal brain was on average about 1500cc, as compared to the modern human brain of about 1400cc, though it was not similar in shape — the neanderthal brain had small frontal lobes and a greater back-brain. If brain size is a measure of intelligence, then they were more intelligent than humans. Neanderthals had larger and hence probably more sensitive eyes, a better sense of smell and more powerful jaws. They would have been superior predators. Their height was similar at around 1.5 metres but their bones were thicker and heavier, suggesting that they were immensely strong, somewhere between two and three times more powerful than humans.[6] As anyone who has ever witnessed a bear in action will attest, such great weight does not mean that it is slow; the picture that emerges is one of a graceful, powerful and intelligent creature, but it would be a mistake to think that the neanderthals were prototype humans; they were not, for they were not human.

The neanderthals disappeared in a wave of extinction beginning in the east and spreading west eventually reaching their last known stronghold, the Grotte du Renne at Arcy-sur-Cure in France. There, resplendent with beads, bone ornaments and all the latest tools (termed 'Chatelperronian') they faded out of existence. The knowledge of their loss invokes a strange feeling that originally we were not alone and that the adventure of life had once been shared. In scientific terms, humans and neanderthals must have competed for the same environment. The ostensible result of this scenario would have been the relatively quick demise of the human population since the weapons and tools available to both would have been more suitable to the larger and stronger neanderthals. This did not seem to be the case. Indeed, simple logic suggests that some level of co-operation, or at the very least a mutual understanding, must have existed between them if they were to live in such close proximity for so long without one causing the demise of the other. The question then arises how, after such a long period of co-operation, could such a breakdown in peaceful coexistence come about?

There is a further mystery locked in this crucial period, one that tells us as much about ourselves as about our ancestors for it was exclusively amongst humans that the budding of symbolic art took place. At first this was a series of abstract and quickly drawn symbols — crosses or lines, shapes and swirls, maybe a system of messages to be read later by other people — but this was followed by three-dimensional representational art: sculpture.

All over Europe figurines appear accompanying cave art and complex burials. Each one is carefully crafted and small enough to be portable; moreover, they are as alike and as recognisable as are the more

Diagram 4.3
From Laussel in the
Dordogne in France and
carved in Limestone the
figurine dates from around
24,000 years ago and
stands 43 cm tall.

modern representations of Christ or Zeus. They are the first genre. These figurines, the vast majority depicting a large-breasted and heavily-hipped woman, attest to spiritual beliefs that were shared by diverse cultures from different regions. The appearance of art, music and religion attest to the radical nature of this change in society. Something or someone must have caused this sociological change in the way that humans habitually interacted with each other. (Diagram 4.3)

For the first time, humans had created a society that resonates with our own modern society and at this point culture, as we perceive it, made its appearance. Yet the bulk of work referring to this period by researchers from all fields seems to mark this change as a physical event, as if humanity had undergone some sort of accelerated evolution producing a new 'species' of mankind. This new species has even been given a name — Homo sapiens sapiens, the 'double thinking man'. What is missed in every argument is that nowhere in the fossil record can it be shown that humans changed physically at all. The flowering of cultural artefacts had its roots in our one hundred and twenty thousand years of history — whatever it was that caused us to suddenly develop had been with us all along. We came into existence with the neanderthals at our side, Cain and Abel born of the original mother, and now it seemed that the death of Abel had liberated not only our creative side but also our destructive one. Standing as an almost universal icon above these events are figurines of the Goddess, the first expression of human art and a direct link to the mythology of the Dingle Diamond.

The disappearance of the neanderthals and the appearance of the Goddess represent the two principal events of the Palaeolithic era. They not only re-shaped our culture, created art, and gave rise to human society but also brought into being the ability to translate historical events into narratives. Given the stable nature of lore and myth in hunter-gatherer and tribal societies, it is quiet likely that the story of the neanderthals would have left an enduring account within the corpus of early myth. It is equally likely that such a story would survive in much the same way as myths marking geophysical milestones — for example, the Flood. As with the Martu, major mythological chapters in the story of humanity could easily have left their imprint firmly embedded in the earliest writings, especially those tales that relate to the myth of the Goddess. These myths, when compared to the archaeological story of the neanderthals, could be read in a new light and perhaps could give us an idea of the events that lead to the appearance of the Goddess and hence to the rise of art. It is a question that can only be answered by searching the legends.

A small number of recently translated Sumerian myths, from about the same period as the *Marriage of Martu*, describe a war between the people of the Goddess and a primitive authoritarian 'people of the mountains'. In this myth, the human population of the 'wild mountains' live with another group of beings, and these are described in exactly the same way as the *Martu*. The Sumerians place these mountain dwellers in a region called Ebih. They are non-human, intelligent, authoritative and powerful, and are only subdued by the intervention of the Goddess. The story that is retold here is taken from several versions of the legend of the goddess Inana recalling her battle with the 'people of the mountains', and from a closely related epic of the Sumerian hero Ninurta, Inana's warrior. I have interpreted and combined the stories in narrative form below, retaining the essential information contained in the original myths.[7] Seen in the light of the human/neanderthal saga, it goes a long way to confirm its impact on our mythology.

Goddess

The people gathered by the mossy banks of a quiet pool where a sparkling brook broke its fall from the high bluff. The ground was damp and they were sitting on woven grass mats placed around a wide stone that made a platform from which a young woman was speaking. Her jet black hair was bound with a headband of yellow and red and a necklace of beads on her bare neck flashed in the late evening sunlight. As she spoke she held forth a slender spear, its stone point bound to the shaft with resin and leather.

"Hear the words of Inana, warrior-leader of the Black-headed People! In my left hand," she turned her palm upwards, "I hold the divine power of the Goddess and in my right, the holy *a-an-kar* spear, drenched in blood. My craft is that of battle leader, planner of conflicts. I ride the power of the lion and like a mighty bull trample my foe. I am Inana from the plains of the north and now I walk in the mountain ranges, bringing the light of the Goddess to the Tribes of the Stones."

A sudden cloud submerged the glade in darkness. Inana lifted her spear, holding it like a staff in front of her. She raised her voice. "There is a shadow over us all. It covers the mountains as the cloud covers the sun. It is the shadow of the non-people, the Ebih, they who are not like us. They dictate to us our every breath. Ever they have sought to hide our freedom from us. In my home, my tribes, too, were once as you. Once, as for you now, the light of the Goddess was persecuted by these clever guardians of our souls."

She paused to let her words take effect and then, in a more subdued tone, continued. "But they would not listen to my voice. My warriors, my lions, were spurned and the battle totem of the Goddess was cast down. The Tribes of the Stones did not come to my aid, they could not come to my aid for the Ebih bound them, the power of the mountains held them, the Ebih of the broad mountains who do not resemble other people, who are not reckoned as part of this world, held them, for the Ebih are an unbridled people, quick-witted but with a dog's instincts and a monkey's features, and their grip on your people is as strong as the ages and as deep as time."

The crowd stirred and muttered, some looked furtively over their shoulders as if they expected to be interrupted. Inana spoke over noise. "The Ebih have shown me no respect. They have not given grace to the Goddess or freedom to her people. They have cast her away like esparto grass in the wind and poured fearsome terror on her holy places."

The Discovery of the Dingle Diamond

Stepping forward, she placed her spear on the ground in front of her audience and, dropping to one knee, continued. "I have come forth at dusk and followed the signs of the Goddess to the Gate of Wonder, the long path to this meeting place that none but the holy ones know. I have come meekly, with no warriors or weapons, to petition the elders of the Tribes of the Stones. I come to speak because you are all of the Anuna, all followers of the Goddess. I ask that you listen to my plea and aid me in my trials for I will fill my hand with the soaring mountain ranges and deliver it over to my terror. Against their magnificent sides I will place my warriors, against their small sides I will place my warriors. Let me storm them and start the game of 'Holy Inana'. Let me prepare my spears and throwing sticks, set fire to their thick forests and an axe to their evil doings. I will spread fear amongst the Ebih and they will honour the Goddess and you will be free." An inscrutable look crossed her face, almost a smile, and grimly she added, "Let me set up battle and prepare conflicts."

An, the leader of the council gathered there, raised himself up and, leaning on a black staff, answered her. "We of the Emery Stone question this. Our tribe has endured the longest and we are the most resolute in troubled times. Yet we question you."

He turned to face the people and pointed a bony finger at Inana. "My little one demands the destruction of the mountains. What is she taking on? Inana demands the dereliction of these mountains! What does she think she is standing against?"

A second of the Anuna spoke. "Because of the Black-headed Men, the Ebih have poured fear on our holy places." She made a sharp cutting motion with the edge of her hand. "Because of Inana's raids, the Ebih have spread dismay amongst the devout of the Goddess. Her aggressive actions have caused dread and ferocity to be placed over this land, her arrogance cries out to the very earth. So say the People of the Flint."

A third stood. "The People of the Bloodstone see ripe fruits hanging in the verdant gardens and in luxury do the Ebih live. Under their guidance, we labour until the magnificent trees are themselves a source of wonder to the roots of the earth. Wild rams and stags roam in abundance and deer couple amongst the cypress trees. The Ebih have all their needs met."

An grimaced as if he carried a burden of great weight and, speaking slowly, replied. "The offerings and the seventh day toil demanded by the Ebih are not easily passed by. And now with your spur, Inana, the Ebih seek to instil dread and fright amongst us. The mountain ranges' radiance is fearsome. Maiden Inana, you cannot oppose them." Thus he spoke.

One by one, the elders of the Tribes of the Stones voiced their thoughts and the debate continued until the dark skies paled and bright Nabir was below the world's rim. A tall hunter sitting near the edge of the glade, who until now had remained perfectly silent, rose. He introduced himself as Ug-gen of the many tribes of the Basalt clan and in a deep voice said, "The throw has already been cast and Fate has moved. Who can stop her? The Goddess has acted and who will oppose her? For now, heaven has seduced the green earth and she has borne him a terror who knows no fear. Asag is his name, a child who knows no father, a ruthless hunter of souls from the mountains, mighty in strength and like a great wild bull he tosses his horns amongst the People of the Goddess. The Flint, Diorite and heroic Quartz Warriors will follow his lead and come raiding to destroy the Anuna and their sacred places. For them, a shark's tooth has grown in the mountains. It has stripped the trees. Before its might the Goddess is humbled. My tribes-people, it is not lying idle! Who can compass Asag's dread glory? Who can counteract the severity of his frown. People are frightened, fear makes their flesh creep, their eyes are fixed upon him. My council, the mountains pay him homage, yet I fear this will not assuage his anger."

A bright-eyed young man stepped up to the platform. Unlike the others he wore his hair cut short. "I know of one who will help us." His words tumbled out of him, eager to be heard. "He is born of the Goddess and he, too, has heaven for a father. The mountains are his home. Mighty Ninurta is his name and many have heard of his feats of strength. We of the Lapis Lazuli have asked for his help, saying, 'Ninurta, not a single warrior can be measured beside you. Who has so far been able to resist Asag's assault?' " He looked sharply at An. "This warrior of the Ebih is beyond control, he is too big, too fast. Rumours of his power constantly arrive at our camp. This Ebih's strength is massive, no weapon can be taken against him. Neither the axe nor the all-powerful spear can pierce his flesh, no warrior like him has ever been seen. The die is cast, we can not avoid our fate. Who, if not Ninurta, can aid us?"

An turned away towards the tranquil pool. "Alas!" he cried, shaking his head. "Alas!" The council broke up at the first rays of the sun and left from the Gates of Heaven with little harmony and no agreement. But Inana and a few remained and vowed to seek Ninurta.'

If the neanderthals were the masters with humans playing the role of servant or serf, then such a relationship could have formed the archetype for the many different human models of class society that we can turn to for comparison.[8] The biggest difference between this proto-type and more modern class divisions is the time scale, which becomes vastly extended. In the Middle East, humans and neanderthals had existed together for at least one hundred thousand years, a tremendous length of time for a society to remain so stable and one that we, with our view of short-lived civilisations, find hard to relate to. When it is taken into account that both humans and neanderthals went through a shared process of genetic evolution — both species arising from a common distant ancestor — then the period is long enough to allow humans to adapt genetically to the social conditions. The two groups would have been culturally and physically very distinct and there may have been little in the way of interbreeding, even if it were possible, yet their societies would have developed together. This type of genetic adaptation is not uncommon in nature — where two species co-exist, both adapt to increase their mutual co-habitability. This process is known as co-adaptation and arises from climatic, environmental, social and physical pressures on the organisms. Such genetic acclimatisation would imply that acceptance of the role of the neanderthal was 'hard wired' into our brains, a process that would occur even if there were no genetic exchange between the two species.

Unlike their brothers in the Middle East, neanderthals in Europe lived exclusively without humans until about fifty thousand years ago. Then, in a sudden surge, humans entered the neanderthal communities of Europe to fulfil the same roles as they had in the Middle East. As they spread rapidly into Europe, the rapidly increasing human population started to reach the point where it became too large for individual clans, each led by their neanderthal communities, to be totally independent. This population pressure could have forced a change upon the society as it increased in complexity and size. The human birth-rate at this time rose significantly leaving neanderthal numbers static, and this must have caused problems for the neanderthals. New methods of living and of interacting would probably have evolved from this pressure.[9] It may not have been possible for the neanderthals to continue to dominate humans without creating a definite social structure to support them. This structure is called ideology and its development can only arise between two socially distinct groups, where one group is dominant. The need for such an ideology could have led to the rise of such class forces as the concept of group identification and an ideological framework for control, probably based on religion or spirituality. One thing is certain: the arrival of art is the signpost for this sea-change.

We have a standard by which we can judge this change. If we examine the structure of the tribal society of those modern humans who did not come into contact with neanderthal/human populations, we see that these class forces were not evident.[10] Tribal structures are in themselves very stable, given that the conditions and environment in which they exist do not alter — the rain forest tribes of Malaysia, for example, still operate a hunter-gatherer lifestyle without the evidence of pottery, writing or the complex infrastructures that are the generally accepted measure of cultural advance. From this comparison it can be seen that such sociological change and development stems from a hierarchical organisation of class forces.

The changes that appeared in Palaeolithic society climaxed in a dramatic conflict between neanderthals and humans, which in less than five thousand years saw the extinction of all neanderthals, bringing to an end the long epoch of peaceful co-existence.

Whatever sparked off this conflict, it spread like bush fire and humans were compelled to fight. Very probably it was the last thing they wanted to do. After the passage of so many aeons of living in harmony, the neanderthals must have seemed a little god-like, beyond question by the likes of human beings. Perhaps this was a time when, in our eyes, the gods did indeed walk the earth and they would have been a formidable enemy. In facing such odds, it is likely that those who met this challenge would have had to do so in secret and in closely-knit groups. If they originated as an underground movement, then it would have been a tendency that sought to unite all humans in a common cause.

To successfully achieve these aims would require a high degree of organisation and communication between different human groups. Signs that could be hidden from the neanderthals would be needed to impart information over time and distance. These signs, as an emblem of the struggle, would have indicated to the knowledgeable the times and places where a meeting, or perhaps an ambush, would occur. Such signs were a very real form of magic, invisible to inquisitive neanderthals or uninitiated humans. Writing, the alphabet and the translation of intent, far from starting out as simple tallies as many anthropologists believe, may have originated out of necessity in the thick of a struggle where weapons of mass destruction were military tactics and the dubious ability to die for a cause.

At the heart of the human ideology would have been a common structured belief, one that could contain and embrace novel concepts.[11] The pillar on which this could have been built would have been spirituality. That spirituality did exist many aeons before humans carved stones can be clearly seen in the carefully laid out neanderthal and human burials with the red ochre decoration and grave gifts. With such a foundation it only remained for this belief to encourage the conception of warfare. In this way, the authority of the neanderthals and the ideological compulsion they held over the human mind could have been effectively contested. The creation of this tanist, or rival, was such a momentous task that it required the invention or discovery of a new form of deity, one who would be powerful enough to challenge the gods who already lived. It needed the Goddess.

Calling a deity into being is a difficult achievement, a deity by its nature having no physical presence, but by using art in its most powerful form, combined with social and political control, the result was a complete success. The link between the unconscious and the material world was forged with social change, but the medium through which it expressed itself was art.

The Goddess would have been the ideal that gave humans the strength and courage to succeed, the power behind the rebellion imbued with all the conditions required to achieve victory. Yet she was only the ideological force in the struggle, a spiritual channel, if you will, that opened the eyes of humans to new horizons. The ideological had to manifest on the physical plane. A practical and very human agency needed to spring from the limbs of the new goddess, one that could achieve the ideals of its practitioners. This agency was the creation of the Warrior, a new class of humans that become possible only through the doctrine of the Goddess. The Warrior and the Goddess occurred in tandem, indelibly linked at their inception by the need to answer to the neanderthals. This presupposes a considerable mythological environment. Direct evidence for a complex body of mythology emerges suddenly with figures such as the Lion Warrior' from Stadel Cave in Germany, dating from 30,000 BC. These pieces would have needed to be portable, easily transported away from danger or hidden from the keen eyes of the neanderthals. This fundamental act of carving an icon on stone contains the root of the power of stones in religious history.

The creation of the Goddess becomes the precondition for our spiritual reasoning, the impetus for our churches and mosques, temples and sacred groves and, conversely, why we have wars and torture, starvation and greed. The initiation of the Lion Warrior becomes the mode by which humans accomplish these aims. This one epoch of human history serves not only to define us but also to inform us about the origins of what we treasure most about ourselves, our ability to conceptualise and create. The history of the carved figurines of the Goddess takes form in these years and the question of how this came about becomes a vital one, not only for the religions of the world but, perhaps, for our very souls.

It is noteworthy that the force that precipitated the end of the neanderthals was female and creative. This speaks volumes about the dark and light sides of the Goddess that we see in later interpretations. It gives us a direct link to the later written mythologies of the earliest civilisations, forming a connection between the unrecorded myths of an earlier age and those of today. It also informs us that the prevalent view of the female principle as passive and submissive was not evident in its origins.

The Goddess was the inspiration behind the new warriors that emerged to meet the challenge of the powerful neanderthal fighters. Organised, disciplined and fighting for the cause of humanity, it must have seemed to the neanderthals as if a madness had manifested in their world. The power and terror of a body of humans (for it would have been likely that both men and woman would have fought in the front line) fighting together, perhaps under the orders of a priestess, can be easily overlooked in our own jaded epoch of wars but thirty-five thousand years ago it would have been the equivalent of possessing a nuclear weapon, a superior tactical advantage that would have left an enemy defenceless.

The Sumarian myths continue to describe this conflict between the Goddess and the peoples who lived in the Ebih. It breaks out into a war, one so terrible that the whole of human society is riven, and out of the ashes a new social order is born. In the course of this struggle the first hero appears. He is given the motif of the lion and instructed by the Goddess, becoming her consort. This hero is able to weld the individual human warriors into a cohesive force and for the first time, we see the origins of warfare and its results.

N inurta was sitting at his ease on a reed mat, talking of the world and of the hunt. Around him the laughter and chatter of a festival, celebrated in his honour, echoed through the forest. The bison hides of his tent were draped with richly woven hangings, a bright fire scented the air with cedar and the smoke spiralled into the blue sky. The midsummer dance had just started and people were twisting and weaving in a graceful pattern to the beat of drums and the soft tones of the reed whistle and bone flute. Ninurta arose to join them, the beautiful Bau, leader of the hunt, by his side. At that moment a messenger from the Anuna burst into the glade. She stopped by the edge and threw her arms wide open, a traditional greeting, and after she had recovered her breath she walked to the centre of the dance and spoke directly to Ninurta. The dancing stopped and a hush settled on the celebration.

"Hero! The People of the Goddess appeal to you. Because of your father, Enlil, because of your superior strength, they are looking to you. Since you are strong, oh hero, they are calling for your help saying, 'Ninurta, not a single warrior can be measured against you.' The Anuna want to advise you about the creature called Asag. There have been consultations with the Ebih. They are seeking to put an end to the Anuna and Asag has taken up their cudgel. Its face is deformed, its location changes continually and day-by-day this terrible force adds new tribes to its cause."

The fire seemed to die down as the messenger continued with her news, her voice punctuated by gestures, her eyes riveted on Ninurta.

Goddess

"You, Antelope of Heaven, must trample the mountains beneath your hooves. Ninurta, son of Enlil, who so far has been able to resist the Asag? It is beyond all control. No warrior like it has ever been created against you, Ninurta. The Asag is your dark brother. It is against you that it fights, it avows to have your soul, you who reach out towards the earth's divine powers. Splendour! Jewel of the Anuna! You are a bull with the strength of a bull. You are a lion with the ferocious roar of the lion. This Asag, though, he is clever beyond all mortal cunning. My Ninurta, whose form the Goddess blessed, what is to be done?"

Ninurta gave a great cry so that the heavens echoed and the very rocks trembled. His face darkened and all the joy of the celebrations flew, like a bird, far away. He stood before the people of his tribe and beat his thighs with his fists. When he spoke it was a single word. "Enough!"

On that day, Ninurta rose and went out to battle. On that day the earth became dark. The Anuna trembled and disappeared over the horizon like sheep. On that day the fate of the Ebih was sealed. Ninurta rode the eight winds with his people gathered behind him. In his hands he wielded the *a-an-kar* spear and the mace. His warriors, armed with clubs, surrounded and beat to death the Ebih wherever they were found. His shaman moved an evil wind to a hurricane — irresistibly it went before him, stirring up the dust, filling up the caves of the Ebih. Under a rain of fire, Ninurta reduced the forest to ashes. Even the earth put her hands to her heart and cried out pitifully for mercy.

Many of the Tribes of the Stones followed Ninurta's lead and in less then three days he had a war party. Without allowing his enemy to prepare for his arrival, he led the warriors through the Ebih's lands. He killed their messengers in the mountains, he crushed their huts and flooded their caves. He tied together their hands with hirin grass so that they beat their heads against the rock. But not all went in Ninurta's favour. The lights of the mountains no longer shone forth and many young men and women never danced the springtime's return. The world became filled with sickness. People gasped for breath, they were ill, they hugged themselves and cursed the earth. They rued the day the Asag had been born, for the hero caused a terrible poison to run through the lands and his lion heart smiled.

The Discovery of the Dingle Diamond

The Anuna were organised. Their messengers crossed the mountain trails bringing news of the conflicts, thus Inana was acquainted with every movement of the Ebih and their leader, the Asag. The reports were not all favourable, for though Ninurta had managed to inflict mortal blows on the Ebih, he had not managed to halt the rampage of the Asag. Inana was worried and informed Ninurta.

"Hero, beware!" she said, concerned. "You have battled gloriously in the thick of the Ebih. Those of the Ebih whom you have killed are Kuli-ana the Dragon, Gypsum the Strong Copper, the Six-headed Wild Ram, Lord Sama-ana, the Bison Bull, the Palm Tree Lord and the Seven-headed Snake. Ninurta, you slew them in the mountains."

"But, hero, do not turn again to do battle as terrible as that. Do not lift your arm of the smiting weapons, do not bring the young men to Inana's dance. Ninurta, do not go to such a battle as this, for the Asag is waiting for you in the mountains. The Ebih were not organised, you took them like a hunter. They were not united, for the power of the Goddess was not with them. The Asag is a different matter. It is cunning beyond all human standards." She stepped close to his side and taking his hand in hers, spoke softly. "You who wear the horn of the moon, who is great beyond all measure, I am full of fear for you, for this time you will not equal the Asag. Ninurta, do not take your war band into the mountains."

But Ninurta, very wise, rose from his contemplation. He shook his head. "This is not a game that I can leave, Inana." Looking up, he glanced towards the glade where the clatter and chatter of preparations for war could be heard. "Your council may be fair, but I can not take it. For good or bad I have my own fate to follow." And so saying, he turned and stretched his legs to join the warriors.

Pressing his advantage he went into the Ebih's lair in the vanguard of the Anuna. And there they met the Asag. It leapt to the head of the battle wielding the stump of a tree for a club, laying to the right and left and leaving a terrible carnage of broken bodies. It was a mad dog attacking the helpless, dripping with sweat on its flanks. It roared at the land and tore the flesh of the earth, covering her in painful wounds. Behind it, leaping and dancing with the frenzy of the fight, came its war band. Ninurta's people were routed and in terror they fled. None, it seemed, could stand against this mighty warrior. The Anuna flattened themselves against the rocks. An was overwhelmed and he crouched, wringing his hands against his stomach. For three terrible days the Asag and his warriors roamed the slopes seeking out the Anuna. The lands of the north wind were reduced to nothing in the whirlwind of the storm. Its people were finished. They had no solution.

But Ninurta was not daunted. He howled at the mountain and flailed about in every direction, seeking the Asag. And like a bird of prey, the Asag looked down angrily from his lofty home. He commanded the lands to be silent and a great quiet fell upon the battlefield. Then, without ceremony, the two magnificent warriors faced each other across the silent land. Ninurta approached his enemy. The Asag approached his enemy. The struggle was fierce, the earth herself cried out. But the Asag was the stronger, and knew it. A smile broke out across its inhuman features. With a swift movement, it swept Ninurta off his feet and hurled him across the plain where he fell awkwardly, taking a few moments to struggle to his knees. It seemed as if he was finished. But Ninurta had unhooked a bone throwing-stick and had picked a slim leaf-shaped blade bound to a stout piece of ivory. He raised both over his shoulder and looked once at the Asag. There was a blur of motion. Nobody moved. Then the Asag abruptly staggered and looked wonderingly at the ivory blade sticking out of its gut as if by magic. The Asag's terrible splendour was contained, it began to fade. Like water, Ninurta shook it; like esparto grass, he uprooted it. He pounded its sides and pierced its liver with his dart and, piling its body like a heap of broken rock, he struck off its genitals. And thus Ninurta conquered the terror of this Ebih.

In the mountains, the day came to an end. The sun bade its farewell. Ninurta wiped his brow and washed the blood from his clothes. He sang the song of victory over the Asag's body and gathered the elders of the Tribes of the Stones about him.

"From this day forth," he told them, "do not refer to the Asag. Its name will be stone, its entrails shall be the underworld, and its valour shall belong to me. The Ebih have been humbled." He turned towards Inana who had stood by his side in the thick of the battle. "I have done all this in the name of the Goddess. For you, now, the mountain meadows will produce herbs, for you they will make ripe fruits. Let the hillsides supply you with rich perfumes: cedars, cypress and box. For no-one else shall the mountain make wild animals teem. You have become an equal to the Ebih. Maiden Inana, you have great powers. May you be exalted!"

Inana looked at him and smiled. The leader of the Black-headed Folk and the organiser of battles smiled at Ninurta. "Great Hero, whose word is like the lion of his heart, you have not fixed the destinies of those warriors that you have conquered. And those that have aided you, you have not decreed their lot. What shall be their fate? Who but you can proclaim it at the head of your warriors."

Ninurta studied the faces of the assembled Anuna. He spoke first to those who had fought on the side of the Asag — the People of the Emery Stone and the Diorite; the Limestone clan, dreadful in battle; those of the Basalt and the bewitching Granite peoples; the Quartz tribe who caused lightning to be directed against him; the Flint and the Obsidian, whose battle cries had caused terror; the trampling Feldspar and the fierce Slate. Ninurta addressed them thus:

"Since you aided me not and caused me harm, your names shall be lower than the lowest. The people will use you as a servant. You will be broken and chipped. Your portion will be the smallest and your place the last. There has been too much killing already; in my mercy I will not have you killed. You will be content."

Then, turning to those of the Tribes of the Stones who had joined his side in the thick of the battle, he said, "You who have suffered the most, whose young men will no longer dance at the festivals of the year, to you I shall give exultation. Amethyst! Carnelian! Lapis Lazuli! You shall be considered great amongst the Anuna. Your names will ring throughout the ages and every person will glorify and treasure you. You are raised up. Where the Ebih once were, so you are now."

Inana was well pleased and went from there with her black-headed warriors of the lion. She travelled to the mountains and addressed those who still remained there. "Oh Ebih, who live in the mountains, hearken to my words! Because of your elevation, because of your height, because of your attractiveness, because you wore the holy garment and reached your soul up to heaven, you did not grant grace to the Goddess. In your arrogance I have brought you low. You are no more. I have put tears in your eyes and lament in your heart. Birds of sorrow are building nests amongst you."

Raising her voice so that the mountain echoed with her power, she decreed, "From this day forth I have changed the age-old rituals. I have moved the old ceremonies. I have imposed my victory on Ebih. No longer elevated, no longer revered, you shall live as all live, in the heart and mind of the Goddess." '

The act of rebellion that humans were compelled to engage in was born of strict necessity — always the mother of invention. The Goddess fulfilled all the needs of her people. She drew them together, organised them and gave vent to their expression and in her final form, cut the umbilical cord of worship that the neanderthals had imposed. The result was nothing short of revolutionary. The Goddess had been unleashed and her power was such that those who could adapted to contain her or they became extinct, and with this extinction died the neanderthals and a way of life that had lasted for over a hundred thousand years. With this loss of the guiding principles of life (ever present in the shape of real beings) Homo sapiens, or at least those who had been in contact with the neanderthals, were cast adrift and for the first time were free to create the world as they saw it, and they saw the world through the eyes of the Goddess. The social forces that had been contained by the link with the neanderthals were un-shackled and any restraints were lifted. Humans needed to unite and the Goddess drew them together. They needed to identify with a strength that could make the break from neanderthal authority, and this they found in her character. They needed to adopt the powers of the earth for their own culture, and the Goddess opened the door. From her came all things that we now consider as human from kings to builders, sha-mans to farmers. She was united with the spirit that flows through all things and was, in a real sense, the final creation of a doomed species.

It was not the Goddess herself who fought the new wars but her warriors, armed with faith and dedication, faith in the movement's leaders and their ability to plan conflicts, and dedication to the cause of the Goddess. It is likely that the neanderthals, strong as they were, had no adequate response to a collective body of methodical and dedicated warriors, willing to fight and die for a cause that was seemingly sense-less. Incapable of organising and paralysed by the brutality they be-came the prey. Hunted to extinction they were mute witnesses to the birth of warfare.

Without the neanderthals' influence, settled societies, human tech-nologies, our religions and hierarchical organisations would have been impossible. It was the unique combination of these cultural advances that gave us the world we have today. With it came our need to follow leaders, to enslave others and fight wars, but this was not the only price that it exacted, and perhaps here lies the root of the feeling that we have of searching for something lost which we have now unknowingly striven to recreate.

It was not pride that prompted Demeter, mother goddess of the Greeks, to declare her mysteries to have been the saviour and civiliser of human kind. She refers, in true goddess style, to a phoenix born from the ashes — the ashes of the neanderthals and of the old ways. The phoenix carries the arcane knowledge of the Goddess, and contains the seeds of agriculture and the arts and the essence of an organised and ordered society bound together by a mythological tradition. This phoenix was born in the Middle East, where humans and neanderthals had existed together longest, and she flew away to nest in the mountains of the Caucasus and the valleys of the Danube in the heart of Europe, the place of the first agricultural communities. But as the Greek legend of Pandora's box clearly outlines, once these forces had been released they could not be called back. This double irony is the mystery in the heart of the spiritual — the destructive forces of war allied to the creative principle of art. It is the icon of the Goddess and the Lion and the mystery of the birth of the serpent from the egg, the story of death and rebirth, of loss and gain. It is the story of the Goddess and her journey into the underworld to rescue her daughter from its grip, and it gives us an answer as to why the Goddess always has a dark and a light aspect. It was into the very caves most sacred to the neanderthals that this human essence descended on her mission of rescue. In the darkest reaches she gave birth to the spirit of humanity, and this spirit was the tool she used to change the world. On returning, she had to sacrifice her age-old lover, the neanderthals themselves. As they died, so in their place rose her new creation, the Lion Warrior. The wheel had turned and a new social force of immense destructive power had been unchained, not necessarily for the worst as from that same destruction a transformation came about.

Before the Goddess, humans had lived under the control, benevolent or otherwise, of a more powerful being. There was no such thing as society, only race and lineage, only the individual or the tribe. The concept of the Goddess gave us our society with all that we arrogantly call our own. The price was the murder of our elder brothers and their loss has been our ever-present drive, the impetus that makes us eternally restless, ever seeking and so inventive.

The origin of the Goddess was in the form of the neanderthal, and here we have the answer to the features of the 'old woman' in the triple-goddess of Old Europe, discussed in the last chapter. Recent work rebuilding the facial features of neanderthals (based on the forensic reconstruction of the skulls of murder victims) has given us a modern and graphic example of her ancient form. Her long nose, weak chin and low forehead appear, as if by magic, under the skilful art of the scientist. It seems that the neanderthal is the ancient role model for this type of figurine, a form that has been faithfully handed down from generation to generation. Here, too, could be the reason why this particular set

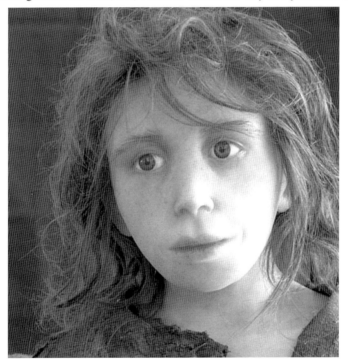

Diagram 4.4: The features of a neanderthal reconstructed from the skull of a young woman by Elizabeth Daynes and the University of Zurich.

of features creates such an impact: it is the physical emergence of something long buried in our racial memory. (Diagram 4.4)

The loss was probably more than purely physical, for it is likely that the neanderthals had a close relationship with the powers of the earth. Anthropologists point to the migratory and hunting habits of these people and, except for caves and other sacred sites, their lack of permanent dwellings. As they appeared first on this earth they could have been our teachers and prophets, interpreting the ways of the earth and guiding our perception of it. Our myths are full of stories of power places around which were constructed sacred sites, many of which survive still as holy places telling of a tradition that was once universal.[12] Perhaps neanderthals could physically see or feel these forces that humans could not perceive. The echo of their knowledge was passed down in shamanic tradition within the framework of the earth Goddess belief.

The Dingle Diamond is located in one such place of shamanic power, a place where the earth forces and their relationship to the changing seasons have been measured and used to direct and control this energy. The builders were people of the Goddess and their tradition and heritage were a direct link to the society that grew out of that first ever war. Through them there is a connection to another way of looking at our world and with the knowledge of the Palaeolithic neanderthal extinction and the rise of the Goddess and her lion warriors, a fresh understanding of the human condition and our seemingly irrational fixation with spirituality can be seen.

Before we can decipher the secrets that we inherited from these creatures, we need to understand the dual-edged weapon that was the Lion Warrior. For this force, once released into the world could not be withdrawn. It was a power that built our world, but it was also a destructive influence that tore into society, uprooting and savaging anything stable. The Lion Warrior was, however, tamed and shackled for a very long time and thus, for a while, the forces of war and greed were subdued and diminished. Just how this was done is the story of the Lion Warrior.

Chapter Five
Lion

"Hail, thou god Tem, who comest forth from the Great Deep, and who shinest with glory under the form of the double Lion-god."
Egyptian Book of the Dead.

From their inception thirty thousand years ago until the present day, the Goddess and her consort, alone of all the icons that humans have used, have retained their original meaning and mythological status. Amongst the myriad of beasts and creatures found in human art across the aeons, these two symbolic forms have remained essentially unchanged. Around their story hover the legends of kingdoms and empires like moths near a flame. Many writers have commented on this uninterrupted central theme in human mythology and have devoted their time to identifying its source.[1] The conclusions that they have reached have allowed us to do little but wonder at its simple motif and its universal appeal to each generation. It is hardly surprising that the understanding of the true meaning of this phenomenon has always been referred to as 'the mysteries'. These were secret initiations, jealously guarded by a barrage of occult wisdom and obscure references, usually in the form of religious ceremony.[2] Those scholars who have endeavoured to penetrate the veils have been rewarded by an incisive illumination of the nature of our universe. It is fascinating to find that nearly every 'great philosopher' has been a student of such lore. Some, like Isaac Newton, who devoted much of his life to the esoteric doctrines, even found answers to questions that became the bedrock of modern science. Others, for instance Jesus or Buddha, endeavoured to blaze a trail into the enigma of life and death. It is likely that the inquisitive nature of all human thought, and the ability to rationalise the world of the seen and the unseen, stems from the story of the Lion Warrior and the Goddess. It is certain that the rise of human culture originated with

Diagram 5.1
Various portrayals of the Goddess associated with lions from different epochs of history.

the extinction of the neanderthals and the beginnings of such conceptual art.

As discussed in the last chapter, the Goddess arose from an experiential requirement that humans had to break away from the dominance that Homo neanderthal held over us. She always carries around her person, or adorning her robe, the symbolic representations of human achievement: music and the arts, hunting and planting, law and judgement — all have separate icons, and all are practical vocations that emanate from her very being. But not all her symbols are as easy for us to interpret. A testament to her power made manifest are those images of her form that commonly appear with lions at her side, a relationship that has been one of the most enduring of all human portrayals. Accepted as an emblem of the Goddess, the association between the nurturing feminine principle and the aggressive male strength of the lion is not often questioned. It is only when her relationship to the Lion Warrior is understood that the implications of her lions become clear. (Diagram 5.1)

The lion has represented kingship, commonly with a military connotation, in every culture and epoch. It was the 'Lion of God' of the Christian Church militant and also adorned the banners of Ali, son-in-law of Mohammed and general of the Muslim army. Effigies on the carved tombs of the crusaders, if they had died in the just cause of a crusade, depict, resting at their feet, a lion. The lion crowns the Judaic kings and lions dance with David and Solomon in the temple. The Roman goddess Cybele was drawn through the streets of Rome on a chariot pulled by lions. Hera, the wife of Zeus, rides on lions as do numerous other Greek and Persian goddesses. On the great Akkadian seal of 2200 BC, the Goddess appears bearing weapons with one of her feet resting on a lion. The Lion and Goddess merge in the form of the Egyptian Sphinx, inscribed to commemorate the campaigns undertaken by Pharaoh Thutmosis IV in 1400 BC. The lion adorns the Mesopotamian temples and ziggurats, and statues unearthed in Catal Huyuk (an ancient city of Old Europe) show the Goddess resting on lions as she gives birth. In China, where there are no native lions, the symbolic and stylised form of the lion is seen as the guardian of law and a badge of rank. The Goddess also appears riding lions in Hindu and ancient Mayan mythology.

The usual depiction of the lion as a symbol of military power is not synonymous with the Goddess; however, she is often associated with it as its mistress or queen and her affinity with it shows that she is capable of summoning, focusing and unleashing its energies. For this reason, we find the image of the Lion Warrior amongst the earliest evidence of human art. Four thousand years before the demise of the neanderthals, around thirty-two thousand years ago, as the wave of neanderthal extinction was spreading from the east, there was a settlement of Homo sapiens in the Lone Valley in Germany. Here in the caves of Hohlenstein-Stadel they left stone tools, pendants, drawings and an unusual piece of art. Known as 'the Lioness', it is a detailed carving of a 28cm long piece of mammoth ivory. Marked with the tattoo of a hunter, this lion warrior stares at us from across the aeons, reminding us that humans had found a way to use the power of the lion, combining it with human form, to create a warrior.

Nor is this lion warrior unique; the Hohle Fels Cave in the Ach Valley in Germany produced an identical, though smaller, ivory lion warrior. This, too, dates from the time of the crucial struggle with the neanderthals around 33,000 BC. (Diagram 5.2)

These figurines are among the oldest pieces of portable art ever found, and convey to us the proposition that humans had achieved the ability to conceptualise — the capacity to create a model of something that has no existence in the real world but, instead, represents an ideal.

Diagram 5.2
Lion Warrior from the Lone Valley in
Germany found in the caves of Hohlen-
stein-Stadel. It is carved from a piece of
mammoth ivory. 33,000 BC

The Lion Warrior came into being with the Goddess. Whereas she was the repository for the concept, the Lion Warrior was the temporal and extremely practical method by which humans managed to win their freedom to develop their own cultural world. The Lion Warrior was a badge of office worn by a select group of people who identified them-selves not with their individual needs, but with a group concept. In Palaeolithic times, those who associated with the Lion Warrior created the first institution that human beings had known, and it seems likely that this was, to put it into modern terms, an army. For the first time, humans were organising their society using these collective groups. Those who could control the ideology also controlled the institutions and, in wielding this power, they were able to shape the nature of their society. The key question was who controlled the army. The Lion was the axe before which the old order fell, but it was also the channel through which the new way of life would be manifested. (Diagram 5.3) The power of the Goddess, the wellspring of human potential, is behind the concept of the Lion. Near Galgenburg in Austria we find her, contemporary with her warriors, carved in limestone; with her left arm raised, she is dancing the sacred dance of the earth.

These figures — the Goddess, crucially accompanied by the strength of the Lion Warrior — represent what are probably the most significant and earliest symbols of a spiritual belief. Having been created, they passed unchanged through three hundred centuries of human history and still, today, emerge as universal symbols and are especially connected with royalty, or with our rulers. These two archetypes are the substratum of all human thought patterns. From them emanates the combined opposites that philosophers refer to as the dialectic, recognised as the basis for cognitive thought. The concepts that branch directly from the Lion Warrior and the Goddess are familiar enough to us. The Chinese concept of *yin* and *yang*, the physical and spiritual nature of humans, intuition and rationalisation, science and art, logic and inspiration, male and female, theory and practice, the earth and the sun — the catalogue is practically endless, yet they all essentially come from the same root.

The Goddess held the source of the concept approached by art and language. But there was other knowledge that, since the death of the gods, needed a home where it could grow and be preserved. The first form of this knowledge was extremely ancient, handed down by shamans and soothsayers from generation to generation. It was a holistic knowledge of how the earth functions, the complex interactions of energy that form the matrix of life and give rise to sophisticated ideas of medicine and healing, that was the legacy of the neanderthals.[3] It could be said that this 'old knowledge' is our true spiritual heritage, unpolluted by deities or gods. The second form was a new science, the observations of the stars and the movement of the planets and, most highly prized of all, an understanding of the seasonal changes in the procession of the year. So the trinity was formed: the goddesses of birth, of wisdom and of the impulse for life. These sisters became part of the repertoire of human knowledge, the framework over which the ancient world was stretched, creating a holistic unified philosophy.

For the people of the Neolithic age it was important to assign the

Diagram 5.3
Dancing Goddess from
Galgenburg in Austria.

conceptualisation invested in these figurines to visible tribal lore. The three faces of the Goddess represented different aspects of a vibrant and vital daily life, reminding us of the three pillars that make up our essential humanity. This process of transmutation — the realisation of the potential of the Goddess — required human intervention, and this took on different sociological forms. The divisions that existed in the tribal life of the people of this time were created from these forms.

They were qualitatively different from ancient tribal patterns in that they were informed by the Goddess and instituted by the Lion Warrior as complex and organised institutions, the hallmark of which we recognise today as 'civilisation'. The models of the Lion Warrior are a reference to a past that is no longer remembered, but they describe why the myths that surround the triple-goddess relate not only to her rank and position, but also to well-defined socio-economic divisions. The link between the human act — this ability to participate and build structure in society — and the concept invoked by the Goddess was contained in the symbol of the lion.

Over the course of the next few thousand years the cult of the Goddess became established across most of the globe, but it was her relationship to the power of the lion that was the key to the kind of society that flourished under her. It can not have been a gentle period in history, for societies take time to adjust to new conditions and these conditions amounted to a complete revision of human history. All that stemmed from them was new and untried, for something that had not existed in the human mind came into being at this juncture, a concept that had not arisen in all the aeons during which the neanderthals had flourished. It was the concept of war and it filled the vacuum left by their demise, creating a duality from which came an impetus that would ultimately be destructive if allowed to reign unchecked. This was the real meaning behind the ancient Sumerian references to the divine plans that had to be recaptured and restored to the seat of power. Such divine instructions may have been a guide, but it was the arrival of art, of the ability to conceptualise, to struggle and die for a cause that was quite literally an aesthetic, which was the real divine intervention.

It was the act of grasping this ideological weapon that was the source of the conflict in the society following the successful conclusion of the war with the neanderthals. As the mythology of the Sumerians relates, the struggle left a power vacuum in the new society and the methods of the old order needed to be re-established, with human beings taking on the roles of the now vanished neanderthals. These roles were the simple practical offices which when imbued with 'power' could create the new world that was the Neolithic, but it took the might of the Warrior at the beck of the Goddess to institute them. The 'lion warriors' — in modern parlance, the army — were a power in their own right, and once invested with the collective strength of an institution they were not easily controlled. The Sumerian legend of Ninurta relates that once the power of the Anzud bird (who represented the wisdom and lore of the neanderthals, and who held the divine plans) had been returned to the Goddess, then the warrior Ninurta, having seen the plans and in full knowledge of his new found power, sought to blatantly take on the Goddess and rule the world. The Goddess retaliated and in this instance defeated and subdued the Lion Warrior, so restoring her power.

This popular part of the legend is complete and is called 'Ninurta and the Turtle'. The turtle was a symbolic agent of the Goddess and has since been used as the representative of the Goddess in many myths, especially those from the New World and the Far East.

After the war the Mountain lamented the loss of the Ebih. In her pain she cried out to the Goddess saying, "my daughters are gone and my sons are no longer with me. What is there to love me now? The authority of the Ebih has vanished. They were a cedar that was rooted in the other world, its leafy crown my wide shade. My voice, my security; they are not here any more, who will take me by the hand?"

Inana heard all that was spoken by the lonely mountain. She saw the chaos in the mountain's soul and she was troubled. Once again she turned again to Ninurta, her lion, for help.

"Hero," she said, "what now for the people of the mountain? What now of the black headed warriors? The authority of the Ebih is gone, the divine link to the otherworld is gone. The people no longer know their way through life. Even the spirits of the ancestors are restless." She placed her hand on Ninurta's shoulder and spoke softly into his ear. "Go into the Mountains, oh peerless one, and there you will find the Anzud bird. She is guardian of the Uta-ulu, the divine plans. Bring her back to me and we will return the Uta-ulu to their rightful place."

At her bidding Ninurta, the greatest of heroes, travelled for seven days until he reached the valley of the 'Gates of the Otherworld'. There, in the Pine Tree, he found the Anzud bird. Its beauty had no equal, its plumage was as bright as the day and its eyes as dark as the starlit night. Around it were seven chicks all with gaping beaks waiting to be fed. Ninurta put aside his mace, he put aside his spear and on his knees he addressed a hymn to the bird.

"Anzud Bird, guardian of the Gates of the Otherworld, messenger of the divine plans of Uta-ulu, you who are the path that once lost can not be found. Why have you flown from the Goddess to hide in this tree?"

And the bird replied: "Cruelly you have treated me, Ninurta. Your mace has gouged my flanks and your dart has pieced my liver. You shook me and buffeted me and piled me up like broken rocks. I let slip the knowledge of the secret marks. The divine plan I let fall, I was stripped of the holy powers."

Ninurta was shocked when he heard these words and gave a wail. "And what of the Goddess? The sacred learning, the Uta-ulu, have not fallen into her hands, she can not exercise their authority. She can not live, like the Ebih, in the otherworld. The mountain cries out for your loss, and chaos is in the minds of the people of the Stones."

As Ninurta watched the bird drove its long beak into its side. Again and again the beak thrust deeply, each time drawing a fountain of blood which the chicks swallowed gleefully. As the Bird fell dying she said, "take you, Ninurta, hero most cruel, one of my chicks and return with it to the sacred places of the Goddess. There the Uta-ulu will return to the otherworld."

So Ninurta did as he was bid, and the bird and he together went back to Inana.

Inana was delighted with the hero and honoured him duly. "Hero! No other Ananu could have acted so. As for the bird which you have captured, from now and forever you will have its power, for you have looked into its pitch black eyes and seen its rainbow plumage. You have the knowledge and the divine plans, all that is and shall be. The power to hold the will of the people, for good or ill, is yours. Even the Goddess will do your bidding. Yours is the place of honour and all will proclaim you their lord. But remember, you are in the hands of the Goddess."

Ninurta was not happy with these promises for his heart had been stirred by visions. Secretly he was not content, for he contemplated great deeds and, in his soul, was rebellious. His mind had set its sights on the dominion of the whole world and he wanted to take that which was not his to take. He uttered the word of power, which he had gained in knowledge from the Anzud bird. The world trembled, and for a while the balance of light and dark was disturbed. The Goddess perceived the revolt, for the chains of the earth had moved. She sent Inana to him. But the hero Ninurta refused to come out and raised his voice against the maiden. "Go from my door and from my path. For I am mighty and cannot be crossed. I wish you no harm. Go from my door."

Inana fashioned a great power, the old power of the Ebih and the Uta-ulu. This power she placed in a turtle that she made from the clays of the Otherworld. Against him she placed the turtle at the Gates of Heaven, then she summoned him forth. "Come walk with me," she said to him. "Let us talk about your design for the world." As they walked, the turtle reached out and pierced Ninurta's tendon from behind and the hero gave a great cry.

Inana feigned surprise. "What is this" she questioned? The turtle scraped the ground until it had dug an evil pit. Ninurta, who was struggling to free himself from the magic grip, managed to turn around and, as he did so, Inana tripped him so that he and the turtle fell headlong into the hole. The hero was not able to escape and the turtle gnawed at his feet.

The maiden looked down at the hero and said to him, "My authority is from the Goddess, she whom you who have set your mind to kill. You who make such big claims: I cut you down, I raise up. You who have looked at her enviously and sought her position: what has your position now seized for you? Where has your strength gone, where is your heroism? In the great mountains you caused destruction, but how will you get out now?"

And so saying she turned away, leaving Ninurta in the grip of the turtle, deep under the world.'

The legend clearly explains how the collective psyche of the societies of Europe and the East might have responded to such challenges from an organised army by instituting a form of social control, an embryonic blueprint for the legal systems of later civilisations. The supremacy of the neanderthals was re-invested in the rule of a sacred king, who was given the symbol of the lion. The sacred king was given the rank and powers of the old neanderthal gods, and the new power to organise and control people in the act of war. So the lion became the symbol of kings and chiefs and, from the Mesopotamian King Hammurabi to the medieval King Richard the Lionheart, the association was universal. Enthroned within this lion was the dark side of human potential, at once destructive and terrible. The Lion Warrior had come of age and a new status was created, that of the sacred king around whom the institutions of society grew and flourished. It was the ability to transform the roles of the warrior and the king into a creative urge that was the crowning achievement of the Goddess and her people.

For good and for ill, humans had opened a channel into the world of the unseen, and through the resourcefulness of the Lion Warrior they had created the means to make this inventiveness a reality. Life was no longer based on an unalloyed response to needs and environmental conditions. Through this channel flowed the powerful energy of the imagination and with it came the necessity to make moral choices. The harnessing of this energy for social and cultural purposes illuminates one of the most misunderstood aspects of ancient society, that of the sacrifice. In many myths there are references to the annual sacrifice of a sacred king.[4] Ethnologists have recorded the practice of killing the king at the end of his term, or when he became ill or infirm, or when a challenger to the throne was successful, right up to historical times. This has been interpreted as the practice of a merely savage people, a confirmation of their barbaric nature, a view impossible to marry with the evidence of the enlightened culture achieved in Old Europe.

As the Sumerian writing suggests, the sacred king was not free to act as he wished but was held under pain of death in the name of the Goddess. Then, in an act that represented both the end of the neanderthal and the physical curtailment of his power, the king was sacrificed to the Goddess. The whole of society took part in this act. Every man, woman and child knowingly created both a pageant of the past and a means to free themselves from the shadow of the loss of their gods. The destructive power that had enabled human beings to take life with impunity was thus held in check.

The roots of the word 'sacrifice' — so misunderstood in the world of today — stem from the Latin *sacer facere*, meaning to make whole and sacred. It is in this sense that the sacrifice of the Lion King becomes a means to restore something that had been lost or broken, so creating harmony and synthesis. The ancient Greek chronicler of mythological history, Hesiod, declared "When gods and men were sundered, sacrifice was created."

Two conditions apparent in their society were met by this ritual. The first was that the deep-rooted tendency to defer to the neanderthals,

Diagram 5.4
From the caves of Cogul in Spain, these nine females dance around a
naked man whilst his soul is carried away by a fawn. 12,000 BC.

which still remained after their extinction, was transferred to the sacred
king, leaving humans free to develop independently. The second condition was that in killing the king in complicity with the shared power of
the Goddess, the ability of any unscrupulous individual to abuse that
position of power was limited to the duration of his reign. Instead of
wreaking havoc, the energy of this novel concept was channelled into
the creative process. The remorse suffered at the loss of the gods was
transformed into a conscious expression of life.

The role of the sacred king was perfectly integrated into the story of
the year, which was intimately connected with the lives of the people.
These seasonal rites measured all of existence, and the earth power was
a measure of the seasons. The spring growth and summer harvest, the
autumn storage and winter sleep were, for these people, the source of
all life.

The Aurignacian cave painting at Cogul in Spain delineates this
relationship. (See Diagram 5.4) Created around 12,000 BC it shows a
group of nine women dancing around a single male figure. Whilst the
women are dressed in flowing skirts, the man is naked and his penis is
clearly drawn. The nine women represent the triads of the new moon,
the full moon and the old moon, appearing as young girls on the left

Lion

and as older women on the right. The last is a hag, dancing by herself. A fawn with a spirit riding its shoulders leaps away from the scene, a common motif in mythology representing a departing soul. It seems fairly obvious that the man is the object of the ritual by the women, and it is likely that after the dance, as is told in countless myths, the women will destroy him.

In this way, the sacrifice of the king symbolically united the final battles against the neanderthals with the death of the year. From the depths of time this ritualistic focus had held sway and as kings were ritually killed after their prescribed period, it made of this death something more. It transformed it into the idea that human society was able to transcend death and, in so doing, created a way to embody the most ancient of human concepts, that of the force that runs through all that lives on the earth, the cycle of life and death itself. The Christian doctrines are clearly identifiable in this story: Jesus is given the power of the lion — he too is elevated to the level of sacred king, son of the sun god, and he, too, is a sacrifice. In this way, those who follow his creed are cleansed of the sins of man.

This concept of sacrifice is completely different to the degenerative practice of murdering a victim to obtain a favour from a barbaric god, or the brutal killings undertaken by later kings to ensure the safety of their realm.

As a collective body of individuals we make up our community and, especially in today's world, we often feel helpless in the face of society's constitutions and decisions, often made in our name. It is not possible for us to live outside this structure. Perhaps it is fitting — before we utilise our own internal Lion Warrior and make a moral judgement on this sacrifice — to briefly remind ourselves of the society that the people of Old Europe created. War was unknown and conflict rare. Money and wealth, power and greed were banished. In a time when the only available materials were stone, bone or wood, these people created a sophisticated and ergonomic society. Perhaps if the vested interests of our institutions had not been passed down the generations, but had been curtailed at the end of a specific period, we would not now have a world where two-thirds of the people starve while the rest live, increasingly fearful, in fortresses of material wealth.

The role of the *sacer facere* was to fetter and transform the authority of the lion, and we find that this is the meaning of the ancient Sumerian

103

tale of the Turtle and the Warrior. This theme — the story of the Lion Warrior and the male aspect of power — has been clearly described in the ancient myths of every culture that was rooted in the neanderthal extinction. They describe how, after he has learned to fight and to kill in the name of the Goddess, the Lion Warrior takes into himself the knowledge by which this is accomplished. In taking this authority, he tries to use it to rule over others. The Goddess responds by curtailing his powers and trapping him in the earth. In this way, the male and destructive elements of the Lion Warrior of the neanderthal era were controlled by the Goddess and by society. It is a moral tale and a warning to those who might misuse the gift of knowledge that had been brought into the human world.

What of the lion that symbolised this concept of aggression and power? According to the myth it had been safely dealt with, and from studying the archaeological evidence of the culture of Old Europe it seems that it has all but disappeared. But the picture is more complex. On the southern Siberian plain by the River Angara that flows into Lake Baikal, some remarkable finds have been made. These date from about 20,000 BC and are accompanied by cave paintings depicting a hunting culture at the close of the last Ice Age. These people also understood the concept of the Goddess, for here we find all three of her forms including the seven-tiered hair net similar to the figurine found at Willendorf from the same period. The skulls of mountain lions were also found inside the remains of huts. The clay and stone sculptures of lions around the kilns of Dolni Vestonice tell us that here, also, its power was recognised. The people of the East, the region that had started the revolt against the neanderthals, had not forgotten the lion.

As the relatively settled and peaceful cultures of Old Europe began to be established, the lion appears less frequently in the myths, icons and figurines. When it does, it is often chained at the feet of the Goddess. In contrast, the nomadic lifestyle of Siberia did not undergo this cultural evolution. On the wind-swept plains it was not the feminine principle of the earth and the harvest that was prominent, but the male principle of the hunt. Although we have no written evidence of the mythology and no description of just how the Lion Warrior escaped from his bondage, escape he did. Perhaps in these northern lands the Goddess failed to reclaim her power. The myths of the Inuit peoples, those who live around this region, tell us only that there was a time of great unrest and quarrelling amongst the people. Those who did not like it left, the quarrelsome ones stayed. The Christian gospel of Saint Thomas has this compelling quote about the nature of the lion, and it is interesting to note that it can only be understood clearly in the light of the theory of the Lion Warrior: 'Jesus said, "Blessed is the lion which becomes man when consumed by man; and cursed is the man whom the lion consumes, and the lion becomes man."'[5]

It would seem that this double-edged principle was quite capable of consuming human society. Gradually, in the wind-swept wilderness of Russia, this male principle of power took pride of place over the feminine, and a rift opened in north-eastern human culture. Control of the sacred king by the Goddess and the tribe was weakened. The lion, emblem of the destructive nature of this power, was unchained and from this time forward, their world took on its nature. This gulf between the lion-harnessed and the lion-rampant does not represent two different cultures, but rather is an emphasis on different aspects of the same theme.

Pity the quarrelsome people of Siberia as their society was wrenched from their collective control by the tidal forces of the unleashed power of the lion. Even so, in many ways, this lion was still only a cub confined to these regions. It would be many thousands of years before this cub acquired the maturity to challenge the established world order.

In the Middle East, another aspect of the Goddess culture took shape. This was the appearance of large communities occupying towns and cities.[6] These first cities, founded as early as nine thousand years ago at Deh Lura Plains, are in Khuzistan Province at the foot of the Zargos Mountains in south-western Iran. Bus Mordeh is the oldest of these cities.[7]

Here archaeologists have found evidence of agriculture, irrigation, animal husbandry and obsidian tools that were traded for goods from the region and further afield. There was also smelting and trading in metals, and metalworking became very important. Here was the start of the accumulation of wealth and, with it, the first evidence of a male hierarchy found in burials and grave goods. The sacred king of the year took on the role of coordinating the complex political activities that these new social structures demanded, and with this came a corresponding investment in the secular power of the individual in society.

In these societies, the idea of the sacred king as an equal of the Goddess rose to prominence. This face of the trinity manifests in the story of the Goddess of the springtime who descends into the Underworld to reclaim her hero from the grip of the old wise goddess of the neanderthals, for she has found that she cannot function without him by her side. In doing so, she gains the secrets of immortality and returns with her lover. But the old wise goddess is the repository of the knowledge of the law, and represents authority and an imposed discipline of social conduct that stretches back through time to the ancient lineage of the neanderthal peoples and as such she can not easily let this human hero go. A gift or offering has to be made to this goddess of the earth. The gift that is given in exchange for the warrior is the all too human knowledge of love and romance, lust and sexual union, represented by a human male who also descends into the old goddess's lair. There he seduces her with his lust and love and, in return, she is forced to release the Lion Warrior.

None of the players in this most ancient of stories remains unchanged by this drama. The old goddess of the earth is fertilised by the human aspects of love and has to give up some of her powers, powers that have been invested in her since the first pre-human expressions of spirituality. The spring goddess has to die and be reborn in a new form, and the Lion Warrior is justly chagrined for his arrogance and made humble by his rescue.

The Sumerian myth concludes Inana's story with a description of her descent into the Underworld. The legend is told and retold in different guises in many religions, some more obscure than others.[8] Here it is told as the legend of the goddess Ishtar, another name for Inana. The story comes from the Babylonian civilisation, some two thousand years after the Sumerians although they, too, have their own version. Tammuz is the name given to Ninurta and the old wise goddess is called Ereshkigal, Queen of the Underworld.

After Tammuz had been taken by the followers of Ereshkigal, Ishtar wandered amongst the willows on the banks of the Tigris. She sat by a bed of wind-blown rushes where the waters of the quiet river slipped past her, and cried for him. She sang a lament, her voice filled with grief. "Tammuz, my lover, my lion, now you are not here the field has no grain. My bed chamber is empty and the meadows have no flowers." Her eyes filled with tears. "The garden has no honey and the grapes have dried on the vine. I miss your embrace and your caress. My honey-sweet, you lie sleeping in the cold embrace of my dark sister Ereshkigal."

For forty days and nights she sat, and the fields were not tended nor the ewes led to pasture. At last she arose and brushed the dust from her hair and robes. Her eyes glinted with purpose and she turned to her messenger. "I have decided that I am going to seek out Ereshkigal." A grim smile crossed her lips. "Go now and tell the people that I am seeking Tammuz and I will not return until he is found. I am determined to go to the Land of No Return, and in the caves there I shall confront my sister. I shall tread the road that is only travelled once and enter the dark house. There, where those without light dwell, those who are clothed in feathers like birds, I shall find him. Though dust is their food and clay their bread, I shall bring him back to the world."

Having told her messenger her plans, she set out towards the distant mountains once more. It was a hard path, and long. She slept by the side of the streams and ate only the nuts and berries of the forest. At last, tired and weary of the road, she approached the mouth of the cave. Around her feet wild poppies speckled the grass and two hoary pillars of rock marked the entrance. Ivy crawled up the lintel, obscuring a small, perfectly square opening. Here Ishtar rested and after washing herself from a small spring that emerged from a crack in the cliff, she put on a fresh dress of white linen and took from her shoulder bag her badges of office. A crown of laurels she placed on her head and around her eyes she smudged mascara. On her ears she placed gold rings. Around her neck she hung her beads of lapis lazuli and on her breast she pinned a butterfly broach. Carefully she wrapped her birthstones around her waist so that they hung in loose clusters, and around her wrists and ankles she put on bracelets of gold and silver. Having dressed herself thus, she took a deep breath and, bowing her head, walked into the velvet darkness.

A short way on, still lit by a faint light from the day outside, an oaken gate barred her way. It was criss-crossed with chevrons and a heavy bolt, coated in rust, locked it shut. Ishtar paused and raising her voice she said, "Ho there, gatekeeper, open this doorway! Let me enter, for if you do not I will shatter the hinges and break the wooden beams. I will split the doorframe and loosen the bolt." Each word echoed in the chamber, reverberating and dying away in the depths of the cave.

"What will you do then?" she questioned. "The dead will rise up and will be freed. They will outnumber the living."

There was a silence in the chamber, then a long hiss of a drawn breath. The gatekeeper spoke, his voice like the rustle of dry grasses. "Wait, lady, do not destroy the gate, for I will bring your message to Ereshkigal." The silence returned and with it the gloom of the cave. Ishtar sat on a shelf in the rock and with only the brooding door for company, meditated on what she had started.

Deep in the winding passages of the labyrinth, stood a temple cut from the living rock, black on black, seven even walls of polished basalt surrounded the round tower of the keep. It was to here that the gatekeeper made his way. At each of the gates he uttered a thin rasping call before passing through. He found Ereshkigal performing the rite of balance and quietly waited until she had finished. When the last of the yarrow sticks had been sorted and the incense lit, he spoke. "Lady of the Dark, your sister Ishtar is at your door."

Ereshkigal froze and turned slowly to face the keeper of the keys. Her face darkened, stretching her thin lips. "What" she questioned, "brings her to me? What has incited her? Who has moved her heart that she makes such an effort of will to come here?" She frowned and whimsically toyed with the smoke from the incense. "Surely it is not because I drink water with the gods?" She shook her head. "I am she who eats clay with the dead and drinks muddy water for beer — Ishtar certainly does not want to dwell with me. I weep for those taken before their time, the loved from the lover, the child from the mother." She stepped towards the gatekeeper and spoke as if she was still making up her mind. "Go back and open the gates for her. Treat her according to the ancient rituals."

The gatekeeper went out from the dark walls and back to the gate. He drew back the bolt which, despite its rusty appearance, moved easily under his hand. The door swung open and he pointed towards the long water-worn passage saying, "Enter, my lady. May the spirits of this world greet you, let the palace of the dark world be glad to see you." Ishtar rose and, concealing her excitement, walked slowly downwards. Dimly, through the shadows and dark solitude, she followed her guide.

At length she came to the first of the gates set into the black basalt walls of the citadel. They glinted faintly as if lit by a pale moon. Here she paused. The gatekeeper reached up and took the laurel leaves from her head. Ishtar allowed him to, but asked, "Gatekeeper, why have you taken my crown of laurel leaves from my head? For though I am the one who sees the past and the future, now I am blind."

The gatekeeper's face portrayed no emotion and instead of answering her question, he assured her that this was the price of entry and part of the rites of the goddess of the earth. Ishtar nodded and they went together to the second gate.

Gesturing towards her head, the gatekeeper held out a white cotton cloth and a small woven purse. Ishtar, wiping the mascara from her eyes and unclasping her earrings said, "Why do you take the symbols of the old powers from me? I am the vessel in which these reside."

"Go in, my lady," the gatekeeper replied, "for such are the rites of the goddess of the earth." The journey through the gates lasted seven days and at each gate the gatekeeper demanded that she pay the price of entry with one of her icons of power. Ishtar, for her part, only asked the meaning of the sacrifice and every time was rewarded with the same platitude. At the seventh door she stopped, for the gatekeeper had asked that she remove her white linen dress. Ishtar shrugged as if it meant nothing to her and slipped easily out of the garment. The gatekeeper picked it up and folded it neatly before placing it in a small closet set into the door-frame of the last gate. With this last protection removed, Ishtar stepped into the gloom naked and without fear. Her mind was set on Tammuz and this stern conviction marked her gait.

Ereshkigal had prepared herself well for the meeting. Around her were the spirits of the dark palace and she sat on a throne of stone, under which a black dog sat on its haunches. The dog barred its teeth at Ishtar, but made no sound. Despite her nakedness, Ishtar did not hesitate. "Ereshkigal, you hag of the world of men, you have taken from me my lover! Because of your serpent-eyed jealousy he lies now in your embrace. Take yourself from that throne! Take yourself away from me, for I am here to bring Tammuz home!" Ereshkigal stepped away from the seat of power and summoned her aides. She pulled herself up to her full height, her features moved and contorted, and gone was the thin hag. Her hair flew wildly about her and her breast was heaving. Larger than life she seemed and when she spoke it was with the deadly authority of the Queen of Darkness.

"You are beyond your place, for here in the Dark World I am the authority. You shall not make any demands on my name, for I keep the souls of the dead. I will bind you and imprison you, for you are yet living in the Land of the Dead, and to all things here you are abhorrent." She raised her hands above her head and her eyes widened. Unseen from the numerous passages came the roar of the elementals as they rushed to their mistress's aid.

"An end to this farce!" she cried. "The sixty diseases I summon to you, against your side, against your feet, against your heart and against your head. In torment your body shall writhe as if bitten by a hundred sharp fangs and in my palace you shall remain." Ishtar staggered as if hit by a powerful blow. She clutched her heart and sank to her knees, but no sound did she make. Ereshkigal slowly lowered her hands and, as she did so, Ishtar collapsed on the marble floor, her perfect skin becoming infested with boils and pus and her hair falling out in dark locks around her head. A second great wind entered Ereshkigal's chamber and gently picked up the prone body to carry it away to her dark prison that lay waiting beneath the room.

The world above that Ishtar had left behind was a world in mourning. The joy in the soul had fled, the bull in the field did not mount the cow, the maidens slept in their own rooms and the young men slept by themselves. Such was the depth of their loss that the very colours of the day were pale and grey. Ishtar's messenger, his head hanging low and tears on his face, went to the earth Goddess and prayed. "Ishtar has gone down into the earth and she has not arisen again. The world has stopped. The maid and the young man do not court, neither does the bull mount the cow." At that moment, a young man whose features were like the glory of the risen sun stepped into the room. His body moved with the lithe grace of a dancer as he stepped up towards the messenger. Golden curls, cropped and oiled, framed his face. "I am the child of the moon and the sun," he said, his voice as soft and modulated as silver. "I shall go to Ereshkigal, and there I will woo her and settle her fears, for she is rightly mine to claim and Tammuz has no place in her affections." As he stepped towards the edge of the sacred glade he reached out and touched a small oak sapling standing alone in the centre and looking back said, "I can pass once only through the seven gates and there I shall speak to Ishtar's dark sister. With an oath, binding and eternal, I shall win the waters of life and free Ishtar from her prison." He walked easily away into the night air, a vision or a mirage, his voice echoing back to the messenger, "For my part, I shall live with Ereshkigal in her palace and Tammuz will be reborn."

And so it happened. Ereshkigal spent nine days and nights with the seemly young man. Her heart and her soul were tranquil. When at last their passion had been sated and they were laying at ease, the comely child of the sun and moon made his request. He raised his head from the silk pillow and spoke. "You and I have fulfilled our destiny. Will you not grant me a boon for the love I have born?" Ereshkigal said, "Choose what you will, I shall not refuse you. As the earth Goddess is my witness, so your request will be honoured."

"Oh, my lady, let me have the waters of life kept in the sacred skin, so that Ishtar may drink from it." The fateful words stirred a horror in Ereshkigal, but there was no way she could renounce her vows, though she reached out to try and silence her lover's lips. She struck her thigh and bit her finger.

"I would that you could call back those words, you snake! You have made a request of me that should not have been made. Go from me! I will settle your destiny and decree a fate for you that will never be forgotten." She rose from the couch and where before there had been harmony, there was now a dark storm as Ereshkigal pronounced his doom. "The sweepings of the gutters will be your food, the sewers your drink. In the shadows of the walls you will live and on the doorsteps you will sleep. Become now a drunken sot!" She turned towards her helpers. The words were dragged from her lips but speak them she must, for her own vow bound her. "Go, now. Knock at the prison-gates, give the gifts of precious stones and place the gold around the altars. Sprinkle Ishtar with the waters of life and bring her back to the world of men."

Ishtar was escorted through the seven gates by the gatekeeper, who gave back to her the icons of her office. From there she left the caverns of the Underworld. The gatekeeper, after sealing the bolt, spoke after her. "You have paid the ransom and given back her lover, a soul for a soul, and it has been matched. Now born again is your lover, your Tammuz. Wash him in clear water and anoint him with fine oils. Clothe him in a red robe and let the lapis lazuli flutes play as the dancers sing their lament." Ishtar responded, "You shall not rob me of my only brother again. On the day when Tammuz appears and plays for me the sweet songs of love, then on that day also the mourners and the dead will rise with him and breath the sweet breath of the living." '

The Lion Warrior was thus reinstated to his proper place and the Goddess was empowered to act again in the physical realm of society. From this legend we can begin to see how deeply the peoples of the Neolithic struggled to come to terms with the complexity that had been released into the human mind in the process that led to the neanderthal extinction. The representations of the Lion Warrior and the Goddess move through the legend in a precise relationship, one that is retold with the passing seasons in a cyclical story that has no end. That their society successfully managed to control and to combine these new expressions of the human potential is a testament to the disposition of human beings. In today's world, we universally attribute war and greed to something in human nature, something that we have convinced ourselves that we have no control over. Our rulers and our philosophers wrestle with the problem, but none seem to believe that there is a succinct answer to the conundrum. It may be that we have something to learn from this tale about this uniquely human gift and its relationship to our society.

The settled societies that grew up in the Middle East had a different agenda from those in western and central Europe. Cities and states replaced villages and tribes as the preferred form of social organisation, and as societies developed, so the people were increasingly governed by the code enshrined in the story of the Goddess and the Lion Warrior.

Then, starting around six thousand years ago, a change appeared in the structures and form of these cities. Into the mythologies and legends came a new figure: the male God. This was, at first, none other that the Lion Warrior promoted to the rank of deity, somehow free from his plunge into captivity and fully able to dominate the Goddess with the powers that he had amassed. Thousands of years later, the bitter fruits of this advance came into being.[9]

The cities of the Middle East which rose to accommodate this process were at first undefended, but by 4000 BC the walled city-states of Sumeria had appeared. The goddess culture, previously so much in evidence, was eclipsed and by 3800 BC, different tribes, whose allegiance lay with a male God, had begun to physically take over the matriarchal territories of Old Europe.

It is impossible to pinpoint the exact moment that a change in quantity becomes a change in quality. At what moment does a fingernail need to be cut or the ice on a river melt? Sometimes a catalyst precipitates a complete reinvention of the old order, bringing with it social change and a new urge to develop. Yet this new regime contains all the manners and outward expressions of the old. Only when the shift is consolidated does it become possible to see the inevitability of the process. This begs the question: just what was so powerful in this new 'religious' form that held such sway over the people?

It was not just the armies of the Lion Warrior, or the fear of retribution or the wrath of the old Goddess which enthralled great numbers into a near slave-like existence. It was an ideological concept that played on the deepest feelings of the human psyche in such a way that people were powerless to resist the combination, and often sought to embrace it with open arms.

Joseph Campbell describes in *The Mask of God* how new-born chicks, still with eggshell on their wings, will run for cover if the shape of a hawk is passed over them. That they have never known cover or the hawk does not seem to matter — they have a built-in memory of this bird. The shape of a duck or pigeon will not cause this reaction, but that of a hawk casting its shadow over them will. It would not matter, says Campbell, if all the hawks in the world had died out — the shape that represents it would still stir a reaction of flight.

The ending of the long hierarchical association with the neanderthals left just such a shadow in the minds of humans. Once the means by which the peoples of Old Europe had obscured it was removed, it became available for manipulation by ambitious kings and priests. They held the 'shadow of the hawk' over their subjects. For this end, a new deity came into the world of human beings. It was not of the Goddess or the Lion Warrior, but it sought to control the latter and subdue the former.

The role of the new solar God was to implant this fear, the representtation of the ancient racial memory of the neanderthal overlords. The control that they had held for one hundred and fifty thousand years of human evolution could then be released from the magical chains tying it to the ritual of the death and rebirth of the warrior and the cycles of the year. His power could be freed from the governing and harmonising forces of the Goddess. With this dubious freedom, the concept of the God began to take form in people's minds.

The Discovery of the Dingle Diamond

Once the kings had severed their mythical bonds, they began to do what all tyrants have since done: they used their power to create fear to cow the people. They invoked the 'shadow of the hawk', activating in the minds of men the conditioned responses to the neanderthals, but twisted, now, to accomplish their own designs, and they used the voice of a male God as their source of authority. The ability to be dominated by a more powerful creature was an attribute that evolved with us, hardwired into our thought patterns as our brains evolved on the path that led us to who we are today.

This is what happened in the cities when the God broke free: into the lives of people was brought the shadow of fear, and it drove them to insanity. It was as much an ideological shadow as it was a physical one of force of arms.

The 'shadow of the hawk' did not arise in the cities of the Near East nor in the hills and valleys of central Europe. The egalitarian citizens of these earliest cities had little use for such a religion, and to the peoples of the agricultural communities of central Europe such ideas were anathema. It appeared like a virus on the wind-swept plains of Siberia.

The tribes of these plains were a people for whom power — symbolised by the lion — had been unchecked for centuries. The power of the old knowledge, here on the plains, was firmly in the hands of the Lion Warrior and, as time went by, he became a God in people's eyes. He wielded this power, this 'shadow of the neanderthal', not with the harmonious balance of the Goddess, but with the drive and ambition of a God. It had become the creed by which life was lived. It was a genie that could not be returned to the bottle.

Horses were important to these nomadic peoples. Tamed and ridden they were a source of transport, wealth, food and drink. Hunting remained a major source of wealth and with it developed the principle of a warrior chief or king. For the first time, a people emerged who did not follow their personal conscience to create their own way of life; instead, they existed as part of the chief's retinue. The symbol of this leader was the lion.

This description of a king as the source of wealth and a giver of rings can be seen in the art of the time. In the halls of chiefs, the courage of the lion and the pull of gold drew men to their destiny. In the imagery found on tapestries and copper casts, the bull, gazelle or goat, seen as representations of the earth, are brought down by the lion. Time

Diagram 5.5
The Scythian view
of the role of the
lion. 100 BC

and again this symbol emerges in the art of these peoples. The practice of burying important people with their wealth, sometimes with their complete court, starts in this period.

The goat sees the world as one large herd and desires only to breed more goats, representing the safe world of the hearth and family. The lion operates on a different principle and needs to sink its teeth into the goat, and so there is a balance. By 4000 BC, as their cousins in the south were settling in new territories to build the cities of Sumeria or migrating to the east to settle in China, the people of the plains were dominant enough to start taking their wealth from the more peaceful and less well protected communities of Old Europe. (Diagram 5.5)

History, it is said, repeats itself. For these people, the forces that conspired to lead them to war with the neanderthals were still free in their society. Hunters, raiders and eventually armies, dominated by the male principle, followed the path of the veiled form of the pregnant Goddess, the Goddess who held the reins of the lion. They trod in the steps of the original soldiers of the lion as they fought the neanderthals, commencing in the east and pushing west, as the lion's authority turned on its mistress, replacing her with the cult of the male warrior hero.

As the ancient world stood on the cusp of these changes, three geographically separate cultures emerged from a single root, each taking on a different aspect of the Goddess.

The matrilineal peoples of Old Europe were farmers in settled communities, working with the earth powers and the lore of the Great Goddess. In their world, the spring face of the Goddess was the most fitting for their lives. She represented the force of creativity tied to the earth and from her came the arts of civilisation.

The people of the Siberian plains followed the path of the pregnant veiled Goddess of the summer, becoming ever more held in thrall by the power of her lions. This Goddess was subjugated, dominated and eventually ruled by this power.

Lastly, in the Middle East, she was the consort of the annual king, the old Goddess who guided their society. Under her tutelage were eventually created the laws of the city.

A critical point in history had been reached. The way of the Goddess cleaved into three separate paths. Three separate cultures sprang from the same root, locked together as history unfolded. The struggle for dominance by these branches decided the course our world would take.

The Lion Warrior, the product of necessity born of the concept of the Goddess, returned with a vengeance. This was not a passive process. The peoples of the steppes actively worked to control the lion, for to control the spirit of the lion was to control the Goddess. That meant power — not power with, but power over the earth. Their shamans and leaders practised a form of magic that catalysed a change in the way that people behaved. The result, though of great benefit to the rulers and the minority elite, was catastrophic for the majority.

The creativity and wisdom that had flowed through society became darkened. The wonder and beauty of their art became ensnared by the glorification of war and by another side of human nature, blind allegiance to a cause. When the warriors toasted the god of war in the halls of the lion, people were no longer truly individuals, for they had surrendered their freedom to choose the life they lived. They spoke with one voice and willingly gave themselves to this new creed. For an individual to go against the word of the god meant death. So surrender of freedom, of conscious control and most of all surrender of freedom of thought, was a prerequisite and with this came a new way of life.

In a world where free thought is dangerous, if not fatal, the human mind takes its shape from other sources: the will of the god and the way of the king. To kill with exhilaration, to rate dominion over others as glory, to consider the symbols of this power — wealth above all else — as a way of shaping the minds of men, and to treat all this as positive, was the madness that was unleashed.

A torrent that submerged the mind swept across the land and with it came something darker, something that has been with us ever since.

After the waters of this madness had swept away the society of Old Europe, they passed through the door of time and into our own world. In every person's mind alive today there are thoughts and decisions which do not come directly from within us, but are those of the 'boss', of the leader or of any deity to which we have willingly surrendered. 'I will take your very souls', is the message of God.

In every human being there are two sets of thoughts. One is linked to the earth and nature, to our joy of life and the sheer wonder of creation. The other is controlled by a belief in something greater than ourselves, an entity that we call 'God'. This duality is really an expression of the same motivating forces that led to conceptualisation and art in human society. Just as these creative forces were accompanied by destructive ones in the form of warfare and the resultant extinction of a whole species, so it is that the Goddess holds the creative aspects and the Lion Warrior the destructive ones. As the old myths have shown to us, neither is capable of existing without the other. But it is perfectly possible for these forces to become unbalanced and to present themselves in our society as a very real injurious potential.

One is left to wonder what is our true self and what energy would be liberated if our minds were genuinely free to chose their own thoughts?

6000 years ago a mighty battle was fought and a second global catastrophe enveloped our species. The Goddess fell, torn asunder by these new forces. Her consort, the solar hero, the god who had accomplished the hunt, now turned on his mother. As with the new city-states of the Near East, waves of invaders changed the balance of power in Europe forever. Wherever these warriors appeared — and this was over the whole of Europe, the Middle East and North Africa, and even as far away as the Far East — it was no longer possible to exist as a peaceful community. Palisades and walls started to appear more frequently. Villagers armed themselves and invoked the concept of the lion to protect them. The cultures changed and those that were not destroyed began to use the language of warfare in their societies. However, the voice of the Goddess, resting on her lions (as pictured in the ancient Middle Eastern city of Catal Huyuk) was not as strong a call to the lion's might as other forms of magic which would more successfully mould it to their will.

This struggle leaves a scar running through the old stories, a scar so terrible that it came to be told as a parable. It bursts into the tales as alien as a meteor. There it remains, embedded in the lore of many different cultures, passed down orally until written on clay and then faithfully reproduced by the world's religions. Its nature is so strange that it has often been dismissed as a fairy story but it marks a point in the legends when humans were no longer in communion with the world. This is the story of the Flood.

Chapter Six
Flood

"Oh man of Shurrupak, son of Ubara-Tutu; tear down your house and build a boat."
The story of the Flood, from the Epic of Gilgamesh.

From our vantage point in the twenty-first century it may often seem that the tangled myths, legends and religions of past cultures are a naive melange of exotic gods and monsters, a brightly drawn stencil of incredible wars and impossible heroes, the creations, perhaps, of primitive people who, in trying to come to terms with a world of perplexing complexity, wrapped their history and beliefs together in one chaotically primitive form. Researchers tell us that humans started their quest to define spirituality by naively worshipping the physical forces of nature — thunder and rain, disease or famine. As if to reinforce this simple picture, we are often reminded that early religious beliefs involved cannibalism and human sacrifice, creating a picture in our minds of barbaric simplicity conducted by a people that we could no more come to understand than if they had been aliens.

The generally accepted theory is that barbaric-primitivism gradually evolved into our present day religions, a model that presents us with a comfortable, slowly advancing sophistication of belief. It is a notion so deeply ingrained in western thought that it is hardly ever questioned, and many scholars, who have spent their lives investigating tribal lore and customs, almost invariably hold to this doctrine to illuminate their way. From Herodotus' *The Histories*, written in the fifth century BC, to more contemporary writings such as Jung's *The Archetypal Myth*, our ancestors have been described as savage and irrational. For these writers, the bedrock on which the faiths of today stand is horrifyingly dark. A primitive savage, whether noble or not, isn't something that we can easily identify with and this can confuse our attempts to understand the

119

spirituality of the times. Perhaps because so many influential thinkers have judged human progress in terms of technology, it is inevitably part of our human condition. Certainly, when the complexities of to-day's 'super cities' are contrasted with the quiet fireside camps of the neanderthals, it is an argument that is irrefutable. However, it does not mean that the thoughts of the camp-dweller were any less or more sophisticated than those of people living in the heart of New York City today.

Those who have a deeply held belief in one of the current 'sophisticated' religions hold that the truth about God has at last been reached, and that the path to this truth becomes visible as an incontrovertible fact. When questioned more closely as to the nature of this path, the usual answer is to refer to an ancient and holy authority, a direct revelation from God. These words, we are told, are not the creation of the human mind, but a full blown revelation from a non-human entity, a revelation that lifts us out of our primitive past and into an enlightened existence. The integrity of this knowledge rests upon the ability to prove that the sacred text has not been tampered with since the witnesses to the revelation recorded them. Such sacred writings make up the fundamental stratum which underpins the world's religions and helps to define our views on what it is to be a religious person. It is a paradox that the religious and pious place little faith in today's slick and sophisticated world, preferring instead to rely on wisdom recorded thousands of years ago by the very people whom they so often deride as savage primitives.

In this way the Koran, the Upanishads, the Torah and the Bible have become the only officially recognised dogmas for millions of people from widely different cultural backgrounds.

The world's sacred books can be classified as arising from common sources. The Torah, for instance, led to the Bible and to the Koran, forming part of one family based on a mutual history. In this particular case, the mutual history derives from early Sumerian holy books. From this family emerge faiths such as Baha'ism and Mormonism, branches offering alternative interpretations. As they continue to develop, these new faiths are looked on with differing degrees of hostility by organisations founded upon a more ancient part of the hierarchy, yet they contain these parent religions, adding fresh tales and retelling the old ones with a distinct flavour of the new. Even today, this process of deconstruction and re-assembly continues apace. It marks one of the most fundamental aspects of legend and myth and is probably as unstoppable as the creation of the stories themselves. It is also a guide to the seniority of the themes, for those that occur early on in the development of religion are the most widespread.

However much new guardians reuse them, the fundamental meaning of these early themes is not subject to evolution since they contain knowledge of a truth perpetuated across the centuries. Students of theology have struggled with this aspect of religious texts. The question as to why they endure — even when the parables and stories within the holy texts are contradictory, obscure or obvious fallacies — has never had a satisfactory answer. Most scientists choose to ignore this ability of sacred texts to preserve the significance of a legend, reducing them to mere fairytales. They are not fairytales, though, for fairytales are harmless whereas the power contained in the narratives of the world's religious books affects the human psyche, and the practical result is daily demonstrated. We are forced to conclude that the longevity of the content of the world's sacred texts is a result of a protocol that invokes a real response in human beings. If this formula were to be too drastically modified it would no longer function. Any given religion is thus contained within the twin confines of the practical consequences of the myths recorded and the need for religious leaders to maintain their control over the faithful. The result is the ability of a religion to transcend individual generations, its message reaching out and affecting humans over the course of history. This immortality is the basic character of any religion.

Religious texts can accommodate a great deal of other information within the structure or formula of their stories. For instance, they often contain genealogical pedigrees. Through them, kings and tribes can trace their lineage back through the centuries. Such stories can be altered to retain the history of the tribe, its battles, struggles and movements. Nothing in a myth is wasted, and these different pieces of historical information are carefully grafted onto the vine of the main motif to display many different stories in one epic. This genealogical history runs concurrently with the creation myths and the history of the tribe to form a single body of lore. The themes that thread the holy books weave a complex spell linking not only each member of a specific religious family, but also different families. To disentangle the true story is to try to pluck out one thread without destroying the overall fabric, a hard enough task without suggesting that the whole matter is the product of an overworked imagination.

An example of the way an ancient event is incorporated into the bedrock of religion can be seen in the legends of the Flood, an episode that occurred early in the development of religions. It is from this story that many religious epics trace their ancestry, for it is a tale of metamorphosis and destruction from which only those who build an 'ark' escape to establish new dynasties. The legend is of particular significance to our story, as the catastrophe seems to have occurred at the time humanity was making the transition from a matriarchal to a patriarchal society. It is an epic that has as much to say of the social changes incurred in this period as it does of the physical devastation of a previous way of life.

To our western eyes the most famous interpretation comes from the Bible — nearly every child learns of how Noah took the animals, two-by-two, into safety. So it came as some surprise to the theologians when the same tale, almost unchanged, was unearthed from the most un-Christian Sumerian cities. In the biblical version of this epic, the ark that Noah built is an almost exact copy of the ark in a tale of the Flood found on Sumerian clay tablets from five thousand years ago. This tale is often included in the epic of Gilgamesh. When the two texts are compared, the similarities are striking. In the Bible, God tells Noah, "Make yourself an ark of gopher wood.... This is how you are to make it: the length of the ark is to be.... And of every living thing of all flesh you shall bring two of every kind into the ark." The legend of Gilgamesh tells us that Ea spoke to Ubara-Tutu saying, "Tear down your house, I say, and build a boat.... These are the measurements.... then take up into the boat the seeds of all living creatures."

The detail shared by these two texts is tribute to the faithful reproduction of the story, despite the length of time separating them. The Bible tells us that the ark came to rest on the top of Mount Ar'arat, and that Noah first sent forth a raven that flew to and fro until the waters receded. Then he sent a dove, but it returned having found no place to rest. Noah waited for seven days and sent the dove out again, and this time she returned with an olive branch in her beak. After another seven days he sent her out again and this time she did not return. By this sign, he knew the water had gone and he was able to emerge from the ark.

Flood

The earlier epic of Gilgamesh tells us that the boat came to rest on the mountains of Nisir and after seven days Ubara-Tutu sent forth a dove, which, finding no resting place, returned. He followed this with a swallow, and finally a raven that cawed but did not return.

The Flood is also a feature of many Native American sacred stories that predate any contact with Europeans. One example, among many, is the story of the Prairie Falcon and his people, told by the Indians of California. In this, we are told, the Eagle followed the word of his chief, the Prairie Falcon, saying, "We shall follow our chief to the great mountain. We will go there so that we may see how the world fares. I hear that a flood approaches. We are all going together." After many adventures and a continual rising of the waters they arrive on the mountain as "water flooded the entire world". At last, Prairie Falcon and Eagle and their people arrived at a piece of dry land. There they found green fruit. Hummingbird told them not to eat the fruit. Then they sent Dove to survey the water and discover how humanity fared. Dove reported that all human beings were dead.

The ancient texts of the Zoroastrian religion from the early part of the first millennium state that the god Ahura Mazda warned the hero, Yima, that floods were coming to destroy a sinful world, and gave him careful instructions for building a 'vara' in which pairs of animals were to be saved. Similarly, the Hindu Vedas tell us that Manu, the first human, saved the life of a fish and in return for this kindness, the fish warned him that a flood was coming and told him to build a boat and stock it with every species. He anchored the boat on a sacred mountain.

Many writers on ancient mythology have catalogued and compared world-wide stories of the Flood. In *The Story of Atlantis*, 1896, W. Scott-Elliot states:

"Suffice it to say, that in India, Chaldea, Babylon, Media, Greece, Scandinavia, China, amongst the Jews and amongst the Celtic tribes of Britain, the legend is absolutely identical in all essentials. Now turn to the west and what do we find? The same story in its every detail preserved amongst the Mexicans (each tribe having its own version), the people of Guatemala, Honduras, Peru, and almost every tribe of North American Indians. It is puerile to suggest that mere coincidence can account for this fundamental identity."

The Discovery of the Dingle Diamond

The Sibylline Oracles, of which more shall be told later, state:

"For from the time when on the earlier men
The flood came and the Almighty One himself
Destroyed that race by many waters, then
Brought he in yet another race of men
Untiring; and they, setting themselves up
Against heaven, built to height unspeakable
A tower; and tongues of all were loosed again."[1]

So common is this story and so geographically widespread — occurring in all the major religious writings — that it cannot be disregarded as the exaggerated retelling of flooding in a small area or a local environment. If it were simply a case of a local report, it would be unlikely that the legend would be repeated so similarly around the globe. The form and detail of these tales, and the fact that they are embedded so early on in the cultural matrix of such diverse religious cultures, are indicators of the importance of the information preserved, for preserved it seems to have been, complete with attention to detail. The only changes that have been made are the characters who took part, reflecting the lineages of the various tribes who saw the need to include the flood in their corpus of religious or spiritual tales. Like the supports of a tower, the story of the deluge finds itself central to the whole religious edifice. Because it is part of this structure, the shape of the myth has to remain the same, but, like the Cheshire cat in Lewis Carroll's *Alice in Wonderland*, the physical reality may not necessarily be the accurate part.

From the lineages of tribes found in their holy texts, and by matching archaeological evidence of civilisations with their reworking of the flood legends, we can suggest a major event precipitating the establishment of a solar God. This event need not be a geophysical one, or even a physical event, but it can be dated. Current research in comparative religion would suggest that the evidence for a date converges on an event in the fourth millennium BC. If we are to take this at face value, then it would seem that there should be a great deal of physical evidence for the Flood, and it should not be difficult to trace back to an historical event.[2] But there is no geological, geophysical or

124

Flood

archaeological evidence whatsoever of a large scale flood occurring around 4,000 BC, the most likely date for the origin of the story.

When we add this to the insistence in the myth of the annihilation of the majority of the human race, it becomes clear that the story is metaphysical. If this were an actual event, then there would be evidence of a bottleneck, a point of divergence in the genetic record. There is absolutely nothing. All this points to the mythological importance of the story of the Flood, rather than it being a physical event, it appears to be a psychological one.

There is an anomaly, or contradiction, buried beneath this discrepancy and it provides a doorway through which we can reach a deeper understanding. If the story is told as an allegory, then the events and characters are symbols or disguises for another affair entirely. That this style of disguise appears in so many cultures is an indication of the importance of the information. The need to hide the real significance as an allegory proclaims that the incident was close to the heart of the religion — it was sacred. Moreover it was codified at a very early point, and in this form was reproduced by later religions. Such a story could only be correctly interpreted by the initiates, those with the knowledge of what really happened. To decipher what may have transpired four thousand years before Christ, we have to look at the motifs that the legends have in common and compare these with events that took place across the planet at that time.

The first thing to notice about the legend is that it is a warning. Time after time we are told of people who annoyed their deities and were eliminated as a result. Sometimes they were too noisy, sometimes they were decadent or sinful. In all versions the people had turned away from the divine. This interpretation is given a patriarchal slant in the biblical story, which tells us that the people had strayed in the eyes of the Lord.

In fact we find, on comparative analysis of the legends, that the 'floods' were caused when the people lost their ability to communicate with the Goddess, who took the form of a serpent or water spirit. This loss of communication was the prime cause of the flood.

The second message in the story is one of rescue by the male God. The water spirit of the Goddess initiates the Flood and the male God plays the role of rescuing the people and putting an end to the disaster. There is a quaint twist in the ancient Egyptian story of the destruction of mankind: Ra, the sun god, relents and halts the rampaging Goddess by getting her drunk. In the Persian myth, the Flood issues from the oven doors of an old woman (the oven doors are the sacred corn shrines of the Goddess). God spoke, 'O Earth, swallow up thy waters and thou, O Heaven, cease thy rain!', and the waters abated.

The fact that in many of the legends, including that of the biblical Noah, the waters appear from both the heavens and the gates of the earth, tells us that it is a story about a war being fought between heaven and earth with humankind in the middle. The earth is represented by the Goddess tradition, whilst heaven is represented by the male or solar God. In this light, the epic of the deluge is transformed into a story of the war between the Goddess and the God. This presupposes that there was a separation between the power of the sky and the power of the earth, where at an earlier time there had been unity.

We find this theme in the earliest creation myths of all traditions that tell this story. "In the beginning," says the Bible, "God created the heavens and the earth." Before this act there had been no separation between them. The Egyptian writings say that the god Shu pushed apart his parents to form the heavens and the earth. The Sumerian clay tablets from six thousand years ago, in the reed impressions of their cuneiform glyphs, give a simpler and more direct version. In these, An, the father, and Ki, the mother, were separated by their child, Enlil, who went on to unite with his mother to produce mankind. The Icelandic Edda records that heaven and earth were once joined, but the child of this bond cut the ligament, separating heaven into many pieces. This created an obscene abyss of fire and ice. The mixing of these two elements gave rise to humans and created order in the world. The Babylonian sun god, Marduk, defies Tiamat, the universal mother, and in a battle full of demons and dragons he slays the Goddess, dividing the parts of her body to create heaven and earth and an ordered universe in which humans can live. The Maoris say that the hero Tane-mahuta pushed apart the universal father and mother because they were stifling the ancestors. The Nasadiya, or creation hymn of the Indian Rig Veda, declares that when the Golden Embryo, the Lord of Creation, was born, he propped up the sky and made firm the earth. A supplication to this god is, "Let him not harm us, he who fathered the earth and created the sky, whose laws are true."

Here we seem to be getting close to a truth buried in the story of the Flood.

Six thousand years ago, before the Flood, there was a harmony of belief and people lived within the protection of the universal Mother. Into this stability was born the solar God, whose new existence split the unity into the heavens and the earth. Unbidden, this entered the minds of humans and created a dichotomy between that which is of the earth and that which is of the realm of the spirit. This was no gentle time, for the Kurgan tribes of Siberia, led by the power of the lion, descended upon the world with their duality, the split between heaven and earth. Humans could no longer follow the path of the earth goddess. She was ruptured, and humans were cast out into the crack between two worlds. This was followed by a period that witnessed great changes in the developing societies. All over Europe and the Middle East we find evidence of the collapse of an early civilisation. Large towns such as Catal Huyuk are abandoned and decorative pottery disappears in what appears to be catastrophic circumstances. It was a vicious struggle between the old and the new world, and in the midst of the destruction of the old way of life a new order arose. Cities, armies and warfare were born from the cataclysm, as was money, gold and the ownership of land.

The legend of the Flood is how the struggle between these two forces was recorded. As the old ways dissolved into chaos and the waters flooded the earth, a new God saved the day and established his order. That the waters were not physical is mentioned in the Rig Veda, amongst other ancient writings. 'He who created the high, shining waters' is a metaphor for the battleground between the so-called demons of the earth and the gods of the sky. It is through this portal that the spirit of the male God appears in the hearts and minds of the people as a path or illumination, taming the spirit that had caused the disruption. The early Sumerian texts refer to the god Enlil as 'water'. "So Enlil, whose will is an enormous flood, sparkling and awe-inspiring, came to a sweet decision."[3]

The illumination that this solar God provided allowed the establishment of a new order and arranged all in its place. The sun and the moon, the stars and the earth, were once again made firm, but this time they were perceived through the lens of a god.

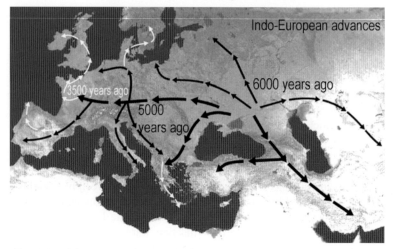

Diagram 6.1
The routes and times of the Kurgan invasions of Europe, showing the predominantly western thrust.

"He constructed stations for the great gods,
Fixing their astral likenesses as their images.
He determined the year by designating the zones:
He set up three constellations for each of the twelve months,
Defining the days of the year by means of
Heavenly figures."[4]

For a people who were drowning in the unchecked chaos of the lion, amid the destruction of ten thousand years of history, this beacon was a lifeline that was eagerly embraced. In their terror and despair, the populations of Europe and the Middle East turned once again to the comfort that the neanderthal regime had instilled, a reversion to the voluntary surrender to another's will. In this way, the rules of a God were inserted into the crack between the worlds. His spirit was obeyed, his will interpreted by the prophets and implemented by the priests. This was the 'shadow of the hawk', for there was no physical god, and certainly no neanderthals, just a path of "right mind and dominion". [5] This iron discipline allowed the rebuilding of the world to begin. (Diagram 6.1)

This process of subjugation of the Goddess, her beliefs and her people, was not as simple as, say, the genocide wrought on the Aztec or Native American. The Kurgan warriors descending from the steppes, descended, too, from a belief in the Goddess. But it was tempered by a male God, a solar God, a God who sought to subdue the Goddess, and from her potency to re-create the world. The relationship between the new God and the mother Goddess is faithfully recorded in many epics.

The Babylonians, who recorded their version of this invasion and of the global struggle for power that accompanied the ascendancy of the rule of God, were quite specific about the division of the spoils. The tale is one of the oldest and bears the name 'Enuma Elish'. A creation epic, it was recorded on clay tablets in the second millennium BC. Most authorities point out that it is a revised version of a more ancient Sumerian epic. This rendition has been culled from the many translations that have been made since its discovery.

A note of warning needs to be sounded before this account is read: it is a tale that is told by the victors, and because of this the moral high ground is plainly taken by the gods and their hero.

It so happened that after Ea, the leader of the tribe of the new gods, had defeated Apsu, consort to the Goddess, he took her symbols for his own. He built a hall over the abyss of the world and there he took to wife the beautiful Damkina. She gave birth to Marduk, the son of the sun. Marduk was without equal and skilled in all the arts of healing, poetry and war, and together with the people of Anu they gave the tribes of the Goddess no rest. One day they would be raiding and carrying away their cattle, the next they would be waiting in ambush for the tribes-peoples as they went across the mountains. There was no respite to be had in the land from these savage peoples of the God.

The ways of the Goddess were disrupted and many peoples were upset. A council was called to which all the tribes who had been afflicted came. No small number, for by now the raiders had widened their scope, and their ambition knew no end. At the council, the priestess of Tiamat, the voice of the Goddess, was persuaded as to the wisdom of a war.

"The Anu has called up from the four quarters the winds of war and they rage in your guts till not one of our people can have any rest. Rise up, our Mother, rise up and render them as the wind."

When Tiamat heard these words she was pleased and she said, "This is what we will do: we will ready the warriors of the Worm, the Dragon, the female warriors and the great Lion warriors. We will bring together the mad dogs of the east and the scorpions of the west, the Kulili and the Kusariqu people, with those of the howling storm." She turned towards the waiting assembly. "Go now to your places and when we meet again it will be under the banner of war. I will pick Kingu as my war consort."

Tiamat went, therefore, to the place of Kingu and gave him the tablets of fate and the badge of the lion, so that he might lead the army. From that place to this she did not rest, but she was gathering supplies and people, weapons and armaments.

When Ea, the war leader of the new God learned how things were with Tiamat he was astonished, and sat in a dark silence till the anger had passed. He thought to collect the tribes of the gods together to seek what could be done, for the tribes of Tiamat were numerous and he had not thought them able to unite. He was also not sure if he could stand against them, for his crown and his flaming coat of leadership were once the property of Apsu, the old consort to the Goddess. He sought first his grandfather, Anshar, and told him of the council of Tiamat.

"She hates us all, Father. Our mother, Tiamat, has raised an army and she travels the lands encouraging all to join her and the tribes are flocking to her call. The ranks grow day by day and by night they plot and plan, a growling roaring rout ready for battle, and the power of the tablets of destiny she has passed to Kingu, the authority that was once of Anu, your son. His word is law and his judgements have authority."

Anshar was silent and bit his lip, his heart was overshadowed by the coming fight and he covered his mouth to stifle his groans. When at last he spoke it was to urge Ea to fight.

"You who have killed Apsu and taken his crown and robe, you who have killed Mummu, now kill Kingu, the battle leader and the commander of her forces!"

But try as he might, Ea could not conceive a plan to accomplish this. Anshar turned to Anu, his son.

"Anu, most powerful of heroes, you whose strength is outstanding, go and speak to Tiamat! It may be that you can calm her lust for battle and avert this war of power. If she will not listen to your words, tell her it is our will that we seek for talks."

When he heard this command from his father, Anshar, Anu went by the shortest road to the tribe of Tiamat. But standing on a hill a little distance from Tiamat's camp, he surveyed the ranks and tents of the army, a mighty sea of warriors and fires, and his heart failed him and his courage also. He turned back and arriving at the hall of Anshar addressed his father:

"My power is not great enough to accomplish this thing."

Anshar was speechless and he stared at the ground before him shaking his head at Anu. Now the tribes of the new gods were all gathered at that place waiting for the news of the parley. At this time they were called the Anunnaki. When they saw that Anu had failed, they were stricken too.

"None of us can stand where Anu has failed. We can not face the wrath of the Goddess and the power of the Tablets; we must surely be undone."

But Anshar stood in all his majesty, and having thought hard, addressed the assembly:

"As Tiamat has Kingu, we will have Marduk as our leader. He who is keen in battle, son of Ea, son of the Sun. It is to Marduk that we will give the divine authority and it is he who will lead the Anunnaki against the Old Hag."

Marduk, his face as radiant as the sun, stepped forward and stood in the presence of Anshar. He kissed his lips and dispelled the gloom, lifting the morale of the warriors waiting there. When he spoke his words were bold:

"I, Marduk, will obtain thy wish. Be not disheartened and raise your eyes. Is this a man I stand against? No? It is but a woman and with a woman's wiles. O my father, my creator, be glad, rejoice, for you shall soon be standing on Tiamat's neck."

The High Lord, Marduk, now turned to face the silent ranks of the Anunnaki.

"Creator of the gods, tribes of the gods, if I will be your avenger, if I will break the power of the Goddess, then I must have the power of the tribes of the gods. Call an assembly, give me precedence over all others and now and forever let my word be law. I, not you, will decide the fate of the world and things to yet be. It is my decrees that will not be changed and never annulled, for my words will last till the end of the world."

Anshar stood and words broke from his lips.

"Gladly will I let this be. Send the messengers to the place of the sediments, the home of the tribes of the old gods. Send them forth that they might hear the word and come to give the world to Marduk."

And so it came to pass. From every corner of the lands, from every island and mountain came the leaders of the tribes and they met in the hall of Anshar to determine the fate of the world. Here they feasted and drank the new-drawn liquor and intoxicating wine, and in this state they settled the fate of Marduk.

A throne was set up and on it Marduk sat, facing his forefathers, waiting to receive the government of the tribes and this is what they decreed:

"One God is greater than all great gods, O Marduk.
Greater than all the honour and fame, the will of Anu.
Great commander of the unfaltering and eternal word.
Where there is action, the first to act.
Where there is government, the first to govern.
His to give glory and his to humiliate.
In truth absolute that none may question.
To you we make a palace of greatness.
To you we give the sceptre and to you
We give the rule of the universe."[6]

As a test the great shamans called forth visions. "Speak the words of power," they said, "and the visions will disappear. Say but again the words and they will appear again. By this we will know of your divine power."

And Marduk, well versed in all the magic arts, spoke, and the visions of the world vanished. He spoke again and they appeared. When his father and all the Anunnaki saw this, they knew they had made the fateful choice and they conferred the sceptre and the crown on Marduk. Also they gave him mighty weapons, matchless in battle. But it was for the bow that Marduk was known. He constructed it and at his side he hung the quiver and arrows. Then he made a mace, mighty in strength. Lastly he created a net of fine mesh, strong enough to enfold Tiamat in. He arose, ready for war.

To his fore, lightning clashed and his body was filled with flame. The four winds of war he stationed, that nothing could escape his will. He brought forth the evil-wind and the hurricane. In his palm he held the healing herb. Thus armed with the four winds, the seven winds, the cyclone and the tempest, he strode forth ready for war. His chariot was drawn by the four horses of the Apocalypse, tireless and versed in the arts of war. Killer, Relentless, Trampler and Swift were their names. Behind him rose rank upon rank of his tribes. As one, the army moved onto the field of battle. Arrayed against them stood the warriors of Tiamat

Marduk rode at the head of his forces, his scouts perceived the plans of Kingu, and Marduk counted his moves. Kingu faced the glory of Marduk and was undone. He did not know the art of war and his orders were confused. The great army faltered in confusion. Marduk moved forward towards the banners of Tiamat. His guard milled around him.'

A new world order was conjured into being. Within it, the heavens became the abode of this entity and the earth was the clay upon which his spirit moved to mould the new creation. Human beings may have implanted the laws by which this entity maintained order in the world, but the God himself divulged their secrets. 'God' is a pure concept and, as such, has no existence except by dint of being part of our collective psyche. However, it is much more enigmatic than this, for in itself 'god' has no realisable form. If the creation of God was a doppelganger for the neanderthals, then it was a concept of something that no longer exists in a physical framework. Yet the social space for a god lives in the very way our brains evolved. Such a 'God' can be responsible for huge changes in people's behaviour.

This paradox is enshrined in every legend and religious epic and manifest in every myth. It is resolved in the coming together of the parts of the religious story to reveal an inner truth, for by following the laws of this discovery, the very forces that do not exist can be made to produce wars and empires, so effective are they at controlling the mind at a very basic level.

The concept of God divided all things and from unity came the dualism of heaven and hell, of good and evil, of wealth and poverty. It is between the poles of this dualism that our present belief system of science and religion with which we have lived for so long operates. It is, perhaps, too strenuous for us to perceive of any other way of thinking.

Poignantly describing a loss of something that humanity once took for granted, the deluge becomes a symbol of that time when we exchanged one way of being for another. The Faustian deal was done and we exchanged the Goddess of the earth for a solar God. For this crime, we became the enemy of the earth, cast out from the Garden of Eden. Such a powerful enemy needed new champions to oppose it, and these new champions were created from the body of the God. Each legend records how the heroes and the lesser gods emerged from the parent. Each fought battles with aspects of the Goddess, until she was crippled and subdued.

Not everything was lost in the mad scramble for power that followed the Flood. It was more a shifting of access to knowledge. Medicine, geometry, astronomy: all the sciences of the day came through the Flood intact. When such skills appear again in the archaeological record, they are in the hands of an educated elite and, just like the Goddess, they are bent to the service of the rule of the God. This protection of a basic core of knowledge and skills is a common theme in the deluge stories, and a clue is given in the attention that the deity pays to the specific instructions about the size and the shape of the ark. Doubtless, people knew how to construct boats, but this vessel had to be a certain shape in order to work. Only in careful symbolic reference to geometry would the people be saved. It was no physical boat, but a spiritual one. The Australian tribes are more specific and tell us that the Flood was in the 'Dreamtime'. The boat is often referred to as an ark, which would have been more readily understood as a sacred container for ancient knowledge.

Such an emphasis is a direct reference to the geometry of the sacred, the roundels and henges of Old Europe, telling us that the key to this mystery was preserved, like the ark, to emerge on the other side of 'the waters' and be incorporated in the foundations of the new belief.

There is another universal feature of this myth. The ark comes to rest on a sacred mountain, a reference to the mountain as a meeting place between the heavens and the earth. It is where the solar energy arrives, like the 'burning bush' of Moses. On its heights, where the air of the earth grows thin, the solar power meets the earth dream and here, between the two, the newly landed survivors emerge. The mountain was not a symbol of the sun god's power before this event. The cave of the Goddess and the sacred grove were the places of divinity before the Flood, but the mountain was not covered by the Flood and remained in contact with the solar divinity, and so it was here that the solar power resided. In every post-Goddess belief system, the mountains are home to the gods. The Flood had made the mountains holy.

The heavens were thus removed from the realms of the earth and became outside our world and hence outside creation. God and his special creation — humanity — were no longer part of the earth. From this moment, the notion that human beings are in some way not a typical part of the process of nature came into being. With this existentialist concept, the things that we do and make become artificial and alienated from nature, as does our concept of what it is to be human.

There is one more piece of evidence that sheds light on this legend. In the Chinese village of BamPo was discovered a continuity of life spanning more than eight thousand years. Early during the excavations, fragments of a teapot were unearthed. On it was written the legend of the tea plant. Here we are told that the people behaved poorly towards the water spirit, a reference to the Goddess, and a dark time came when the world was turned upside down. This reference to a sociological change is in keeping with the more prosaic nature of Chinese stories. As a result, the people were made sick and relationships became chaotic. Only by talking with the mountain spirit could they discover the remedy, which was to drink tea. This is one of the earliest legends discovered and refers directly to the analysis of the later Flood stories that we have looked into.

This identification of a power that was non-physical, that had no material existence and yet had a reality, is the secret revealed in the legend of the deluge. In taking this secret and marrying it to the vacuum that was the legacy of the extinction of the neanderthals, a great mystery appears. It seems as if the vacuum represents a channel through which a compulsion, greater than the individual, could speak. The space through which it spoke was jealously guarded by the peoples of Old Europe, and perhaps it was only when these guardians had been removed that its voice could be heard.

Whatever the interpretation of these events, it was, primarily, the harnessing of the power of conceptual thought in the mind of humanity.

The result of this can be seen, according to the archaeological record as the collapse of a world order, the descent into chaos and a dark age.[7] Into this black chasm sprang the 'entity' and his voice was called 'God' by those who heard him.

However, God was not an invention of a mind of either genius or madness. This power had a shape that had to be conformed to. It would not work unless the lion of the Goddess was invoked, creating the warrior bands that were needed to physically dominate and bind the people to the will of this new God of creation. For this to happen the old beliefs could not just be forgotten, they had to be incorporated and controlled. Unless the explicit ideology of the 'shadow of the hawk' was fulfilled it could not control the minds or souls of a people. Mere force could not contain or subdue a population. In this was hidden the twin aspects of punishment and reward, fear and ecstasy.

Thus a path was shaped. That which was outside our physical reality could enter and become part of this world. Now arose the foot soldiers of this voice, the priest and the prophet, those who studied the shape of the 'shadow of the hawk' and applied it to the world. This new and powerful class would fashion the path of the 'right-minded' which even kings were obliged to follow. It is irrelevant whether the entity in whose name they did this was real or not. Before it appeared it had no existence, and after it had come into being, its message had to be complied with. The key to this was the necessity to surrender free will in order to conform to a social conjuring trick that was both greater than the individual and which followed a road that was not of human making.

All this brought with it new needs and new demands, and the greatest of these was the lineage of power.

The few families who took control in the cities of the plains and of their adjacent farms and fields clung jealously to their privileges. The earliest archaeological reference to this revolution is seen in what is now present day Iraq, and occurred around five thousand five hundred years ago. The image of the 'Tree of Life' comes into being in this period, for the tree is not born into this world fully grown, but is constantly growing and changing. For this it needs a sheltered garden to be protected from the brief passage of its frail human guardians.

The solar God not only required a temple of stone, it also needed a temple of the mind that could be passed on unchanged. It needed somewhere to contain its immortality, and this power was invested in the king. It linked the generations, in a bloodline that royal families could trace back directly to the godhead.

The new kings, ensconced in their cities, needed to make sure that their families would continue in the role of kingship. The earlier matriarchal clan system had ensured that the source of the kings' strength was periodically destroyed, and though it was ever renewed, it was inhibited from evolving and growing past this generational barrier.

An heir to the throne became the most important objective. A woman was to become simply a breeder of sons to carry on the male line. Wealth was amassed, empires arose and fell and were replaced by others, but these same families endeavoured to maintain their control. It would seem that today we live in a world that is also controlled and dominated by a few very powerful families in the form of corporations and even presidential dynasties. Some of these we hear about, and in their own convoluted way they, too, can trace their origins back to the Flood and claim to have been sons of Noah.

These emergent ruling families also needed something that would act as a symbol of their lineage, something that would last longer than their individual lives, for though they believed in eternal life, it was the next generation that would have to wield this new social power in their stead. Therefore they sought something tangible that represented their mastery on earth and spanned the mortal generations of human existence, to solidify and represent their line. They chose gold, perhaps the first symbol of the authority of the gods. Incorruptible, immortal, known as the 'tears of the sun', it represented not only great ritual power but, for the first time, wealth and temporal authority. The longstanding connection between gold and authority started at this time.

The birds sent out from the ark were the first attempts to bring order to the chaos. They were a symbol of transformation. Seen on the cave walls of Palaeolithic France and on the totems of shamans, they represented freedom of spirit and metamorphosis. They are the soul of shape-shifting. The dove in the flood legends is the heart of man which has been altered to take in the new power of the God as it is pierced by the light of the solar energy. The raven is the familiar of kings and magicians, and with its scratchy cry represents this new office. The branch of the olive, the tree of reconciliation, is a sign that the emerging society had to come to some compromise with the old beliefs in order for it to survive. But the mountain was the symbol of this new solar God and from it, his rays dominated and transformed the Goddess.

The ark, we are told, circled the Garden of Paradise seven times, once for each day of the solar week, weaving the spell of the new order into that of the old. There is a legend of this ark in Islam, for it carried not only the survivors of the deluge, but also a stone of tremendous power. This is the story of the Black Stone of the Ka'aba, now preserved in the holy city of Mecca. Every year millions of the faithful walk around it as they pray for forgiveness. The stone is the piece of primordial matter that God gave to Adam when he absolved his sin of eating of the apple of knowledge from the Tree of Life. This apple that had created the image of the Goddess and the lion, the war and destruction waged against the neanderthals, had grown on the tree that had sprung into existence from this seed of knowledge.

This black stone was not a rock of the earth but a meteor from heaven, and, as meteors do, it fell to earth from realms that do not have a physical existence. It fell from the realm in which the concept of the Goddess had been usurped and replaced by a God. In this world it represented a seed which would be the source or embryo of all that was to come. It was from the Garden of Paradise, from a time when humans and neanderthals lived in a world of natural order that the Black Stone of the Ka'aba came. Preserved for all this time as a source of great power, it was threatened by the Flood and was moved to the sacred mountains of Sirat near the holy city of Mecca.

Of the three estates of the Goddess — the lion in the north, the stone in the east and the knowledge of the west — it was the stone of the cities that best expressed the control of the lion. As the first Goddess figures were carved in rock, so stone was the carrier of their secrets.

It was in the embodiment and transformation of stone that the Goddess appeared and it was in the black stones that the source of this power was said to have been stored. The echoes are hard to ignore — it is in remembrance of this that the stones are held sacred. Long is the memory of stone, the bones of the earth Goddess on which is carved the will of man. For this reason, it was in stone that later kings carved their God-given laws. Moses was not the only one to do this.[8]

The nature of the people who provoked this mutation has been extensively studied. Archaeologists call them 'Kurgans' after the burial mounds that they left behind. The numerous remains of their houses, communities and artefacts have now been catalogued and a picture of their migrations, and hence the events of this time, has been painstakingly drawn up.

Where these people of the lion appeared, more ancient cultures disappeared. Time and again the archaeological record shows the delicate pottery and design of the people of central and southern Europe being suddenly replaced by rough corded beakers and new clumsy decoration. The graves and burial rites of all earlier peoples cease and instead we find mounds, or Kurgans, replacing them. In each of these, with whatever wealth they had pillaged, were the remains of a powerful king or chief.[9]

During this time of social upheaval, displaced tribes migrated in their thousands, fleeing their homelands to escape the waters of chaos that had been released into the world, as the lion marched triumphantly over the wreckage of a civilisation. Tales of bravery and despair, of power and glory are told in the myths and legends of many countries. This is the period of the epic, a time of legendary rulers and powerful priests. It is also a time when Ireland, sacred to the Goddess as her last haven in the West, comes into the mythical picture. The genocide of the Native Americans or the Aborigines provides us with a modern equivalent of the annihilation of Old Europe, allowing us to understand the situation in more detail.[10]

The Enuma Elish, the Babylonian creation epic, has a lot to say about this process of invasion. We re-join the story after Ea, one of the principal leaders of the self-styled 'new gods' has defeated Apsu, the consort of the Goddess, and has taken from him the symbols and attributes of jurisdiction. With these he has become a political authority in his own right, and the people who hold him as their lord have upset the delicate balance of power. It is a graphic tale of the war between the Goddess and the God, disclosing how the disparate bands of the Kurgan tribes united under a single leader, Marduk, the Lord of Lords, the highest one to take the field against the Goddess. However the constant allusion to 'the Mother and her children', and the sheer power and awe that the Goddess was capable of engendering, leads us to believe that she is the source of all things. It is this power that the victorious gods use as the foundation for their 'new world'. The story serves as a reminder that those who are victorious are the ones who write history.

The Discovery of the Dingle Diamond

The mountains abruptly left the hot plains, rising in purple ranks against the blue sky. From her vantage point in a cave, at a considerable height, Tiamat could make out the ranks of men and woman on the plains below. The colourful dress of her warriors stood out in the bright sun, each surrounded by a sea of blue and black, the uniform colours worn by Marduk's coalition. They were locked in a dreadful combat and it was clear that her people were being slaughtered. She covered her face with her hands and turned away to compose herself. For months they had been preparing for this battle. Never before had so many tribes come together and this morning they had gathered at the foot of the hills, a many-coloured field of warriors, and sworn to make a stand. No longer would they be hunted down, one-by-one, like vermin. They carried an eclectic mixture of home-made weapons adapted from hunting tools: maces, sticks, spears and bows, no two were identical. There had been brave songs sung that night as the bonfires consumed the last of their stocks of wood. But, as the first rays of sunlight woke the sleeping people, a quiet determination had replaced their elation. Tiamat knew, had known always known, what was to come. She was directly acquainted with Marduk's army and she realised that they carried superior weapons. Moreover, they outnumbered her five to one and were drilled and organised. By contrast, Kingu, her young lover and war king for the battle, was inexperienced and overly confident. By the trunk of a palm she had sat up all night and contemplated the fate of her brave warriors. Now, after the battle had been finalised and the speeches had been made, she had nothing to do except watch as the tableau unfolded.

On the plains below men and woman were fleeing, being pursued and hacked down. The clamour of the battle echoed around the cliffs, eerily adding to the terror of their screams. The sun crossed the sky, treading its path until the shadows lengthened. The tumult subsided and Tiamat wearily raised her eyes. She smoothed her dress and tightened her leather jacket and walked out of the cave and down to the plains below. Beside her were seven of her guards, tight-lipped and panicky. Below her, a tight circle had been formed around those of her people who were left standing. Ropes had been brought and they were being bound. By the base of the cliff she halted whilst a small group of black-robed soldiers dragged Kingu behind them. His feet had been hobbled and his wrists were cruelly bound and his face was a sea of blood from a gash on his head. A thickset young man, his head almost welded to his shoulders, led the group. By his side walked two of the biggest men that Tiamat had ever seen. They had blond hair which protruded from a leather hat, something Tiamat was not familiar with. The soldiers halted a spears cast from her and Marduk stepped forward. He was smiling but his eyes, glittering like coals in his dark complexion, held hatred and in his hands were a polished stone mace and a wide-meshed net. Tiamat spoke first. Her voice, though soft, carried tremendous force.

"Marduk, upstart! Do you think yourself so great that you can hold the whole world in your hand? Are those you have ensnared scurrying now from their holes to hold you high?" Marduk shook his head, turning to spit into the sand before he answered.

"Why are you so proud, why do you not recognise the way of the world? Why did you not submit when you first saw the might of my will? You have been an endless thorn in our side. Mother of All Things, why did you have to fight this war?"

The way he accented 'mother' made clear his sarcasm. With a sneer he stepped up to her and raised her chin in his hand. "You made that boy, Kingu, your consort and gave him powers that challenged our own. You have abused the gods of my ancestors. You have grouped your forces for war and I have struck them down." A brief eddy of wind whipped at the sand around his legs and he walked back a few paces before abruptly turning to snap out a challenge.

"Stand up alone and we will fight, you and I alone in battle!"

But Tiamat was ready, and it was a different vision of the Goddess that Marduk now saw: taller and more terrible, she seemed cloaked in an electric blue haze. Her battle cry, an appalling, high-pitched keen to the earth, echoed from the rough cliffs as she began her battle ritual. Her feet dancing in the sands she intoned the spirit of death, focusing her energy on Marduk's weapons. Marduk stepped forward to meet her, raising his mace in a whorl about his head and looking for an opening to cast his net. For a brief time they were perfectly matched: Marduk, the most powerful of the gods, and Tiamat. Whilst the fight continued, one of the fair-haired warriors stepped around the combat and, coming from behind, launched a thrust at Tiamat's head. Although she avoided the blow, it was enough to give Marduk the space he needed. The net snaked out and wrapped itself around her legs, pulling her to the ground. One of his henchmen offered Marduk a bow and taking it, he notched an arrow. A single arrow, enough to change a world, it hung for a second from his hands and then he let fly. The shot pierced Tiamat's stomach and passed into her womb. She gasped once and put her hand to her wound. For a moment she was quiet, her expression beckoning Marduk, it seemed. Then she folded her arms and was still.

Marduk, then, called his guards around him and walked over to the huddle of prisoners trapped like birds in a snare.'

There was to be no safe haven from the beginning of the new concept. Once one body of people had given themselves to this new set of beliefs, then all paradigms changed. In the name of the new God, in the name of right and might, the 'evil' ways of the serpent — manifestation and symbol of the Goddess — were destroyed. The old cities of the East weathered this crisis. Here, the new laws flourished and armies could be raised to meet the conflict, forming small oases of stability. For the people of the Goddess, who were farmers, herders and people of the forests, there was no safety, only flight.

The memory of this period, probably the darkest in all history, was thus burned into the psyche of humanity.

Even as the last of the burial mound builders, the Kurgans, were setting up their halls and walled villages, the final waves of refugees were fleeing and having to fight for new lands to settle. These new lands were often on the edges of the then developed world, or were regions protected by natural barriers, and were places where generations of the people of the Goddess had been settled from earlier times. The island of Crete,[11] defended by the ocean, and the mountain haven of the Basque Country, were typical.

Other tribes, such as the Tuatha Dé Danaan, or the Brigantes, became wanderers, restlessly moving from place to place in search of a homeland. In doing this, they lost much of their lore and adopted a melange of ideas from the peoples that they met. These tribes learnt much from their wanderings through Scythia and Egypt and, eventually, Spain and Ireland.

The city dwellers of the East, at least those who did not leave their homes and travel elsewhere, developed a brilliant defence and achieved a metamorphosis that has never been matched in any period of history. With their focus on the earth, and the transformation of the Goddess in

her journey through the underworld to achieve resurrection, they culti-
vated a different path.

Between 5,500 and 5,200 years ago — almost overnight in archaeological terms — in the cities of Sumer, the temple complex appeared.
This was no gradual evolution from the water gardens and fields of the
pastoral and agricultural folk who lived before the deluge; instead,
replacing houses we see a fully developed complex of ziggurats
(temple mounds or pyramids) with walls and dwelling places for a
hierarchy of priests, and at the top of the pyramid, closest to the sky
god, was the priest-king, God's mouthpiece on earth. A new religion
had mustered and channelled the power of the lion and enslaved the
population. All the power of gold and the wealth of kings was needed
to put the Kurgans to flight as they swept like a hurricane around the
cities.

The voice in the ears of the priests was closely obeyed by the few
ambitious families who took this power. It was called the ' religion of
the right mind', or of the sun, or of the light.

"I who will invoke thy discipline as the mightiest of all
At the outcome, when I shall attain immortality
The Dominion of the good mind and the straight paths of right
Wherein dwells the wise lord."

So spoke Zarathustra, one of the earliest recorded prophets of these
new methods of ruler-ship.

The new skill of writing was used to immortalise the battles and
struggles of these peoples, and they leave us a story of the taming of a
land, of the bringing of water and the planting of fields.

Such a sudden arrival of this fully formed concept of religious hierarchy is probably the most startling testament to the understanding that
the priest kings must have had of the power of the 'shadow of the
hawk'. They understood both how to wield it effectively and what gave
it influence over the masses. They understood and grasped the essential
power of this concept, applying it with a will not matched until the rise
of the Roman Empire some three thousand years later. For these reasons the world's religions have taken, as the root source for their holy
books, the stories that first were shaped by the 'shadow of the hawk' in
ancient Sumeria and the cities of the East.

The Discovery of the Dingle Diamond

The keepers of history deliberately muddled the narrative to create a moral-bearing legend that could only be understood by those with the correct knowledge. These priest-kings could thus keep the powerful secret out of the hands of others. George Orwell, in *1984*, tells us how the present can be controlled, and the future shaped, by secretly manipulating the past. Such an elite still exists in a powerful enough form to exercise control over our minds. In this way, the magic hinted at in the 'great works' does indeed wake sleeping devils. It is almost as if an entity had broken into the human psyche. That it has been given, and still has, many names — not all of them religious — does not obscure its nature. The source of this power, held to be a direct communication with God, will be discussed in the following chapter. For now, because this voice of command is so polymorphic, and to keep things simple, its titles — the solar God, the godhead, a male God or just plain 'God' — I have labelled collectively as the 'Entity'. I hope that this label will encourage a certain freedom from the fog of pre-conceived opinion, allowing us to approach this delicate subject with eyes open.

The shamanic lion of the Siberian plains-people faded, a distant echo of a primitive anger, though it later became a potent force to threaten the ordered world of European and Eastern rulers. Over time, the Kurgan hordes became the enemy without. This presents us with the contest of a twin belief system, the poles of which are similarly matched, lion versus lion, one wild and one tamed, and far fiercer in the fray is the wild lion. The principle of its taming was not to pacify it but to enrage it, and to harness its energy in a just war. The Shakespearean phrase 'Cry havoc and let slip the dogs of war' succinctly describes the carnage.[12]

The doctrine of freedom and resistance invoked by the Goddess is still very much with us, and still persecuted by those who wield the 'shadow of the hawk' and the power of the lion.

It was an epoch of change and wonder and a time of horror, the beginning of the nightmare years and then five thousand years ago, shortly after this nightmare had begun, a magical people, fleeing the destruction in Europe, arrived at a small sanctuary in Ireland. They were a people who would plant a seed that would grow to form the root and branch of the culture of western Europe. It was the time of tribes like the Tuatha Dé Danaan, vessels of hidden knowledge, tribes that the religious authorities of the Entity tried in vain to eradicate. Not without destroying the 'shadow of the hawk', and thus eliminating the source of the priests' power, could it be permanently erased, for the concept of the Goddess was born as part of the duality of human culture. Like a doppelganger it followed, dogging the rulers' attempts to enslave and exploit and build. Thus the knowledge of the Goddess became occult lore, passed on in secret by the few who knew that the truth of the world could only be understood in this light.

In failing to eradicate the old knowledge, the authorities of the new world order labelled it the bogeyman (or woman), the fear in the night and of the unknown. So the ideas and concepts went underground, starting a process that led through occult societies and culminated in the New Age ideology of today. The process of demonising the truth became one of the chief crusades of the new rulers as they sought to control their society. It was a very useful tool in their armoury and a key plank in the ideology of manipulation. By invoking this fear some of the worst crimes of civilisation have come about, for this fear has been a tool powerful enough to start crusades and pogroms, wars and genocide.

The Entity required a new social structure to contain it and, surprisingly, this was rooted in a solid and enduring material object: the temple.

Chapter Seven
Temple

"And they saw the Wheel of His power made of one circle, three layers, sixteen parts, fifty spokes, twenty counter-spokes, six groups of eight, three paths, one rope of innumerable strands, and the great illusion: the illusion which sees the ONE as two."
The Svetasvatara Upanishad.

By 4000 BC there was little left of the once widespread agricultural Old European society. In its place, civilisation flourished in small walled cities. These tightly knit communities operated under a radically new social structure and within these precincts, the sacred meaning of art evolved into a form of ritual magic, a magic whose true significance was its concealed genius in controlling society. This process was so powerful that it became the dominant blueprint for the next six thousand years, yet here at its very inception it was childishly simple. Through control of this ritual art a few individuals could become powerful rulers, creating and affecting the ideas and concepts that, even today, we all live by and rarely question. For this reason strict censorship of artistic expression has always been a primary policy of dictators and tyrants alike. Time and again, in myths and religion, we are told that it was an entity that was the architect behind this order. He alone, the myths tell us, put the ideas for a new social structure into the minds of men. And it seems he did this in an ingenious way, as a bargain — the original Faustian tryst. In return for the loss of their individual will, the selected few would receive a very practical guide to wealth and power. Zarathustra, one of the earliest prophets of this new way of life, explained this bargain as a simple trade:

"He also, O WISE ONE, shall receive from Righteousness the cattle Promised with the Dominion of the Good Mind, by his power shall he make the neighbouring lands prosper for himself."[1]

Europe after the Kurgan invasions must have been a nightmare. The lions had been let slip. In the aftermath of the violence, ransacked abandoned villages and burnt and devastated lands stretched from Siberia to Africa. The complete chaos resulted in a breakdown of the established order and the old traditions were in a state of flux. There was no going back to the past, no way that humans could return to the simplicity of Eden. The Flood had taken everything, leaving in its wake a kind of madness.

Yet phoenix-like from the ruins, a new world of order did arise. The cities of the East, islands amidst the devastation, led this metamorphosis with a new generation. Instead of elders and shamans, there were kings and priests. It was into this crucible that the divine inspirations of the solar God, the Entity, were poured. The control of the precise dictates of the Entity and the unique energies of the Lion Warrior required a Herculean effort, and the struggle to stabilise society was recorded in detail in the mythology. The emerging leaders of these societies required a base from which they could safely pursue these aims, a secure stronghold from which they could dictate the path that society needed to follow.

In short, those who wanted to reorganise the world in this light needed the Temple.[2]

"Esigala, the earthly temple, symbol of the infinite heaven... beautiful Esigala wherein is performed the liturgy from which the universe receives its structure, the occult is made plain...earth as a mirror of the heavens."[3]

In the earlier stages of their development, temples were devoid of embellishment and, like Bauhaus architecture, had a minimalist form. (Diagram 7.1) Standing four or five storeys above the mud houses, these structures were the hubs of the earliest cities, but they were no mere stage show or empty ritual, nor did they only exist on some mythical plane of complex ideology. The formulae used by the king, and the procedures invoked by the state apparatus of the holy city, were prosaic and dedicated to a fundamentally materialistic end.

As guardians of the temple, a hierarchical caste of priests was

Diagram 7.1
A Ziggurat built by the Sumerians. Its design and scale were far in advance of anything that had been previously built. 3500BC.

created. This body sought to change the whole structure of society in the name of their god. It was a process that from the start was intensely political and it marks the advent of organised religion. Regardless of its outward form, from the Egyptians to the Christians, every later priesthood would closely follow the 'Sumerian Temple' blue-print. It was an incredibly elaborate and ambitious vision, systematically bringing into being separate but organised groups of people, each practising a craft. Some of these groups had to master totally new social skills such as writing and reading, counting, measuring and architecture. All of this was co-ordinated from the fortress-like structure of the temple with military precision by the priests.[4]

This frenetic hive of activity turned the temples into practical working instruments, and it is generally accepted that the economic and cultural life of the region centred around them. There is no doubt that these edifices must have been radical, imposing and powerful and judging by the prosperity of the city, they seem to have succeeded in their aim of creating a new order. The immaculate genesis of the temple has confounded modern historical analysis: the problem is that archaeologists have no theory to describe its origins. The earliest temples, known as ziggurats, have no precedent and appear suddenly, fully formed, at the beginning of Sumerian civilisation. The plans, architecture and building skills — not to mention the organisational methods of this new 'church' and the social bodies of the guilds that surrounded it — were all unprecedented. Yet the stories are very clear about its origins:

it was the Flood that allowed the plans of 'God' to be realised, and the voice of this 'God' dictated his divine plans. The first act of the priests of the Temple on behalf of this entity was to establish the kingship as separate from the priesthood.

The huge temple ziggurat of Eridug was built around 3500 BC in Mesopotamia and is listed in the Sumerian King Lists, which describe the separation thus:

"After the kingship descended from heaven, the kingship was in Eridug. In Eridug, Alulim became king; he ruled for twenty-eight thousand years."[5]

Along with the template for kingship are given detailed and often complex guidelines describing not only the physical structure of the temple buildings but also the form and roles of the political institutions based around it. The document is adamant that these instructions came directly from a conscious, non-physical force that only exists outside of our physical world.

The story of the building of this first house, the first temple, is recorded in great detail on the 5000-year-old Mesopotamian clay cylinders discovered by archaeologists and recently translated.[6] It relates how the god Ningirsu gives divine advice, in the form of a vision to a shepherd, on how to build the temple. The visionary power of shepherds is attested to in many later myths, including the biblical nativity.

The opening stanzas make it clear to the shepherd that he is witness to the unfolding of a plan, and in an eerily practical way this entity introduces the temple:

"There was… a warrior. His arm was bent, holding a lapis lazuli tablet in his hand, and he was setting down the plan of the house."[7]

As the shepherd recounts his vision we are made aware that he does not understand the concept, for there is nothing in his world with which to compare these ideas:

"He spoke to me about building his house, but I could not understand what he exactly meant, then daylight rose for me on the horizon."[8]

Temple

The shepherd is forced to ask for help and he does this on a spiritual level. The stories tell us that the mother Goddess interpreted the dream and in this way the temple could be built.

"Nance, mighty lady, lady of most precious powers, lady who like Enlil determines fates, my Nance, what you say is trustworthy and takes precedence. You are the interpreter of dreams among the gods, you are the lady of all the lands. Mother, my matter today is a dream."[9]

References made to the divine source of inspiration — the godhead or Entity — are common in legend and in ancient manuscript. The story is often the same. A shepherd receives the wisdom of the Entity and persuades the leaders of the society to adopt these protocols and instructions. But what is often over-looked is that these instructions have to be interpreted by the Goddess. The temple becomes an extension of the much older tradition of building roundels and henges that performed a similar communication with the other world in earlier times. This implies a need that the Goddess be the translator of the instructions, so that people may understand them. The Christian version of this act serves as a good example of the need to incorporate this protocol into the establishment of a new religion. Jesus Christ, who specifically said that he was building a new Temple — a temple that was not physical, but in the form of his body — was heralded by angels who told shepherds of his coming. These shepherds took the message to Mary, who in a very real way translated the Temple of Jesus into human corporal form. Thus the Goddess is given her place in the scheme of things. She has become an interpreter of the voice of God, a channel through which the spirit can manifest itself in physical terms. It is a role that she has always played but here, for the first time, she surrenders her power to the over-lordship of a God.

More prosaically, the Entity lists the benefits of the Temple:

"Laying the foundations of my temple will bring immediate abundance: the great fields will grow rich for you, the levees and ditches will be full to the brim for you, the water will rise for you to heights never reached by the water before. Under you more oil than ever will be poured and more wool than ever will be weighed in Sumer."[10]

151

That the benefits of such a Temple were not slow in appearing is clearly shown:

"The ruler gave instructions to his city as to one man. The land of Lagac became of one accord for him, like children of one mother. He opened manacles, removed fetters, established ... rejected legal complaints, and locked up those guilty of capital offences. He undid the tongue of the goad and the whip, replacing them with wool from lamb-bearing sheep. Nobody could make the ruler building the E-ninnu (temple) let fall a chance utterance."[11]

Not only were the instructions for building this temple precise and in considerable depth, but the role of the priests, their everyday duties and their separate offices are also given. In the story, the shepherd is in communication with a source of power that seeks not only the creation of a physical building and its staff, but also a method by which the whole of the society of 5,500 years ago could be radically re-organised. In doing this, the Entity makes it plain that this power can only be held by a few individuals.

Clearly outlined in this amazing instruction manual is the need to make the central sanctuary for the symbolic and real trophies of power as secret as possible.[12] Hidden here is the symbolic geometry that has been the subject of thousands of written words, poems and songs. It is often described as the hub of a wheel from which the spokes radiate.

"The twelve-spoked wheel of order rolls around and around the sky and never ages. Seven hundred and twenty sons in pairs rest on it," says the Rig Veda.[13]

The spokes are regarded as a calendar reference; for example, the symbols of the zodiac, the twelve hours of the day and the twelve months of a year. This imagery hides a practical application connecting the spiritual with the mundane, for the wheel also describes the assembly of twelve advisors of the king who formed the council of the city — the political arm of the priests. Each spoke also describes a socio-economic bastion of the new ideology: the law courts and lawyers, the merchants and bankers, the landowners, the craft guilds, the army, the

Diagram 7.2
The wheel of the temple, in this case from a temple wat in Asia.

farmers, the shepherds, the builders and the nobility — in short, the institutions. All branched out from the priests in the temple, each aspect holding in place the rim of the wheel, the total circumference of which was the society. This was the Temple in all its manifestations. (Diagram 7.2)

This symbolism survives today in all religious temples, Gothic cathedrals being a good example. Often above the entrance is an arc of carvings depicting the medieval crafts and guilds as a wheel surrounding the godhead of the temple, in this case Jesus Christ. (Diagram 7.3) The rim of the wheel took the whole weight of the carriage of God from which emanated the voice of the Entity, whilst the hub was the ever-rotating, ever-changing connection between the rim and the fixed carriage of the Entity. As long as the wheel turned, the carriage could move onwards in a single straight line. This simple metaphor translated the ancient philosophy of the 'circle of life' into a linear progression of time. The Entity, the source of the concept, could be moved over the 'dream of the earth'. It literally moved through time projecting itself and its institutions into a future that was far longer than an individual's

Diagram 7.3
The wheel survives in the arch of a Christian Church, hanging over the
entrance and depicting the trades people.

life span. Since the Entity came from outside the earth, man gave it the
badge of the sun. For this reason, past cultures have represented this
carriage with the 'wheel of the sun'.[14] The ancient Hindu hymn in the
Atharva-Veda puts it succinctly:

"With seven wheels does this Time ride, seven naves has he, immortality is his axle. He carries hither all these beings (worlds). Time, the
first god, now hastens onward." [15]

Seen in this way, the symbol of the 'wheel of the sun' becomes a
simple and direct instruction manual, a guide to the physical steps necessary for any society to follow the path of the Entity and successfully
introduce the 'shadow of the hawk' to its people. The result was always
the same: money in the form of gold became the mainspring of the
society, land-ownership became a source of power and a hierarchy

subjugated the masses to its will.

From the word of God, a precise hierarchical society organised around a religion was created. Since the physical centre of this was the temple buildings themselves, the plans of these institutions would have been kept here in much the same way as a constitution is kept in a modern democracy. These records are found as a peculiar kind of 'roadmap' in the form of a tree dedicated to the vision of the priests.

Protected by the temple, as if in a garden, the Tree of Life could flourish. This tree exists in every religion and it has many names: *Yggdrasil* the Scandinavian Tree of Heaven, the Tree of Life of Mesopotamia and the Tree of Knowledge in the Garden of Eden, are just a few. The roots of the tree are in the material structure of the temple, but its branches and form are shaped by the ideological vision of the Entity, represented by the sun. The tree represents the growth of knowledge and understanding of the sociological structures necessary to hold a society together: the law, the art of war, banking, masonry and science. It is also the expression of the earth, the source of all things, which gives birth under the power of the sun. The Tree of Life shown on the gold ring of the Mycenaean King Nestor, from 1500 BC, describes this well. Here, the branches represent the guilds and trades. Its roots, deep in the underworld and symbolising the mysteries of the initiated priests, are guarded by the dog. The lion sits caged by the tree, its armies no longer rampant but orderly and disciplined, and amongst its branches the people enjoy life. The Goddess and her consort, the king of the year, standing on either side of the tree are the key figures in the myth. They are the farmers who guard the tree and harvest its fruits and, whether these are the hazelnut of knowledge or the apple in the Garden of Eden, it is made clear that only a few will be able to consume them. The Tree of Life holds a clear message from God: only by following in the steps of the Entity can the human concept materialise in a useful way and the fruits of the tree be harvested.

In this way, new arts and lore were created and maintained so that the world could be stood on its head. The old paradigm of the trinity was swept aside and into the world, into the hearts and minds of human beings, came that which has no physical existence, overriding the original concept of the Goddess as defined by a supernatural Entity and shaped by the new castes.

A concept only occurs in the human mind. It is something that has no physical existence but yet can cause change, can change one thing into another. It is a process that has no name but as long as a standard set of rules is obeyed, then the concept can be made to function. A simple example is the exact circle. Try as you might, it is impossible to exactly measure the circumference of a circle, as a slightly better approximation can always be made. In the mind, though, a circle can exist and can be given a precise size. This could be thought of as a human invention, but this ideal circle has its own eternal laws and geometry which prohibit being able either to define the diameter of the circle — in which case the circumference becomes an approximation — or define the circumference — wherein the diameter becomes only an approximation. Because the circle has no existence other than in the human mind yet does not obey humans but follows its own logic, it is often used as a metaphor for the emergence of this form of godhead, and the appearance of the wheel in the art of ancient civilisations tells of its arrival. The Entity is equated to these geometrical laws of the universe, the mystery of both considered to stem from the same source. For this reason, geometry is a main pillar of occult lore and most church lore as well. Through the application of its principles, the minds of people, of the masses, can be channelled, controlled and organised to produce the coherent and linked bodies of knowledge that have given humans their unique ability to control and manipulate the earth power.

This creation of a body of esoteric knowledge was, and still is, part of the rules of application of the concept of the solar God. The majority has to believe in the rules governing it and the traditional formulae used by the temple engender this faith. This is the meaning of Socrates' statement: "It is best that you have understanding, lacking this you need faith and lacking this, have a trade." Both belief and trade are pillars, or spokes, of the Temple.

Knowledge is power, and power lies in the hands of the few. If this knowledge were to be handed back to the masses it would cease to be power. Socrates was not sentenced to death because he was asking awkward questions, he died because he wanted to share his knowledge. The wheel of life, the mechanism of the concept's ability to materialise or direct the physical world, is thus at stake. The dichotomy between the need to pass on knowledge and the need to keep it hidden from the masses has meant that there has been an ever more complex system of disguises in the form of religion. These disguises have proved very successful, and in trying to penetrate them more than a few great minds have become lost.

It was the genius of the Temple that separated the king from the priest, allowing the divine power of the Entity to move throughout the people of the kingdom. It also freed the king from the incumbent duties of earlier priest-kings. In the main, this meant being sacrificed at the end of a specific period, often as short as one year, something no kingly lineage could stand. This ritual thwarted the designs of the Entity, for each time the king died the cycle began again and the progress that the monarchy desired was held in check.

Thus the Temple freed kings and allowed their royal dynasties to be created. The priests took over the burden of the ritual killing of the king, for someone had to die to mark the turning of the wheel and to ensure that the 'shadow of the hawk' was maintained in the minds of the people. An era of sacrifice, animal and human, came about, to create the fear that enabled ruler-ship. This accomplishment was an expression of complete surrender to the will of the Entity. It was in every way as total a control over the souls of the people as the more ancient tribal obedience to the king-priest. Once acts such as the ritualistic taking of life are embarked upon, so then are the people involved tied to the awful splendour of the act.

There is, however, an important distinction to be made between the sacrifice demanded by the Entity and that offered by the sacred king of the seasons. The former was not a sacrifice willingly participated in by the sacrificial subject and the people. In fact it was the very opposite. The bound and gagged victims were brought into view of the horrified and spellbound citizens. The priest, dressed in his robes of high office and surrounded by armed guards, would plunge his knife into the chest of the victim and extract the still beating heart. The victims were neither of value to the society nor to the king seated close to the altar, they were slaves or criminals or enemies captured in war, aliens from another land. In this way, the sacrifice was a display of power and a warning to those who thought they might break free. It crushed the spirit and allowed the thoughts of the city, the will of the king and the dictates of the priests to become the thoughts of a people. The horrors perpetrated by soldiers whose humanity had left them were enough to crush the individual. They could and did do this because of their total surrender to the temple.

Acceptance of a life of drudgery devoted to the glorification of a line of kings and their entourage was now not only possible but also essential. Any other choice was madness.

The Temple and its austere practice allowed the will of the Entity to break free of its prison of mortality, and like a demon it fled across the generations. The sacrifice of blood was a libation to its soul, which allowed it the continuity necessary to surpass ordinary mortality, making it immortal. Generations could build upon generations, each more complex and involved than before. Society, not the individual, was the beneficiary of the sacrifice. This was the nature of the immortality grasped at by the ancient kings, as their priests tried to capture its essence in the physical world. Truly, the gods had become immortal.

The shadow of the neanderthal is very long indeed, and its place in our psyche firmly rooted. Aeons of kinship with our cousins forged the landscape of our minds. The vacuum left by their disappearance and the knowledge that we were responsible for their extinction shapes and dictates our sub-conscious creating desires and yearnings not in our conscious minds but in our very souls. Because we have forgotten the roots of these desires we are no longer able to choose the method by which we can placate them. The genius of the Temple was in its manipulation of this legacy, in the way the priests and kings laid down the new social order, artfully guiding the human intellect until the 'shadow of the hawk' was evoked in our minds. Unlike in previous epochs, the elite of the priest-kings actively sought to bind humanity to their will. To achieve this trick, the priests of the Entity needed to establish three key pillars in their society.

Firstly, there are the laws of the Temple. The authority of God replaces that of the neanderthals, aiming to reinforce the collective acknowledgement of an ancestral guilt, the cord by which we are all tied. By playing on this and, if certain rites and conditions are met, offering a path to salvation, the priests sustain and strengthen their social grip. It is a method so powerful that even our dress code, sexual mores and eating habits are curtailed and dominated, establishing social 'norms' of behaviour.

Secondly, there are laws of the state, which depend upon the king's authority coming directly from God. This is achieved by replaying the act of neanderthal genocide in the form of a sacrifice — not of the king but in the name of the king — to placate the anger of God. When the population takes part in this bloodletting, the people become accomplices to the act thus giving their power to the king, ensuring that the majority accepts the laws of the land, the ownership of property by individuals, and the legal right of the state or the king to enforce laws. This is the iron fist that threatens us. It is an act of obedience required by the state and enforceable by the king's men.

Thirdly, there are the laws of the heart, the authority of faith, the acceptance of God as an individual expression of the society's collective interest. This is the promise of reward for obedience and of the three laws it is the most powerful. In the name of faith, acts of terrible savagery and barbarity are not only carried out but also supported and condoned by many. It is an act required of all of a nation's people, to display obedience to the temple and the king.

These are the practical aspects of the Temple — the laws of the Temple itself, the laws of the state and the laws that govern the hearts and minds of individuals. That we have replaced kings with statuary leaders has not changed the effectiveness of this formula in any way. The laws are still as relevant today as they were at their conception, and deep down under the pomp and ceremony, under even the thought of 'God', lies the loss of the neanderthals in the social lives of men.

When first formulated these laws were simple and prosaic. They are succinctly stated in the tablets of the law that Moses brought down from the mountain:

"You shall have no other Gods before me. You shall not kill. You shall not commit adultery. You shall not steal. You shall not make gods of silver to be with me, nor shall you make for yourselves gods of gold. An altar of the earth you shall make for me and sacrifice on it your burnt offerings and your peace offerings. In every place where I cause my name to be remembered I will come to you and bless you."[16]

Two thousand years earlier, the establishment of Hammurabi's laws under God affirmed the same message (Diagram 7.4):

"Then Anu and Bel called by name me, Hammurabi, the exalted prince who feared God, to bring about the rule of righteousness in the land. Who provided large sacrificial offerings for the temple of Ningirsu. If any one steal the property of a temple or of the court, he

shall be put to death. If a chieftain or a man (common soldier), who has been ordered to go upon the king's highway for war does not go, then shall this officer or man be put to death. If a man violate the wife (betrothed or child-wife) of another man, this man shall be put to death. If a man put out the eye of another man, his eye shall be put out. I have in Babylon the city where Anu and Bel raise high their heads, in E-Sagil, the Temple, whose foundations stand firm as heaven and earth, in order to bespeak justice in the land, to settle all disputes, and heal all injuries, set up these my precious words, written upon my memorial stone, before the image of me, as king of righteousness."[17]

The setting in the Koran is the same:

"This is the book, a guidance to the god-fearing who believe in the unseen. God is all embracing, all-knowing. There is no God but God. Surely we have given thee abundance; so pray unto the Lord and sacrifice. Do not covet that whereby God in his bounty has preferred one of you above another."

Diagram 7.4 Hammurabi's laws as given by the divine, carved on a pillar of stone.

And again in the Torah:

"Ye shall not make with Me— gods of silver, or gods of gold ye shall not make unto you. An altar of earth thou shalt make unto Me, and shalt sacrifice thereon thy burnt-offerings, and thy peace-offerings, thy sheep, and thine oxen; in every place where I cause My name to be mentioned I will come unto thee and bless thee. And if thou make Me an altar of stone, thou shalt not build it of hewn stones; for if thou lift up thy tool upon it, thou hast profaned it."[18]

In the Zend-Avesta (the sacred text of the Zoroastrians), in the scripts of the Egyptians and in the guides of the tales in the Rig Veda, each holy book describes the laws and the paths to follow them in almost identical terms.

The Christ of the Roman Catholic Church, Christ the king of heaven, son and one part of God, is an exact retelling of the above stories. Born as spirit, he is sacrificed for our sins, the sins of Adam and Eve, the sins of knowledge and of the gaining of our powers to be as God. It allows God to be saved and elevated to power, to become the one true path by which we can fulfil our eternal longing. The power of the Roman Catholic Church and the power that millions of believers hand over to its representative on earth, the Pope, is tangible and real. In the name of such a faith, multitudes of barbaric acts have been perpetuated down the centuries. The very birth of the Roman Catholic Church was one of fire and politics. Yet that has not always been the case with Christianity. There is another interpretation of the life of Christ, and this is held by many outside the Roman Catholic Church. It is the story of Christ the Son of Man, born of woman. In this he is the sacred king who was sacrificed to the Goddess in the age-old methods that sought to free us, not enslave us, from this collective guilt. If you have ever wondered what the great difference is between Christ the Son of Man and Christ as God, and why so much blood has been spilled over it, the answer lies here.

By marrying the Temple with the concept of the Entity comes the ability to shape and control the earth forces that flow through life over the course of generations, and because of this the earth itself can be mastered and owned. Broken forever is the link that made us a part of the earth dream where the sacred spirits of the earth and the turning of the year created a unity in which humans participated.

Those dominated by its will were able to defile the earth in the name of their lord. They were able to kill and to destroy without going mad with guilt. They were to look to the acquisition of wealth and to commit murder and even genocide to obtain it. For this reason the Temple also represents the ideal of good and evil. This was not always successful and then the forces of the lion ran amok. Libraries would burn and city walls fall, but always the phoenix rose from the ashes, and from dark ages new and more secure branches of the Tree of Life would flourish.

A power was also harnessed, a power that once was shared but when gathered up into the Temple, it left those who were subject to it bereft of their birthright. This power exists in the process of transferring the concept of the Entity into the actions needed to manifest it in society. As Zarathustra puts it, "I will harness for you, O wise One with Righteousness, By the spur of your praise, the swiftest steeds, Broad and strong through the Good Mind, Upon Which you shall Draw near. May you be ready to aid me!"[19]

This was the power that inspired the prophet to dedicate his life to deciphering the needs and the words of God and convincing those around him to take up this power and apply it.

There is a point in any process at which one thing becomes another. It occurs in every human mind and is the process by which a thought becomes manifest and moves the material world. It cannot be said to reside in any cells of the brain or to be visible in any process, yet it can intervene in the physical laws of the universe to produce change. This process occurs at the borderline where the knowledge of the earth's ways and the realm of the spirit meet. Almost all of the ancient writings, the Gnostic texts and the most modern scientific research have failed to even find a name for this process, but the blindingly obvious fact remains that every minute of every day, human beings perform this miracle of conscious manipulation of the material world.

Serious investigation has reached two opposing opinions on the nature of this process. One acknowledges the process as part of the divine nature of things and declares that the only way to understand it is through direct experience. This path has given rise to Gnostic understanding and is the subject of Zen Buddhism and of mystical inspiration. The other is planted in precise definition and holds that events are purely mechanical and exist outside of our experience. This is the doctrine of order, where everything has its allotted place and has given rise to objective science. Both roads lead to the same conclusion. The act of thought is a concept, something that can have no true explanation.

When we make a movement, however great or small, it is an act of will imposed on the physical world and we believe that we have choice in this action. No one likes to think that our minds are controlled or that our actions are not of our own volition.

The secret of the power of the Temple was to wrest this will from us, surrendering it to a greater cause, thereby making it seem as if the actions were our own, when in fact they were the bidding of the Entity. There can be no mistaking the strength of this power, imbued in the Entity, when used to command the will of the people. This power is still in the hands of the priest and king. Not only does it command obedience, creating the idea that we follow it by choice, but it also frees us from the burden of the results of our actions. To take the life of another without this protection is a very powerful act, it can make people go mad. To remove the responsibility by absolving the perpetrator in the name of a higher cause, such as king and country, is one of the sources of the power of the Temple.

In nearly every account of the origins of the Temple, this power is described as lying in the stone upon which the sacrifice is made. This stone, as the religious texts point out, is unhewn. It becomes the translator of the concept of the solar God and in the right setting can transfer the concept into a practical manifestation. When the Druid Amergin led the invasion of Ireland to wrest power from the strange gods of the Tuatha Dé Danaan, he said, "Who but I knows the secrets of the unhewn dolmen?" This stone is the heart of every Temple: the black stone of the Sybil in which the future and the past were made manifest, the unhewn stones of the circles and henges, and the Stone of Fal which was, historically, the coronation stone of Ireland and later the power of the throne of Britain. There is no doubt that this stone, either symbolically or in a real sense, is at the heart of the power of the prophet and the priest and is the object around which the Temple is built, conjuring up the 'shadow of the hawk' over the people. In Christian terms it was Peter who became the rock upon which the Temple of Christ was founded.

Whatever we believe, this hidden knowledge is faithfully recorded in the symbol of the ray of the solstice sun as it enters the circle of the temple to illuminate the stone. Whether the temple is a circle of stone, a ziggurat or cathedral, the presence of people who have completely given themselves to the concept of the Entity allows this incoming power to be transformed and released into the world, a world created by people but under the dominion of the Entity and all the physical attributes that go to make up his kingdom.

If we are to find out how this Entity has come into our lives and how we can retake control of our own will, then we have to study the Temple in its basic form. In this way, we can perhaps determine the nature of this force that pervades our world today. For the old kings it was simple, for it was communicated directly in dreams. Even so, dreams often carried new and confusing ideas that were not at first grasped, as the following excerpt from the Sumerian text, in a wonderful description of the Entity, points out:

"In the dream there was someone who was as enormous as the heavens, who was as enormous as the earth. His head was like that of a god, his wings were like those of the Anzud bird, his lower body was like a flood storm. Lions were lying at his right and his left. He spoke to me about building his house, but I could not understand what he exactly meant, then daylight rose for me on the horizon."[20]

When we question why two-thirds of the world is starving, why we are killing the earth, why wars and curable diseases kill millions of people each week, why we are spending more on weapons than on benefits, why the potential of so many human beings is crushed before it can flower and why, when we have the choice, we become accomplices in this, we are asking these questions from a position of despair and powerlessness. In our rational world, the Temple and the king still play a pivotal role that can move the minds of millions.

The Dingle Diamond is an ideal and powerful candidate to explore this riddle, for the Tuatha Dé Danaan, the people of the Goddess, created it, yet it is a true Temple and was designed not to rival the Temple of the Entity but to heal the divisions it had caused, and to bring harmony back into the minds of men. To discover how this was done, we need to find out why it was built and what the myths and legends are that surround it. For there is, in the theme of the Temple, another form that the sun God can take, identical in its features and attributes to the Entity but imbued with a very different intent. To discover who this challenger to the voice of the Entity was, we have to travel back to a time when Ireland was first inhabited by refugees fleeing the power of the Entity and his manifestations of war and nationhood as they spread through Europe. We have to go back to the first years of the New Stone Age.

Chapter Eight
The Gift

"Behold that I have not laboured for myself only, but for all them that seek wisdom."
Sophia speaks in the Book of Ben Sirach.

A catalogue of catastrophes, it seems, powers history. Some are natural, such as the vast volcano that destroyed the heart of the Mycenaean civilisation, but many are human conflicts, generated from sheer ideology. A titanic clash of opposing ideals appears to annihilate all that has gone before. But if this is so, then the past is equally generated by synthesis. The new can not completely obliterate the old no matter how forcefully that objective is pursued. Probably the most fervent example of this is the mighty religious crusade fought by the Roman Catholic Church over the indigenous peoples of South America. Not only did these unfortunate natives have to contend with economic slavery but they were also faced with zealots who, unlike the early Christians in Ireland, had only one mission: to eradicate the pagan civilisation. This was accomplished by the destruction of many hundreds of thousands of books and manuscripts along with the martyrdom of thousands of pagan priests. So vast was the scale of this inhuman mission that even the few remaining stone-carved hieroglyphics are not fully understood. Against these odds, it is a remarkable testament to the longevity of tradition that the stories and the culture have grown up again and, piece by piece, been resurrected. Stemming from a cultural root that was old before the first words were written, the legends survive with the folklore of the peasants and farmers even when the written word has been extinguished. Into the ancient themes came new stories from Iberian culture, merging and synthesising with those of the native peoples. Where there was once conflict, a form of harmony that extends into today's world was created.

The Discovery of the Dingle Diamond

A similar process probably occurred forty thousand years ago with the occurrence of the first war. It is likely that the extermination of the neanderthals saw elements of the old human/neanderthal culture being absorbed and modified by the new exclusively human society. The Lion Warrior and the Goddess were substituted for neanderthal hierarchic functions and would have retained many of their characteristics. From this synthesis came the ability to make art and to act and think as a collective. For the next twenty thousand years this gift of belonging, of being part of a cultural heritage of a tribe or nation, was subservient to the mother goddess. And it witnessed the emergence of radical new ideas: agriculture, towns, advanced aesthetics, literacy and engineering — all were a signature of the peaceful development of a people who had safely created harmony from two opposing social forces.

When the Kurgans, led by their warlords and moulded into a cohesive army, crashed down on the world of Old Europe there occurred a clash of beliefs that led to the dismantling of the indigenous customs. Yet even as the victors were consolidating their gains, the old teachings were adapting, changing and re-emerging. This process of assimilation and synthesis in turn rebounded and modified the doctrines of the conquerors. The archaeological finds demonstrate that this phenomenon was in full-swing only a few generations after the invasion. Depending on the locale, the typical pottery and weapons used by the Kurgan invaders take on the form and styles of the indigenous people. The ideological war, it appears, continues long after the physical battles have been won or lost. When radically opposed cultures meet, there is little common ground. For the citizens of the scattered villages and towns of Europe it must have been an almost impossible task to understand the motives of a people who killed for metal and took joy in slavery. The bewilderment was probably mutual. A campaign of resistance to and assimilation of ideas replaces this initial phase. The Tuatha Dé Danaan played their part in this psychological warfare. It is symbolic that they were outfaced, for it would have been impossible to repel such war-like invaders without eventually becoming despotic themselves. In order to survive, the peoples of Old Europe fled to the outer-reaches of the known world, migrating to China and the New World as well as into the north and west of Europe. The Dé Danaan were successful in their northern flight, for the society in Finland was, in 3500 BC, similar to their own. The carved figures and the ancient legends of these northern

*Diagram 8.1
The similarity
between
Neolithic stone
monuments
from Norway
and Ireland.
Top two:
standing stones
(left Ireland,
right Norway).
Bottom two:
dolmens (top
Ireland, bottom
Norway)*

tribes describe a deeply-rooted matriarchal belief system and as we have seen, the buildings, megaliths and designs were almost identical to those of the Dé Danaan. (Diagram 8.1) When they arrived, they are reputed to have built four cities or strongholds and here, amid the mountains and the snow, they rested and built up their strength. At the core of their beliefs lay the culture of the Goddess based on Mother Earth, but war and self-protection had created as well a role for the solar king and the realms of heaven, for they brought with them the doctrines of the Kurgan hordes. The way that these two cultures wove together created a synthesis from which emerged a new spiritual belief.

From northern Scandinavia they moved, *en bloc*, to Argyll in Scotland. At this point they were no longer a band of desperate refugees. A decision had been taken to move. Doubtless, they could have stayed, but there was a strong reason for this move. In answering the question as to why the Dé Danaan left the comparative haven of Scandinavia to engage in such a perilous venture, we can clearly see that they had a purpose in mind that reached beyond their immediate physical comfort.

It is recorded that the Tuatha Dé Danaan spent seven years in Argyll training for the invasion of Ireland, for they arrived on her beaches fully prepared for war. The Irish version of *The Chronicles of the Scoti* makes no reference to them, declaring that the sons of Milidh (Miled), who took Ireland from the Dé Danaan, only occupied Ireland after a great battle on the mountains of Slieve Mis where they fought with the Fomorians and a 'host of demons'. The Book of Invasions has more to say:

"Thirty years after Genand
Goblin hosts took the fertile land;
A blow to the vanquished people of bags
Was the visit of the Tuatha Dé Danaan."
"It is God who suffered them, though he restrained them
They landed with horror, with lofty deed,
In their cloud of mighty combat of spectres,
Upon a mountain of Conmaicne of Connacht.
Without distinction to discerning Ireland,
Without ships, a ruthless course.
The truth was not known beneath the sky of stars,
Whether they were of heaven or of earth."

"If it were diabolic demons
The black cloaked agitating expedition,
It was sound with ranks, with hosts:
If of men, it was the progeny of Bethach."

The authors of this history made it quite clear that when the Tuatha Dé Danaan landed in Ireland nobody knew which side of the great conflict they supported. They were neither worshippers of the sky god in heaven nor were they devotees of the earth Goddess. It concludes, however, that they were ordinary men and that they came from the tribal roots of the Goddess. It would be difficult to decipher this riddle were it not for the fact that they are said to have brought with them certain sacred objects. These tell us that their intentions were more than a simple invasion and occupation of a new land.

The histories describe four treasures that the Dé Danaan carefully brought with them to Ireland, one from each of the four fabled Finnish cities. The first was a stone brought from Filias, known as the 'Great Fal'. The second was the spear of Lugh from Finias, said to be able to kill by its great light. The third was the sword of Gorias, creator of law. The last was the symbol of the Goddess, the cauldron from Murias; in other words, four great icons paralleling those of the 'shadow of the hawk' — the stone of the Temple, the spear of power, the sword of the lion and the cauldron of knowledge. However, of these only the stone is mentioned in the Annals.[1] It is probable that the rest of the treasures, and perhaps the cities, were symbolic references to the status of the Dé Danaan, yet these were powerful ritual objects that do not appear in the story by happenstance.

The stone depicts the heart of the Temple, the power on which the king had to bind himself, and the mechanism whereby the will of the sun god was transferred from the realm of the concept into the physical world. When the Goddess emerges from the underworld with her consort, the solar king, he is crowned on the authority of this stone, which is associated with the Celtic festival of *Imbolc*, celebrated at the beginning of spring.

The sword represents the emblem of royal power wielded by the king's champion. Legend has it that it could separate the sky from the sea at the coming of the sun. This is a reference to the undoing of the unity of the Goddess in allowing the Entity into the world. It is also said that it was the power that could carve letters in stone and it represents the implementing of law and order. The sword is associated with the Beltane festival at the start of the sun king's reign early in the summer.

The spear wielded by the Celtic sun god, Lugh, is the badge of the army. It is often represented as the shaft of sunlight at midsummer's dawn, and is also associated with the festival of *Lughnasa*, which takes place at the beginning of August.

Lastly there is the cauldron, the symbol of knowledge and the power of the earth Goddess. It represents the collective wisdom of the Great Goddess and is part of her celebrations at *Samhain*, the change of the year when the world passes into its winter sleep.

The four symbols each guard a point of the compass on which all temples are planned, each one having a specific role in the design. Two icons come from the culture of the Goddess — the cauldron and the stone — and two come specifically from the God — the sword and the spear. These were tools designed to lay the foundations of a new society, a new Temple, and this is the first time in history that we see these opposing symbolic references brought together. The Tuatha Dé Danaan wielded them for a purpose, a purpose it seems they were highly aware of.

In short, the Tuatha Dé Danaan did not arrive by chance. They were on a mission to establish a new Temple in Ireland, the like of which had not been seen in Europe before. From this base they planned to challenge the dominion of the Entity and the Lion, and they came equipped with the tools for the job. The new Temple took the power of the Old World, of the society of the Goddess and her rule over the sacred king, and merged it with the temple structure that was at the heart of Persian society, creating a new form of social guidance. It was nothing short of an alchemical marriage between the God and the Goddess and it must have involved a considerable degree of ideological research on the part of the shamans and lore-keepers to forge it.

That the Dé Danaan were the direct descendants of the peoples of Old Europe, complete with the beliefs and culture of those peaceful agriculturists, is evident in the names attributed to their gods and goddesses. The first acts of these deities were characterised by unity, contrasting dramatically with the situation on the European mainland where persecution and destruction of the Goddess was the chief characteristic of the tribes of the God. The triple-goddess Dana had three daughters: Banba, the goddess of wisdom who married Mac Cuill, the hazel god; Fótla, the summer goddess of the corn, married to Mac Ceacht, the god of the plough; and Ériu, the spring consort of Mac Gréine, the sun god.[2] The focus of these stories is on the various aspects and characteristics of the marriages of the God to the Goddess.

We are left with a vision of a people of the Goddess understanding and embracing new concepts, and with all the paraphernalia needed to establish a new theology. It is in this odd marriage of the temple culture and the goddess culture that we start to see how momentous this mission was, for the Dé Danaan were trying to do nothing less than close the rift between the earth and the sky and create again the harmony that had been their birthright. On one side was the law of the Temple and on the other was the strength of the human spirit. The constant conflict between these diametrically opposed forces was the destructive driving force that had enslaved the human race. Here was a chance to bring thesis and antithesis together to create synthesis. The problem was how to amalgamate these polarised forces of the God and the Goddess. If the method was remarkably simple, it was also hoary with age. It was envisaged that the old Goddess and her implacable foe, the king of the old ways, would be sacrificed to create the space needed for the new generation. In this ancient version of the Christian mission, the sacred king had to die for the sins of man. As with the Christian religion, this tactic probably resulted in the new creed quickly establishing itself in the psyche of the people of Ireland. However, the Dé Danaan not only needed to forge an ideological space, but they also needed a physical land in which they could bring these ideas to life. For this they had to fight.

When the king of the Tuatha Dé Danaan, Nuadu Airgetlam, waged war against the Fir Bolg in Connaught, hundreds of thousands were said to have been killed.[3] This was a clash of ideology as much as it was a struggle for the land. The Dé Danaan emerged victorious and from this success immediately moved to establish a political truce between the tribes. They did this using a tried and trusted method that would ensure an integration of cultures. The Dé Danaan's chief, Echu, took the wife of the defeated Fir Bolg king as his spouse. Her name was Tailltiu, and to legitimise this royal marriage, the child sun king, Lugh, was given to them to foster. This act of reconciliation demonstrates how far from a true matriarchal society the Dé Danaan were prepared to go to realise their vision. Lugh's adoption represents the first recorded intermarriage of a royal lineage to protect a bloodline, for he was the son of Eithne, the daughter of Balor of the Evil Eye. Balor was the king of the sea pirates, the Fomorians. Into the royal family of the High Kings and Queens of Ireland were now merged the bloodlines of the Fir Bolg, the Fomorians and the Tuatha Dé Danaan.

The Discovery of the Dingle Diamond

The origin of the lineage of Lugh is one of the first inklings we have of the method that the Dé Danaan employed to unite the Temple with the earth Goddess. They would have had direct experience of the extent of the power of the Entity over Europe; they would have known that to win a direct fight against such a powerful enemy would have been impossible, so they avoided any direct confrontation and further war by using this process of family bonding described in the detail of the myth.

Balor, the Dark Lord, had an only daughter, Eithne, and some said she was the most beautiful woman that ever lived. His shaman had told Balor that he would meet his death at the hand of his own grandson. So to avoid his destiny, he locked Eithne in a tower on the island fortress that was his home. He put twelve women in charge of her and forbade any man to come near. Thus freed from the fear of death, he used every opportunity to go to war, robbing and pillaging at his whim. Balor, the dark lord and champion of the Temple, was a solar god in his own right. That he tried to contain the power of the Goddess with twelve rather than nineteen female guards tells us that he was of the same lineage as the European Temple and an implacable foe of the Goddess.

The Tuatha Dé Danaan did not want to oppose Balor and the powerful Fomorians with arms, and so had to find another way of defeating him. The opportunity arrived when Balor stole a sacred cow, the symbolic representative of the Goddess, from the Dé Danaan. Deprived of this power, their Lord of the Land, Cian, decided to go on an expedition to retrieve the lost cow. But his druids had warned that no one could get within sight of Balor's evil eye and remain alive, a remark that sheds light on the power of the Temple to control the minds of the people. Cian engaged the help of Birog of the Mountain, a powerful priestess, who disguised him as a woman and took him over the water to Eithne's castle. Once inside, Birog put the guards to sleep, and Cian met Eithne. They fell in love and conceived a child. Thus the power of oppression is lulled, and from the body of the imprisoned Goddess emerges the solar hero, Lugh. Balor, finding out about Eithne's offspring, was incensed and to thwart his prophecy of doom he had the child thrown into the sea. Birog, who already knew what would happen, rescued Lugh and brought him safely to his father. This tale of the lost or hidden child shows the pedigree of this new being. Moses, Osiris, Zeus and especially Arthur were all similar solar deities who had to be hidden away from the wrath of their father or grandfather.

In this tale, Cian gives the young solar god to Tailltiu to be raised as her own son so that the Fir Bolg and the Fomorians are made complicit in an act of creation that would lead to their own undoing.

Lugh later become the heroic representation of the sun god and a great king of the Tuatha Dé Danaan. He is held responsible for creating chess, ball-play and horseracing, games that are still held during the festival of *Lughnasa* each August in honour of Lugh and his mother, Tailltiu, at Telltown, the modern name for her home place.

When the Tuatha Dé Danaan landed on Ireland's beaches Egypt was still young, Greece had yet to be and China was only just realising its potential. Mesopotamia was still in its infancy and Rome, the aggressive and powerful future bastion of the Temple, had yet to be conceived. Up to this point, across all of Europe and the East a vicious and merciless war to dominate and control the Goddess was being fought. Everywhere there was direct confrontation, the serpent of the earth Goddess was vanquished and her people forced to flee. In fomenting this dualism the dominion of the Entity established its power, and its enemy was the serpent. From these roots of conflict the Judaic religion, founded in the Mesopotamian struggles, emerged complete with its serpent-killing saints. Even today this religion still wears the colours of this conflict. As the penalty for offering the apple of knowledge from the Tree of Life to Eve, the Judaic God declares to the serpent:

"You are cursed… upon your belly shall you go and dust shall you eat, I will put an enmity between you and the woman and between your seed and her seed."

This telling quote from Europe's most influential religious book clearly outlines the attitudes of the priests of the Temple. The power of the Entity, incarnate in the vast military power of the kings of Mesopotamia, was ruthless in its aim. The seed of the earth Goddess and that of the earth spirit had to be separated, for they were the pillars on which the trinity of the earth Goddess — the spirit/serpent, the mind/Goddess and the body/humanity — had held the forces of the Entity in check for so many millennia. As we have seen, the story of the defeat of the Goddess as told in the Enuma Elish, the Babylonian creation myth, was a remorseless war between the people of the goddess Tiamat on one side and on the other, a coalition of gods, and it is categorical in detailing which of the two powers is the stronger. In the telling account of the ensuing power struggles, which are the hallmark of societies ruled by the gods, one god emerges as the most able to defeat Tiamat. His name is Marduk and the price for this victory is that he alone was granted ruler-ship of the universe, the right to order the world as he saw fit. Before this time there had been no single god with absolute power. To face the battle, Tiamat raised up her sacred king and champion, Kingu, to fight for her, but at the moment of confrontation Kingu could not face the Entity. He was simply not powerful enough to combat the new God. Tiamat was left alone to face her nemesis.

Both the tribes of the Tuatha Dé Danaan and the priests of the Temple knew that the Goddess couldn't be killed, for she represented knowledge essential to the Temple. From her earliest appearance she was the wellspring from which the accomplishments of civilisation rose, and she represented the channel whereby the voice of the Entity could enter the minds of men and hence the physical world. But she could be imprisoned and enslaved. The power of the king and the army, the power of the priest and the Temple, rests upon this knowledge. The Rig Veda explains it thus:

"I am the queen, the confluence of riches, the skilful one who is first among those worthy of sacrifice. The Gods divided me up into various parts, for I dwell in many places and enter many forms. I stretch the bow for the solar king so that his arrow will strike down the hater of prayer. I incite the contest among people. I have pervaded sky and earth."

The Enuma Elish makes this clear when the victorious Marduk dismembers the body of the Goddess using each part to create the basis of his new world order. Tiamat does not die but is transformed into the raw material of this new world.

"And unto Tiamat, whom he had conquered, he returned.
And the lord stood upon Tiamat's hinder parts,
And with his merciless club he smashed her skull.
He cut through the channels of her blood,
And he made the North wind bear it away into secret places.....
Then the lord rested, gazing upon her dead body,

While he divided the flesh of the body, and devised a cunning plan.
He split her up like a flat fish into two halves;
One half of her he stabilised as a covering for heaven.
He fixed a bolt, he stationed a watchman,
And bade them not to let her waters come forth.
He passed through the heavens, he surveyed the regions thereof,
And over against the Deep he set the dwelling of Nudimmud.
And the lord measured the structure of the Deep,
And he founded E-sara, a mansion like unto it.
The mansion E-sara which he created as heaven,
He caused Anu, Bel, and Ea in their districts to inhabit."[4]

Only in Ireland, under the guidance of the Tuatha Dé Danaan, was there a principled struggle to end the terrible war. In the place of division they sought to create unity. Where the priests of the Temple endeavoured to disempower the Goddess, they aspired to rebuild her authority. Instead of trying to destroy the God of heaven, they were seeking a way to elevate both him and the Goddess to a new position. In terms of the society that was produced this meant that the feminine and the masculine were given equal stature, something that was an anathema to the aristocracies of Europe. For the priests in the Temple, the Goddess was a power that needed to be harnessed and taken captive, to be exploited and controlled by the Entity — in fact, their treatment of women reflected this role. For the Dé Danaan, conversely, she was an integral part of a still living tradition, and the high status of women in their society expressed this. For these reasons, the Dé Danaan chose to challenge their oppressors from within, hamstringing them with their own mythology. It was nothing less than an attempt to establish the reign of the ancient sacred king of the year within the guiding principle of the Goddess. It was a successful format and was to appear time and again throughout history. Here, around three thousand years before the birth of Christ, we see that the power of the Goddess is not one of the might of arms or the force of law, or even the material manifestation of the Temple, it is simply the active choice of healing over destruction and wisdom over ignorance. The Celtic legends of Cerridwen, the goddess of wisdom, underline this ideological offensive. She could not kill the hero Gwion who stole the three drops of knowledge to become the sacred king. But she could bring into the rift between heaven and earth the quiet balm of restoration, and in this way subdue and control the terrible will of the Entity, transforming righteous anger into constructive love.

This remedy was the defining act of the Tuatha Dé Danaan, dimly recorded in the annals of Irish history. For this reason they are remembered as the people of the Goddess.

The ability to use the enemy's own weapons against him can be most clearly seen in the medieval legends of King Arthur. These legends, told and retold in many forms, weave and encircle the myths of the Tuatha Dé Danaan.[5] Although they are often dressed in the vestments of the 'Knights of the Temple' of medieval times, they are in fact the direct heirs of the Tuatha Dé Danaan. King Arthur has his roots in Irish mythology, all of which stem from the acts of the Dé Danaan. The many parallels between the stories, separated by almost four thousand years, are proof of how successful the Dé Danaan were in instilling their philosophy into the framework of the Temple. The ancient themes of these stories tell of a band of warrior monks or knights, dedicated to using the power of the Temple for the good of humanity. The tasks they undertake and the feats they perform are at the bequest of the feminine, and in this they are a rival to the armies of the Temple and a force of change in society, representing the use of might in the cause of love.

"I shall challenge," said King Arthur when he drew the sword of kingship from the stone of the Temple, "the notion that might is right."

Lugh, like Arthur, is credited with surrounding himself with a band of warrior knights, each representing a facet of the royal rule. It was called the art of assembly.

"Lugh, son of Eithne, a cliff without a wrinkle, with him there first came a lofty assembly."[6]

The *raison d'être* of this group was to manifest the specific functions needed to support the sacred king. Between the time of the Tuatha Dé Danaan and that of the Knights of the Holy Grail arose the most famous of these assemblies, the Twelve Disciples of Jesus. This assembly was also brought into being for the task of undermining the Temple from within and to use its power for the benefit and freedom of mankind.

In one of the most poignant legends of the Dé Danaan we clearly see parallels with the later stories of King Arthur, and it is also the simplest

The Gift

and most direct mythological analogy of the dilemma involved in taking on the 'right of might'. This is the legend of Bres.

Bres was the son of Ériu, one of the Dé Danaan's goddess trinity and consort of the sacred king Mac Gréine, the sun god. But Bres was not the fruit of this union, for Ériu had been visited by Elatha Mac Delbaith, king of the Fomorians who had 'gone a trysting'. Bres is thus intimately connected with Lugh. His father is Fomorian and his mother is a goddess. In this way, the Tuatha Dé Danaan sought to cement peaceful ties with the Fomorians. Both Lugh and Bres were fair to look upon and had the grace and stature that declared them solar kings but in their destiny was a symbolic parting of the ways, for Bres represented the dark side of this power.

In the battle with the Fir Bolg, Nuadu, the king of the Tuatha Dé Danaan, had his arm cut off. Since he was no longer perfect in body he was denied the right to rule and after the battle, in a deliberate act of conciliation, Bres was given the kingship.

"Seven years of Bres which was not a white space," states *Lebor Gabála Érenn* in an aggrieved tone. "Through its fair prospect for the song abbot, in the Princedom over the plain, generous in nuts, till the arm of Nuadu was healed."

The meaning of this elegantly cryptic verse is that Bres was a vicious tyrant. He taxed the people of the land heavily and he enslaved the Dagda, the good god, and put him to work building his version of the Temple. Ogma, the god of knowledge, was made to carry firewood, and the warriors of Ireland were reduced to servants. Bres dominated and enslaved the people and for a while it looked as though the Dé Danaan's mission had failed. That Bres was not a great solar god is seen in his meanness. Corpra, the druid referred to as the 'song abbot' in the Christian verses, who visited the royal household and found neither meat nor ale, composed a satire against him:

"With food ready on a dish, without milk enough for a calf to grow without shelter, without light in the darkness of night, with enough to pay a story-teller: may that be the prosperity of Bres."[7]

'Generous in nuts' suggests his people 'worked for peanuts', in modern parlance. His meanness was the weakness that led to his downfall as the tragic consequences of his greed played themselves out. Nuadu had a new arm made for him by the physician Dian Cecht. This was made of silver, and ever after he was called Nuadu of the Silver

Arm. The Tuatha Dé Danaan were all too glad to have Nuadu back and Bres was asked to relinquish the kingship, which he did with a bad grace and went back to his kin, the Fomorians. Reminding them that he was an heir to their throne, he outlined his grievances and persuaded his grandfather, Balor, the dark lord, to raise an army and avenge him. Balor was forced into a fight, something he had no wish to do as he knew that his invulnerability was compromised when Eithne gave birth to Lugh. This second battle with the Dé Danaan was also fought on the plains of Mag Tuired. Here Nuadu is killed by Balor, whose one look was said to slay a man. The slaying of the great king is a sacrifice in this Temple. Nevertheless, the Tuatha Dé Danaan prevailed.

More than one hundred thousand are reputed to have died in this battle and it destroyed the dominance of the Fomorians forever. In an act of clemency after the battle, the Dé Danaan gave the survivors one fifth of the land of Ireland to live in. These people chose to move to the north and from there many of the future stories of conflicts in the land arose.

Bres represents all that is wrong with the god of the Temple. He is the greedy king who rules by oppression. He is a representative of the God of the Old Testament and of the Mesopotamian epics, creating war and disharmony. His counterpart, Lugh, presents us with a new image of the power of the concept, one that could, if tied into the earth force, create harmony and happiness. Both are really the opposite sides of the same coin but Lugh, the voice of the sun in the minds of men, unites with the power of the earth, creating a marriage of harmony between the sundered body of the Goddess and the solar hero, between the heavens and the earth. He does this in precisely the same way as the people of Old Europe, by sacrifice, as per the previous role of the neanderthals, thus stifling the voice of the Entity.

Usually, sacrifice means to take something of value and then give it up to honour a principle. As we have seen, this was the case with the sacrificial kings of Old Europe. Through their sacrifice, the power of the lion and the dominance of the principle of might and subjugation that had been awakened were held in check. The 'king for a year' was a willing participant in this act. But the concept of the Temple changed the meaning of the sacrifice. The Entity, enthroned in its holy centre demanded bloodletting and this display of force both subdued and made accomplices of the participants.

The Gift

If this travesty were to be broken, then the meaning of the sacrifice would have to be stood on its head. The act had to be one of willingness on the part of the doomed king. In this way, the spirit of man overcame the brute force and might of arms of the Temple's lion. The willingness to die for this cause became the creed of non-violence. If there is any doubt of the power of this philosophy to affect human collective consciousness and to radically alter the course of history, a brief look at the myth of Jesus will allay it. The key message of the New Testament is that Christ was willingly sacrificed, in full knowledge of what he was undertaking for the 'sins of man', meaning, in this case, the administration of the Temple.[8]

The history of sacred kings who, like Nuadu, have been sacrificed is lengthy. Attis, the consort of Cybele, dies and is reborn; likewise, Adonis, Christ, Dumuzi and Tammuz. This betrayal of the Goddess leading to the death and rebirth of the God plays a pivotal role in challenging the rampant dark power and transforming its energy into light.

Within it is played out the theme of betrayal. In the Welsh version of Lugh, Llew Llaw Gryffes of the Lion Hand was knowingly betrayed by his goddess; similarly, the fall of Samson at the hand of Delilah, and the betrayal of Christ by Judas, clearly show that the sacrificial subjects had to knowingly surrender their power through betrayal.

When this act is analysed a surprising fact becomes evident: the occult meaning of the crucifixion of Christ. When a god is sacrificed to himself, it points to the existence of a greater power than himself, a power that controls the destiny of the universe that even the gods are subject to. This is the power of the Goddess, she who was before all else came into being. It is this power that transforms the sacred king into an immortal. The Tuatha Dé Danaan, and later the early Christians, acknowledged the existence of this power and treated it with great caution.

In nearly every collection of Irish myths from all the cycles, this theme of surrender is apparent and it lays the ground plan for the attempt of the Christian religion to alter the Temple. The main point of difference was that the Tuatha Dé Danaan built a physical temple to achieve their aims, whilst the Christians constructed the same temple in the minds and souls of men. This is probably why the Irish took so readily to the Christian faith before the new dark force of the medieval Church of Rome made its successful bid for power.

179

Coming back to Lugh, who at the conclusion of the fight with the Fomorians took the kingship and with a mighty thrust of his now all-powerful spear fulfilled the prophecy and slew his grandfather, Balor — Bres, on the run from the conflict, was hunted down and pleaded for his life. Lugh spared him and the score was settled. This act of mercy is in keeping with the ethos of the Tuatha Dé Danaan's strategy. Lugh went away but did not die. He appears as the sun god to those in need.

The epic of Arthur's anti-ego — his son from the incestuous relationship with his sister Morgan — is a future echo of this strange conflict. The result is that, with full foreknowledge of his impending death, Arthur has to fight his final battle. Like Lugh, he does not die but is carried away to a land in the west to return when he is most needed.

Thus we are for the first time confronted with a new model for society. It contains two identical solar gods, the twins who are rivals for the voice of the Temple and the power of the Goddess. One is the wrathful god of the sun, the Entity. His splendour is not of this earth and he is the eternal foe of the Goddess seeking to subjugate and imprison her. The other is the Goddess's champion and lover, or consort. He stems from the earlier sacrificial king and his is the 'way of the wild wood'. They are sons of the same parent and their tale becomes the basis of a thousand myths.

Great confusion arises from this because it creates a bipartisan outlook — it depends on which side of the fence the tale is told as to which side is good and which is evil. A look at the legend of Lucifer makes this clearer. Lucifer means 'light' and his realm is that of the material earth although he comes from the concept of heaven and uses knowledge and understanding to bring his message into the world. Jehovah, by contrast, is the jealous and angry God using the force of law to bring about his will. His kingdom is outside the earth in an unmanifest realm. Both have their place in the Temple but they can create very different forms of societies and are viewed very differently by those who follow either the left hand or the right hand path.

The corpus of legends on the subject from this period is too extensive to cover here. Suffice it to say that all the themes of the once and future king are to be found in the story of the Tuatha Dé Danaan.

The foundations of the Arthurian myths occur in this new vision of the Temple that the Dé Danaan brought to Ireland, and also contain the embryonic form of early Christianity. They lay the basis for the secret

The Gift

orders and monasteries of the Christian monks through which the education and behaviour of feudal Europe was to be ordered. The great cathedrals — the new temples — and the secret orders that arose were the foundations of a power that the Roman Catholic Church would struggle to bend to its will for the next thousand years. But these cataclysmic events were still three thousand five hundred years in the future.

For the Tuatha Dé Danaan the struggle was to end in tragedy, but their ideas lived on in the faerie mounds and the minds of people. Ideas cannot easily be killed and the ripples from the stone that they dropped into the heart of Ireland spread despite the best efforts of the lion to subdue them.

The source of this ripple was found in the idea that free will — individual control over one's thoughts and actions — was a prerequisite for the healing of the Temple. The *awen*, the knowledge of true reality, could not be the possession of a few of the elite but was a common birth-right. The energy that could be freed by removing the voice of the Entity from the mind of humanity would in itself transform the world.

In order to achieve this transformation, the tribes of the Dé Danaan had to make manifest the Temple. In a real sense, its power was the mirror-image of that of the Sumerians and the Babylonians who rivalled them. The Dé Danaan settled at Tara and constructed the temple of Newgrange, 'An Uamh Gréine', the 'cave of the sun'. The kidney-shaped mound covers an area of over an acre. At the end of a nineteen metres long passage they constructed a three-roomed chamber that welcomes the first ray of sunlight of the winter solstice dawn. They covered its sides with white quartz, banked it with ninety-seven kerbstones decorated with megalithic art and built around it a great circle of stones. The quartz came from almost forty miles away in the Wicklow Mountains to the south. Around sixteen-hundred granite boulders are used in the structure, most of which were brought from the nearest source in the Mourne Mountains, also many miles away. It is estimated that the construction of the passage monument at Newgrange would have taken twenty years for a workforce of at least three-hundred men.

This, and its sister sites such as Loughcrew, the 'palace of the sun king', have been documented by archaeologists, who have catalogued the increasing complexity of the monuments climaxing in the present day reconstruction of Newgrange. The Tuatha Dé Danaan sought out and built thousands of megaliths, stone circles and dolmens, and installed in them their vision of Lugh. For a thousand years they re-established the old order in the land, and the *Annals* tell of their achievements.

Yet the greatest and most powerful of their works was also the most closely guarded secret, namely, the Dingle Diamond. Here they divined the strong forces of the earth dream and constructed around them a temple that stretched across the energy lines. They aligned it with the rising midsummer sun and placed the Stone of Fal at its heart. It became the hub of a new wheel and for hundreds of years it was the centre of a direct challenge to the order of might and the sword. The society that grew around it was peaceful and creative and during this time Ireland became a cultural oasis in a desert of destruction. During their reign, the chaos of the war between the Goddess and the God destroyed Old Europe and from its ashes, new empires began to be established under the influence of the un-manifest God, the Entity. Like water in a desert, the influence of this learning spread far afield from Ireland's shores, and its stability and durability allowed a new paradigm to grow in the hearts and minds of the people.

The keepers of this knowledge were men and woman of learning, which caused a schism between the Temple priests and their control of the powers of the earth. Into this gap flowed the *awen*, the knowledge of true reality. Three thousand years later, the links between the Irish Gnostics and those of the Near East bore fruit. This fruit was the doctrine of Jesus the Nazarene. Both beliefs challenged the might of the Temple not with force of arms but with love. The parallels between this creed and that of the Dé Danaan are so striking that they lead to the almost heretical question: were the Tuatha Dé Danaan the forerunners of Christianity?

This act made them immortal, their vision the warp and weft of the Temple, an intimate part of a chimera that could not easily be removed. Its people were freed from the Entity and took this culture with them in their travels to other lands. All hailed their learning and wisdom, yet this same wisdom also invoked a challenge and sounded a harbinger of doom in the ear of the dark god. Such a mighty provocation to the creation of the Temple could not be ignored or left to grow, for the defiance was ideological and therefore potentially lethal to a society that based its structure on an illusion of power.

The Gift

A long time passed before this challenge was answered, for struggles and wars, the rise and fall of empires, and the establishment of the voice of might and law in Eurasia meant that the Entity was not yet powerful enough to threaten this bastion of the Goddess. But the storm clouds were gathering in the East, and the lightning bolt of the God was heard more frequently as his power waxed. There came a time when it could reach out its arm in the form of a people who were followers of the lion, who were quite capable of taking Ireland by storm.

Chapter Nine
Seasons

"Man models himself on the earth,
The earth on heaven,
Heaven on the Way,
And the Way on that which is naturally so."
Tao Te Ching

If you were to stand on the rounded summit of Mount Brandon, on midsummer's dawn, you would just be able to pick out the small church of Ballyferriter. With the sun at your back, you would be looking straight along the solar leyline, the main joist around which the temple of the Diamond is constructed. This intersects the true north leyline at an angle of exactly 52°10' of arc. This unique signature defines the precise latitude of Ballyferriter at the centre of the Dingle Diamond. If it had been built a few degrees further north or south, the solar alignments would fail to fit the perfect triangular geometry of the temple and there would be no harmony between the earth Goddess and the solar God. Only at this precise geographical position do the ground plan of the temple and the movements of the solar year marry. (Diagram 9.1)

The Tuatha Dé Danaan accomplished this remarkable feat of engineering with a precision that modern surveyors would envy, combining knowledge of mathematics and astronomy with the art of surveying and an intimate awareness of the earth. This painstaking alignment has to be present in every solar temple of this type. That they possessed this knowledge a thousand years before the building of the Pyramids compels us to redefine our views of the abilities and wisdom of the very earliest peoples of Europe. Almost every later culture created solar monuments that embody the idea of marrying celestial events to the passage of the seasons. Stonehenge, the Pyramids, the Aztec and

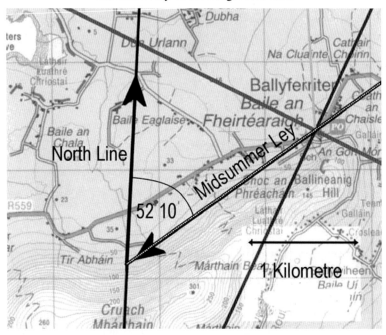

Diagram 9.1
The angle at which the midsummer leyline crosses the north line is
exactly the latitude of the Dingle Diamond.

Peruvian monuments, the mounds and earth sculptures of native Americans, *feng shui* in China, the European Gothic cathedrals and the temples and wats of Asia all share this common theme. Contrary to popular archaeological opinion, it is difficult to believe that these later temples were built in ideological isolation. Their elaborate construction, together with a corpus of communal mythology, is indicative of a common earlier source. From this, it is possible to draw the conclusion that the knowledge of the Temple of the Tuatha Dé Danaan was the predecessor of all of these structures.

With this in mind, I started to look at the archaeologists' ground plans for the first temples in ancient Sumer on the banks of the Tigris and Euphrates rivers in Iraq. The structure of the Dingle Diamond appeared, time and again, as the basic geometry around which these ziggurats were built. Like the Diamond, they too seem to have been constructed around two equilateral triangles forming a cross. But there was one difference: a second key point was used by the ancient Sumerians. This was the exact middle of the triangle and it was used as a centre point for another arm of the cross. The plan of the twin cross fitted perfectly in the Dingle Diamond, its upper bar neatly defining the most western point of the Three Sisters, co-incidentally defining the place where the great north line crosses the Diamond — the lower arm forming the main Ballyferriter church leyline. The ancient Sumerian architects were probably very aware of this ground plan, for the symbol of a two-armed cross appears in Sumerian hieroglyphics as the symbol *Kad*, where it denotes the title of king, thus there is a logical connection between the role of the king and the basic plan of the Temple. Whilst I was pondering the significance of this structural link between the temples in Iraq and the Dingle Diamond, my colleague produced a small silver cross almost identical to the symbol *Kad*, whose geometry corresponded to exactly to the plans of the temples and to the Diamond. 'It was given to me in Spain,' he said. 'It's the Cross of Lorraine.'

The Cross of Lorraine has a long history. As we have seen, its earliest recorded appearance is as a Sumerian hieroglyph denoting royalty but its background is firmly linked to the occult. It is deeply entwined with the Cathars, a medieval Christian Gnostic sect who trace their ancestry back to the ethos of the Tuatha Dé Danaan. The word 'cathartic' means 'to heal two separate parts', namely the soul and the spirit, a reference to the function of the Dingle Diamond. Condemned as heretics by Pope Innocent III, the Cathars were nevertheless well integrated with their Roman Christian neighbours in their heartland of Languedoc in the French Pyrenees. In 1209, Pope Innocent III began a thirty-five year crusade to exterminate the Cathars by sending an army to attack the town of Beziers, with its mixed population of over twenty thousand people. They committed genocide on a scale so terrible that it still casts a shadow over the people of that region. This is indicative of how ruthless the Temple, in whatever guise it takes, can be in its attempts to eradicate such an ideological challenge. The Pope's command was: "Kill them all. God will recognise His own". About fifty thousand people were slaughtered and Pope Innocent III himself announced that "neither age, nor sex, nor status was spared."

The Cathar Cross of Lorraine proved to be the illumination needed

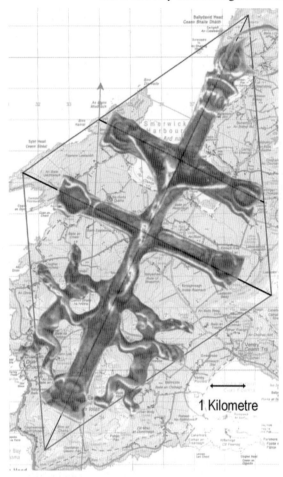

1 Kilometre

Diagram 9.2
The Cross of
Lorraine fits
neatly into the
form of the
Dingle Diamond.

to decipher the riddle of the Diamond.

The cross I held was double-sided. On one side was a crucified Jesus with a strange serpentine body, and on the other an image of Mary. Above her is the word CARAVACA, which is Spanish for 'cow face'. This is an allusion not so much to the Christian Mary as to the earth Goddess herself. The symbolism goes back further even than the bulls' heads that decorate her temples in Catal Huyuk and Crete, and which have been found in great numbers at the sacred sites of the neanderthals. The cross is a representation, in Christian guise, of the Lion Warrior and the earth Goddess, united on the same Tree of Life, echoing the countless images of this tree throughout history. A cross of any form can be a symbolic representation or map of a sacred geometrical landscape. It could be that the Cross of Lorraine contains a secret concerning the geometry of uniting the Goddess with her solar hero. With this in mind, we applied it to the Dingle Diamond. (Diagram 9.2)

The geometry of the cross fitted perfectly into the Dingle Diamond, showing the calendrical significance of the double bars. Its centre lies in the middle of Smerwick Harbour, where local legend locates a lost city of the Tuatha Dé Danaan.[1] The link between this ancient symbol and the Diamond was confirmed.

By this extraordinary piece of serendipity, we were able to unlock the story of the Dingle Diamond and to answer the riddle of *Lughnasa*. Yet there was another piece of the puzzle missing, and this was supplied by the stories and legends associated with the key features of the Diamond.

We are lucky to have careful records kept by Christian monks of the mythology that was used to construct the Dingle Diamond. From this we can begin to see that the stories, and the festivals connected with them, were all part of a single body of knowledge that linked the people to the earth.

The legends tell us that the Celtic calendar divided the year into eight parts. The four major cross-quarter days of the year are Yuletide, the mid-winter solstice, when the sun is furthest away from the earth and the day is shortest; *Ostara*, the spring equinox, when day and night are of equal length and the days are lengthening; the midsummer solstice, when the longest day occurs; and lastly, *Mabon*, the autumn equinox, when day and night are once again equal. Between these are four major festivals associated with the Goddess: *Imbolc, Beltane, Lughnasa* and *Samhain*. We will look at these and their relationship to the Temple more closely later, but for now the relationship between *Lughnasa* and midsummer demands our attention.

Lughnasa is the celebration of the victory of the sun king, Lugh, over his adversaries Bres and Balor of the Fomorians. It is celebrated at the beginning of August as a fair with games and races; using the Dingle Diamond as a calendar reference places it on August 5th. About this time of the year, also, is the pilgrimage to the summit of Brandon Mountain, mentioned in the first chapter. It is surprising that the festival of *Lughnasa*, the consummation of the victory of the sun, was celebrated on the solar leyline of the Dingle Diamond some forty-five days after the midsummer sunrise — two solar events, one mythological and one physical, taking place on the same mountain. With the added proviso that they had 'Lugh of the Shining Brow' in common, it was unlikely to be chance that united them.

This ability to relate the physical events to a known mythology gives us a clue as to what has been missed in the analysis of all similar solar temples to date. From Stonehenge to the Carnac alignment in Brittany, researchers have concentrated on mapping linear relationships to the rising or setting sun, concentrating mainly on the physical alignments. The Dingle Diamond reveals how celestial events, tied into the earth's energies, are exhibited in the mythology. It is like having an instruction manual allowing us to go beyond an elementary understanding of how the stones mark out celestial events, although it is a guidebook that has been written in an ancient style and format, unfamiliar to our more prosaic age. The guidebook tells us that the year was divided geometrically and that the festival of Lughnasa occurred forty-five days after the solstice. So, using the Cross of Lorraine as a guide, the forty five day gap was measured as forty-five degrees on the map which pointed exactly at the apex of the Dingle Diamond at Ballydavid Head.

The midsummer solar ley neatly divides the east side of the triangle into two equal parts, separating the northern apex from the burial ground of the priestesses at the hill of Leataoibh. The solar ley is represented in the mythology by the festival of Lughnasa, which falls exactly between the summer solstice and the autumn equinox — a forty-five day interval. Where the solar ley crosses the circle centred on Smerwick Harbour, it marks a point exactly forty-five degrees from the apex of the triangle. This tryst between the angles and the number of days stands out from the story like a bright star. (Diagram 9.3)

In a manoeuvre similar to the 'star gate' of popular science fiction, all we had to do was to rotate the solstice line by forty-five degrees, one degree for each day after the solstice of June 21st, thus locking the solar ley into the exact localities of the Diamond and allowing the myths that surround the sites to be read in their correct orientation to celestial events. The result was that each day of the year can be seen as

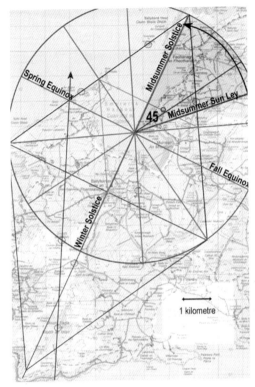

Diagram 9.3
Where the solar ley
crosses the circle cen-
tred on Smerwick Har-
bour, it marks a point
exactly 45° from the
apex of the triangle.

one degree on the circle that surrounds the cross. Back at the drawing board, it took only a moment to define the centre of the Cross of Lorraine, allowing a circle to be drawn around it that passed through each of the corners of the main triangle in turn. The solstices and the equinoxes were placed first around this circle, each marked by a significant point of the triangle. Then the four festivals were designated; again, each one rested on a significant point in the triangle. We had in front of us a circle that represented the turning of the year. On this circle were the places that the Tuatha held as sacred, each site linked by mythology to its correct function for that time of year.

The circle of the year, drawn around the northern triangle of the Diamond, perhaps has no existence other than as a guide. Without it, the Dingle Diamond is an impressive temple of the sun by any standards. With it, the Diamond is transformed into a calendar marked out by the hills and sacred places that make up its features. To engage the earth power with that of the solar ley, it is only necessary to turn the dating ring round, like the lock of a safe, by forty-five degrees. This way, the sacred points of the earth become specific to each day of the cosmic year's cycle and the mythologies of the key stations of the Celtic year can be revealed. As the Dakota Indians say, 'The year is a circle around the world.'

The significance of forty-five degrees as the link between the heavens and the earth is not to be missed. The sciences of alchemy and geomancy, as well as astrology, say that by turning forty-five degrees a doorway to another realm can be opened. From investigations into the symbolic 'cycles of being' conducted by Yeats in *The Vision* to the diagrammatic representations of the Buddhists' 'eightfold-path', the movement of this line crosses the spiral of life and takes us into another sphere.

The reason why there has been complete bewilderment among those who seek to understand the purpose of ancient monuments is due to the significance that their research gives to a purely lineal relationship between seasonal and astral events. The relationship is not linear, nor is it logical. The physical path of the sun on Midsummer's Day is transmuted through the medium of myth into the landscape. For this reason, the stones and monuments that celebrate the events of the year do not directly correspond to the sites that mark its turning.

The Dingle Diamond gives us a graphic example of this. On the crucial day of Midsummer it is neither the church of Ballyferriter nor the Black Tomb that experiences the merging of the solar and the earth energies, but the apex of the triangle on Ballydavid Head. Here the fires of the solstice would have been lit, and the ceremonies performed. The stone and the church — or the seven slabs which predated it — are needed to transform the solar energy as it passes through them. Consummate with the myth of the underworld, once the energy has travelled into the earth it is transformed, emerging from within the earth with a precise geometrical shift. It is here that the rituals connecting the shaman with these forces are made real, and the doorway to the other world is opened. This secret has been only dimly remembered, and there is still great confusion in the minds of those who try to grasp this truth. The Celtic formula used to enter the faery realm is a good

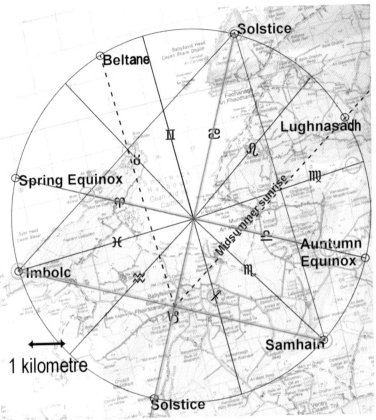

Diagram 9.4
The Dingle Diamond creates a holistic geometry out of both the thir-
teen months of the Goddess and the twelve months of the God, merging
them to fit in with the seasonal solar events and the landscape of the
earth.

example: 'turn sideways to the sun.'

The discovery that the Dingle Diamond was not designed geometrically, but rather depended on the number of days in the year, allows us
to investigate the Celtic seasons. According to the placing of the sacred
sites around the Dingle Diamond, the cycle of the year appears to be set

up around a repeating unit of twenty-eight days. These lunar months, of which there are thirteen in the year, make a total of three-hundred and sixty-four days. Traditionally, this is the 'witches', or Celtic, lunar year, and it has a long history. The significance of thirteen as 'the witches' number' stems from the seasonal divisions. Robert Graves describes a calendar ' alphabet of the trees' as having thirteen consonants, one for each month. Irish and Welsh lore make constant references to the number thirteen: 'thirteen wonders of Britain', 'thirteen prison locks', 'thirteen precious things', and so on. Thirteen lunar months leaves one day over in a solar year of three-hundred and sixty-five days. This is the 'year and a day' of fairytale and folk legend, the magical day of the birth of the Lion Warrior as the divine child or the solar king who can challenge and defeat the dark power. The three-hundred and sixty four days of the witches' year, plotted around the wheel of the Diamond, are punctuated by the eight seasonal festivals and the twelve houses of the zodiac. These form a symmetrical geometry within which the year and the temple are divided into twelve months. Dividing the year into twelve is a tradition of those cultures associated with the Kurgan Indo-Europeans, the people of the male god. It is this tradition that we have inherited today. The Dingle Diamond creates a holistic geometry out of both the thirteen months of the Goddess and the twelve months of the God, merging them to fit in with the seasonal solar events and the landscape of the earth. (Diagram 9.4)

To help us grasp this potential, the Dingle Diamond offers a traditional interpretation of the seasonal changes. Although this is the most superficial of the Diamond's functions, it is also the most well-known. Millions of people around the world are familiar with its pattern. For this reason, we present a 'round the circle' tour of the Diamond and the sacred places that mark it out. It is a measure of how well the Neolithic peoples of Ireland were able to trace the flux of the earth magic as it shifts and changes, like the tides of the sea, following the cycle of the year.

The circle of the year turns around the Diamond. (Diagram 9.5) It starts with the traditional opening of the Celtic year, *Imbolc*, the festival of spring and the time of the return of the Goddess from her journey to the underworld. The Dingle Diamond accurately marks the place of this festival as the tor on Sybil Head, overlooking the rocks known as The Mother and The Crow. The Celtic name for this high point is The

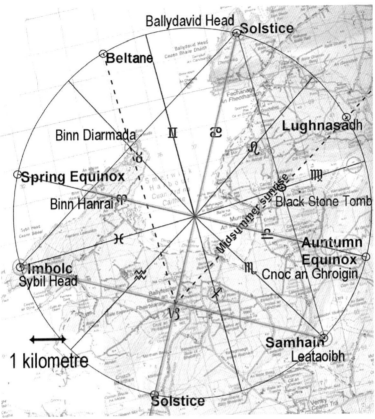

Diagram 9.5
A 'round the circle' tour of the Diamond and the sacred places that
mark it out.

Altar of Fire, a direct reference to Bríd's, or Bridget's fire from which
all the neighbourhood fires were lit at this time of the year. In Ireland,
Bridget's fire was attended by nineteen vestal virgins. Nineteen nuns
now busy themselves with the same task.[2] It blazed on The Mother
headland as a symbol of the turning year welcoming the quickening of
the earth force in preparation for spring. The Diamond tells us that
Imbolc, the festival of the arrival of the non-manifest, actually occurs,

195

fittingly, on February 19th.[3]

Imbolc marks the release of winter and thus the festival is about fire and light and marks the point in the year when the Goddess returns from her journey into the underworld. She brings her lover, the solar hero, back with her, just as she once produced his earlier reincarnation, the Lion Warrior. The most significant point in the old myths is that something comes back from the underworld — the Sumerian Inana or the Greek Persephone — and is made manifest in our reality. This force brings with it a power that originates outside our world and plants it in the physical realm. The earth dream, having been inactive for so long in the realm of the un-manifest, is returned to this world where it initiates creation itself. This is the station of the year of the phallic Goddess of Old Europe with her large buttocks. In her is implanted the serpent's egg, the seed and embryo of all life.

Imbolc falls in the Celtic month of *Nion*, named for the ash tree, the 'tree of rebirth'; *Yggdrasil*, the Scandinavian 'tree of heaven', was also an ash. Most of all, the ash represents the power of pagan Celtic magic and its opposition to Christian mythology. This was marked in 665 AD by the felling of the five magical ash trees of Ireland.

The vernal (spring) equinox is pointed out by the southernmost of The Three Sisters, a hill called Binn Hanrai. Binn Hanrai, as it is called on the ordinance survey maps is, in fact, more correctly called Binn Na Rí, The Hill of the (sacred) King. This is the time of conception and a celebration of love. The sexual rites that accompany the festival are between the sacred King and the Goddess. The equinox was marked in Greek mythology by the dances of The Muses, the Celtic version of which are the Three Sisters of fate, who represented the Goddess in all her aspects. The hills of the Three Sisters are an appropriate place to hold this festival.

The celebration of *Beltane* follows this at the beginning of May. The date of May 1st is artificial, having been decreed by Caesar in the year 46 AD when he rationalised the Roman calendar. All celebrations of the 'bright fire' that mark this marriage between the reborn God of the year and the Goddess would, henceforth, be carried out on this date throughout the Roman world. The Dé Danaan, three thousand five hundred years earlier, celebrated this unity of being around May 6th. It is on Binn Diarmada that the spring fires would have been lit, a fitting hill, indeed, for it was here that Dermot bedded Gráinne. The sword brought to Ireland by the Tuatha Dé Danaan from its home city of Gorias also features in this festival. The young sun king, Lugh, draws from the stone the mark of his office, the sword of the law.

Midsummer, the great solstice, follows. On June 21st the sun is nearest to the earth and is at the peak of its influence. It is at this point that it enters the temple. Symbolically, it is a force of change coming into the context of the earth, merging with it and infusing it with the celestial powers. It is the time for a manifestation not of the material world. At this time of year the barrier between what is fixed and what is yet to be is removed, and the world becomes pregnant with possibility. On the most prominent peak of Ballydavid Head, the mystery of midsummer would have been witnessed. Here a huge fire would have been lit, allowing the sun to complete an alignment that stretches from The Sleeping Giant through the hill of the mother Goddess, across The Three Sisters, and on to Ballydavid Head, linking seven significant hills.

Warm summer months yield ripening crops at Lughnasa. Now the sun settles into a new role and it is a time of stability. The world has been fixed again after the flux of midsummer and the changes it brought are now established. The path set out by the midsummer ley is followed to its conclusion. This is a point in the cycle of the year when knowledge is obtained of the future and the past, and wisdom is brought to fruition. The Tomb of the Black Stone marks this point on the Dingle Diamond as taking place on August 5th. As we have seen, Lughnasa is the festival of the sun king, Lugh, who wields the spear brought from the city of Finias, holding the balance of power between creation and destruction. Into his hands at this time is given control of these forces, and the world holds its breath as he takes on the role of the Lion Warrior, for he has the choice to use it for good or for evil.

The autumn equinox is the special time of fruitfulness when the Goddess and the God are ripe and full and, like a seed, ready for transformation. This is the time of the harvest king. The conception of the winter solstice has now come full season and is ready to appear in the world. It is a time for the enjoyment of the material and the physical. It is also a time when the physical appearance of vegetation undergoes a metamorphosis, becoming the seed of new life. In agricultural communities, the first ears of corn to be cut have, from the earliest times, been made into a corn dolly that is buried so that it might sprout again next year.

The Discovery of the Dingle Diamond

The Dingle Diamond marks the autumn equinox on the summit of a prominent round hill called Cnoc an Ghróigín. This is similar to *ghroíbháin*, the Irish word for 'labyrinth', or 'maze'. At this time, the harvest king is traditionally sacrificed to the Goddess, treading the path of the maze as an initiation into the other world. This sacrificial king must complete the maze if he is to return and be reborn in the womb of the Goddess.

The grain harvested at this time of year represents the Goddess changing her form and travelling into the underworld as the earth goes to sleep at *Samhain*. The leaves have fallen from the trees and the physical world goes into the dream.

The Goddess in the earth is graphically represented by the Diamond, when on October 21st, the burial place of the priestesses on Leataoibh hill is highlighted. This is directly opposite the rock called The Mother, or Sybil Head, and marks the direction of the midwinter sunrise. *Samhain*, the traditional witches' festival, celebrated around November 5th, represents the old wise woman, or the hag. Between these dates, the doors to the other world are said to be open and it is possible to pass through into a different realm. Cerridwen, or Cessair, or the old neanderthal Goddess are all different manifestations of the wise old woman, and they keep this wisdom in the form of the cauldron. Here we can see the seasonal meaning of the cauldron brought to Ireland by the Tuatha Dé Danaans' from their Nordic city, Murias, and it can be correctly placed in the story of the year at this time. Its influence in Irish mythology is all-pervading and it appears in many guises and in many stories.

The 'turning of the wheel', *Yule*, is marked by a series of stone beehive towers sprinkling the fields at the base of the Diamond. It lies outside of the wheel of the year, just as the Goddess has to travel out of this realm and into Hades, the underworld. Innana in Mesopotamia, Persephone in Greece, Anath and Isis in Egypt, Astarte of the Canaanites, Ereshkigal of the Babylonians, Etain in the Celtic tales — the list is too long to reproduce here. Each tale is the same: the Goddess leaves this world and travels into the realm of the un-manifest, the concept, the unreal, or the underworld. Here she is transformed from an old hag into a young virgin who gives birth to a miraculous child, a son. This is the child of the year, the future solar God. The birth happens at this time of year for good reason; the solar energies are weakest at this point in time when the sun is furthest from the earth. The result is the conception of ideas that can be born into the world and are ready at this point in the cycle of the year to take root and grow. The Goddess gives us a gift from which hope is born. It is not for nothing that Christmas, a time of giving presents, marks this date. The God is reborn in the Goddess, and the Goddess herself is transformed.

This, then, is the sacred landscape of the Dingle Diamond, a journey around the sacred year, merging and uniting the celestial dance of the universe with the seasonal changes of the earth. It is an ancient theme, one that has been echoed in a thousand myths. However, the order of the year, turning in step around the circle, mixed up the different myths of the Goddess. The theme of the story of the Goddess and the Lion Warrior, as laid out in the Sumerian legends and echoed in the Celtic myths, does not follow the simple path of a circle around the year. For a while, this deliberate veil obscured the Diamond's most significant function, which would be revealed when we uncovered the final secret of its mythology. (Diagram 9.6)

Diagram 9.6
The sacred landscape of the Dingle Diamond includes the islands. This is Inishtooskirt, The Sleeping Giant.

Chapter Ten
The Secret

"Do not be ignorant of me anywhere or any time. Be on your guard!
Do not be ignorant of me."
The Thunder, Perfect Mind.

Imbolc, *Beltane*, *Lughnasa*, and *Samhain* mark the four festivals alternating between the cross-quarter days of the solstices and equinoxes. To narrate the story of the year, it would seem a salient choice to begin with spring and conclude with the winter solstice — the seasons, after all, are sequential, for obvious reasons. Yet the time-honoured legend of the Goddess does not fit easily into this schema. A significant number of writers have attempted this synthesis but in order to accomplish it they have had to rearrange either the legends, or the sequence of the year. The most unfavourable commentators resort to concluding that our ancestors had limited ambitions and did no more than report on the changing of the seasons. Miraculous as this may be, the seasons are events that have occurred every year since the dawn of creation and it is doubtful whether such ancient and powerful themes, many of which are the bedrock of our spiritual faiths, describe only the logical events of the seasons. Nevertheless, each of the stations of the year has a mythology associated with it and these combine to form the legend of the Goddess. The Dingle Diamond, though, presented this association as a plan of the year around which the mythology of the landscape was drawn. The legends were quite clear: the whole temple had been constructed to unite the story of the year with the legend of the Goddess. Could it be that there was something in the plan or struc-ture of the Diamond that was the key to the puzzle? Maybe there was something in the map that I had been missing.

Taking up a pencil and compass, I sat at my writing desk and once

*Diagram 10.1
The four points and
cross, engraved in
ancient rock art in
Sweden.*

again drew the circle of the year, putting the stations in their correct place. If you were to sketch this pattern you would use a cross to represent the four stations of the year and you could use four dots to represent the festivals — a logical choice, as the solstices and equinoxes are astronomical events, whilst the festivals are mythological. What stood out on the paper was an ancient symbol, one that I recognised, for I had seen it etched in stone from the very place where the Tuatha Dé Danaan had spent so long in their fabulous four cities. (Diagram10.1) It was a very early image of a cross, in a form that appears as part of a widespread iconography.

The cross and the four points have a long history, but are most often associated with the spiral and the labyrinth, as they form the template around which these patterns can be constructed. In fact, it is the method used by the creators of what archaeologists call 'the Troy Maze', after its most famous incarnation. The spiral and the labyrinth are really two aspects of the same thing, as one can be deduced from the other, both based around this archetypal motif. These symbols — the cross, the spiral and the labyrinth — can be seen together in temples and churches around the world. In Chartres Cathedral, for example, a ray of the midsummer sun is channelled through a space in the beautiful stained-glass window dedicated to Saint Apollinaire.[1] It falls, dramatically, on a specific white gilded stone in the cathedral floor. Chartres is also famous for the labyrinth pattern set in the floor of the nave around which barefoot pilgrims walk. At Newgrange, similarly, the midwinter sun crosses a spiral carved stone before illuminating further spirals deep in the passage chamber.

In many myths, the pattern of the labyrinth occurs in association with the number seven, said to be the most secret of the mysteries of the temple builders. Traditionally, both the spiral and the labyrinth have seven turns for seven is the magical number that joins the temporal to the spiritual. There are seven sacred planets, the seven days of creation and days in the week, and seven ages in the life of man. The three great Jewish feasts last seven days each and every seventh year is the Jewish sabbatical. In the stories that were researched for this book there were many unexplained references to the number seven; for example, seven gates through which Inana had to pass to enter the underworld, the ark that circled the mountain seven times before coming to rest, and the seven sides to the church mosaic in Ballyferriter. Both the Pythagoreans and the Egyptians held that the four festivals of the witches' year and three of the points of the solar year come together in a marriage of harmony in the number seven. The eighth point, the winter solstice, brings return. This last point is marked on the Dingle Diamond by the beehive monuments at Slea Head and does, indeed, lie outside of the other seven points of the year.

A labyrinth, when constructed using the cross and the points, has seven windings that have to be followed before the centre is reached. This unique association is an allusion to the Troy Maze, examples of which are to be found across the world from South America to northern Russia and in Australia and Africa. The Hopi Indians call the labyrinth 'Mother Earth' and say that the path is the universal plan of the creator. The Old Europeans decorated their pottery with it and the Zulus draw it in the sand after smoking hemp. Coins from Knossos and the floors of the Gothic cathedrals exhibit it. The Romans painted it on their walls, and their historian, Lucretius, comments on it. The Etruscans show the solar God leaving it, bringing with him a fabulous mythological creature. The Indian epic, the Mahabharata, states that this pattern forms an impenetrable wall guarding the secrets of the earth, which only the chosen can reach. It is also the most famous universal symbol of the Goddess culture. (Diagram 10.2)

There was a frustratingly large body of evidence building up, suggesting that the unresolved mystery hidden within the simple calendar of the Dingle Diamond might help to explain the muddled seasonal legends. Like other solar temples; the Diamond has a precise cross-shaped ground plan, a ray of solstice sun pierces it and the legends associated with it are similar. In a great many solar temples the path of

The Discovery of the Dingle Diamond

Diagram 10.2
The classic Troy Maze
labyrinth from an ancient
Greek engraving.

the labyrinth and the mythology were linked; in some places, such as the labyrinth at Knossos, the archaeological evidence of the maze is matched by the mythological story of the Minotaur. Like the esoteric principles of the spiral, this mystery was concealed in the physical form of the Diamond creating a secret that could only be known by the initiated but, once revealed, it under-pinned the whole ethos of the Temple and illuminated the history of the neanderthals.

As is often the case, the clue was written in the landscape. There is an ancient pilgrims' way in this part of Kerry, set up by the first Christians in the time of Saint Patrick. It is one of the strangest of Christian pilgrimages, marked on the ordinance survey map as the West Kerry Pilgrims' Way. In the sixth century, the churches and dwellings of those who came here to practise their faith marked the route. It twists and winds around the peninsula, visiting first this holy place and then that, in much the same way as the coils of a labyrinth.

Although it was unlikely that this old pilgrims' route was the remnant of a spiral path, it gave me the idea of employing the construction of the labyrinth as a path around the myths. Using the computer, I constructed the maze pattern, based on the cross and dots, and superimposed it on the points of the Dingle Diamond. It was almost as if I had placed a filter over the image of the Diamond. Clearly outlined was a method of traversing the seasons that put the seasonal story of the year, and each of the sacred places on the Diamond, into its correct place. The chronicle of the Goddess and the Lion Warrior suddenly leapt out

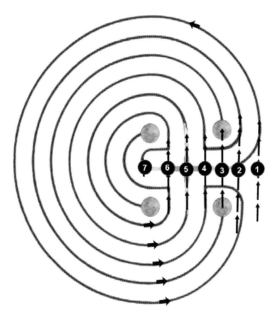

*Diagram 10.3
Seven windings
around the spiral
of the labyrinth
pass through
seven gates, or
veils.*

from the map.

Set into its true place in the temple of the sun and the earth, the Diamond becomes the pathways of the labyrinth, and its steps describe one of the most sought after secrets of mythology.

As we have noted, the labyrinth pattern is based around the symbol of the cross. The arms mark the four quarters of the year and in between these are the four festivals of the Goddess around which the paths of the maze turn. The Dingle Diamond exactly mirrors this construction. Tracing the path of the labyrinth, from the entrance to the centre, creates a journey passing along, or around, these points. If a pilgrim were to complete this tour of sacred sites, it would have taken seven years. In doing so, the pilgrim would pass through seven gates or veils, which make up the seven coils of a spiral that wraps itself around the centre point of the labyrinth. (Diagram 10.3)

The evocation of such a route is in itself typical of an arcane expression: *'Seven years and seven turns through seven gates.'*

It is this path, or journey, that the sacrificial sun king, consort of the Goddess, has to tread in order to obtain immortality or rebirth in the

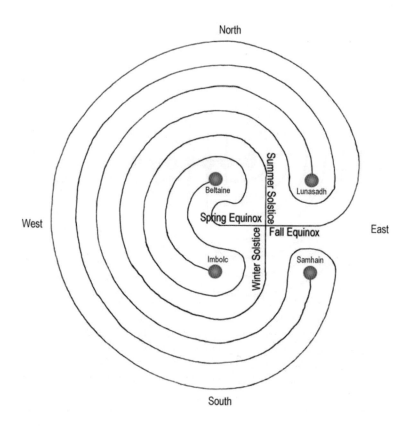

Diagram 10.4
The festivals of the seasons marked out in the form of the labyrinth.

womb of the Goddess. This odyssey is described in mythologies from lands as far apart as Greece and China. From Jason and the Argonauts to the early Irish legends of the Sons of Tureen, and in a thousand and one similar tales, the hero follows the precise dictates of this spiritual quest guided by the form of the labyrinth and facing the challenges posed by the seasonal year. The journeys undertaken by these mythical heroes are often defined by the path of the sun through the heavens.

The Secret

This trajectory is called the zodiac and the constellations on its route have always been given a special place in mythology. The zodiac has been charted and defined for at least five thousand years. When the labyrinth is united with the zodiac and the myth of the sacred king, we discover just what this story entails. A secret path that delineates the journey precisely could be traced out around the Dingle Diamond. For the first time, the sun king illuminates not only the myths of the Tuatha Dé Danaan's temple, but every other legend involving a solar hero. The labyrinth was the cipher that brought together the story of the year and the legend of the Lion Warrior and the Goddess, and it did this with an almost audible click. The account weaves a pageant that takes us back across the ages to a time when the neanderthals still influenced our culture. In a way, they still do. (Diagram 10.4)

The schema that we were facing was a remarkably simple answer to the question of the seasons and the ancient myths. It bears repeating as a summary. As the year progresses and the sun travels through the constellations, the route around the labyrinth is accomplished. In the myth of the sun king a spiritual journey is embarked upon. It is a journey that takes seven years, passes through seven gates and seven stations of the year; the eighth, as the Greeks said, brought return.

The fact that these labyrinth points are also represented physically in the landscape suggests that the sun king's journey could be applied on a personal level, perhaps as a spiritual or initiatory journey for pilgrims. It could be that if someone were to follow the Dingle Diamond, travelling through the stations of the maze, each in due season, they would be transformed. Certainly, as the seven-year cycle suggests, a physical alteration would occur since over the course of seven years the human body replaces or regenerates every cell. What the effect would be on a person spiritually is open to conjecture, but the myths are particular on this point stating that some form of spiritual re-birth or enlightenment is attained.

There is a word of warning here. It is a warning that has been written into mythology, for the knowledge can be used with wisdom or for evil. If the sun king's story could be used positively as a tool for liberation, it follows that perhaps it can also be used negatively. It is in the psychological elements that we can discern the myth's negative effect on the mind. The labyrinth path is so fundamental to the secret of the 'shadow of the hawk' and the arrival of the Entity that it's narrative spreads out from the pages of legend and into every aspect of our modern world. The story that unfolds, as the labyrinth visits each point in the Dingle Diamond, is identical in structure to that used by the priests of the Temple in co-ordinating their new society. It is the liturgical format that creates faith and holds the meaning and emotion in all religions, and it holds a heady attraction for the human mind. Strangely enough, this configuration also forms the plot of nearly every successful book, play or film ever written. It seems to affect the human mind at a very deep level, allowing it to be deceived and convinced unconsciously, playing like a virtuoso on human emotions. In a similar way to a radio signal, the will of the Temple can then be subtly broadcast.

Sometimes, in fiction and drama, this theme is not always clear and some stories, perhaps the best, cleverly disguise the labyrinth and its characters. But the more mundane tales blatantly push them forward and are easily recognised. Sometimes, only a single aspect or turn of the path is highlighted as a detail or enlargement. Sometimes the male figures are replaced by female, or vice versa, but always it is set against the backdrop of the seasons amidst the twists of the labyrinth. It is a canon that has never changed, and it is an irresistible tool that affects the will of human beings. This ability to influence particular parts of our minds lies close to the secret story of the Temple and the challenge put to it by the Tuatha Dé Danaan, for it is by this means that our individual wills are interfered with, and why the thoughts that appear as a consequence are adopted by us all as our own.

The Temple is not a creation of the human mind, but an exploration and decoding of the way that the human brain has evolved to deal with consciousness. It is a process that occurred within the energies of the earth and the sun and by the side of our neanderthal cousins. The pathway of this process is the twists of the labyrinth and it is the key to the way our minds work. Any person with this key holds great power, for the myth of the solar king is an extremely powerful psychological tool: it is the means by which we interpret our lives within the Temple. If we willingly hand-over our control of this energy to the 'higher' authority of an institution such as a church, then we relinquish the right to choose our own destinies.

The hero, the sacred king, treads this path to reclaim his power and win the love of the Goddess, but it is also a path that brings him face to face in a life and death struggle with his alter ego, the Entity. The

Goddess aides him, as in the Greek myth of Theseus and Ariadne, who gives Theseus a silver thread to navigate the labyrinth of Knossos. It is also the path that the Knights of the Round Table encounter as they search for the Holy Grail to transcend the boundaries of life and death. It is the road that Christ embarked on before being transformed by his crucifixion. In short the path of the labyrinth can free our moribund spirituality and restore to us our command over it.

Each particular station of the year is a marker describing a key event in the journey, and the path takes the traveller around all eight stations creating twelve points. This is probably why there are often twelve disciples who surround the enlightened or chosen one. It is also a reference to crossing the boundary between the earth and the heavens, as the twelve points are also a reference to the twelve constellations of the zodiac. (Diagram 10.5)

The sites of sacred power forming the Dingle Diamond are carefully visited in their turn by the path of the maze. The four stations of the solar year, the equinoxes and the solstices are met with twice, once arriving and once leaving, whilst the festivals of *Imbolc, Beltane, Lughnasa* and *Samhain* are circled only once. The seven years needed to

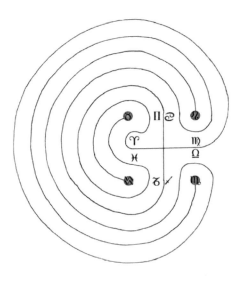

*Diagram 10.5
The Zodiac laid
out as a path
around the laby-
rinth, passing
through or around
each sign in turn,
explains the true
order of the
Zodiac.*

complete the seven windings of the spiral that form the labyrinth proffer the order in which these seasonal events occur. In successfully completing the pattern, the mind and the body undergo a physical transformation, and perhaps an 'at-oneness' with the earth dream is attained. Possibly here, too, is the meaning of the well-known phrase, 'seven steps to heaven.'

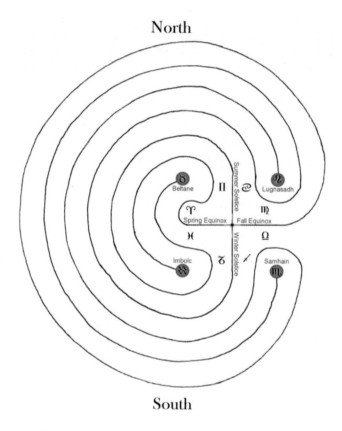

North

South

Diagram 10.6
A labyrinth to follow as the story of the year unfolds.

The Archetypal Myth of the Labyrinth and the Sun King
(Diagram 10.6)

Year one
1. The Father and the Mother **Libra**
The labyrinth of the Dingle Diamond is entered from the east, where the sky glimmers with the daylight's promise. It is the autumn equinox, when the world is in balance, a harmony of light and dark, of male and female and it is the ancient, time honoured, start of the year. The season is marked by the zodiac as Libra, the scales of balance, where the forces of fate that stand behind all things are weighed and judged. Into this timeless state came the Goddess. The natural equilibrium of massively ancient forces are disrupted by the birth of the Goddess. As she enters the mystery she undoes the status quo and the process of creation is started. The Enuma Elish describes this remote time:

"When in the height heaven was not named,
And the earth beneath did not yet bear a name,
And the primeval Apsu, who beget them,
And chaos, Tiamat, the mother of them both
Their waters were mingled together,
And no field was formed, no marsh was to be seen;
When of the gods none had been called into being,
And none bore a name, and no destinies were ordained."

Over one hundred thousand years of human/neanderthal relationship are disturbed by her act, as the gift of human consciousness, in the form of the Goddess, is brought into existence to become a powerful force in our evolution.

The stage is set. The distinctions between 'them and us' that developed in the long relationship with our neanderthal cousins are invoked. It is a strong appeal to ancient forces deep in our psyche, and leaves us with a sense of destiny.

2. The Virgin Birth of the Divine Child **Sagittarius**
The labyrinth now turns to exit the Diamond through the south, the winter solstice, when on that magical extra day of the year the divine child is born. This child is, of course, the Lion Warrior, the offspring of

the Goddess, representing the birth of human consciousness. The child is the seed of the active principle. As the Goddess has yet no consort, this Lion Warrior is a Divine Child born of a Virgin. His father is of heaven and his mother of the earth. The birth of this future hero disturbs the fates and his birth is usually foretold as part of an older prophecy, one that heralds the coming demise of the dark power. The dark forces, knowing this, attempt to escape their destiny by killing the infant whilst he is still small and helpless. The child represents a new force of human consciousness. The harbinger of change for the old ways, his very presence upsets the old order. The chaos that he brought can be seen in a remarkably concise reference near the start of the Enuma Elish where the old gods are complaining about the activities of the offspring of the Goddess:

"Their ways are truly loathsome to me.
By day I find no relief, nor repose by night.
I will destroy, I will wreck their ways,
That quiet may be restored. Let us have rest!"[3]

The child symbolises a new power, the first spark of a distinctly human awareness of the universe, which changed forever the old relationship that we had with nature. In physical terms, it was the creation of the Lion Warrior as a precursor to the sacred king. The story now draws us into another reality, one of struggle and war. Into this milieu is born the child of the Goddess, the soul of humanity, and immediately it is threatened by a dark power from deep within our oldest fears. We are left with hope and given secrecy and cunning.

Sagittarius is the sun sign for this part of the journey, for he is the keeper of the seventh circle of hell, the passage out of the underworld in the form of a labyrinth. Chiron is his Greek name, the King of the Centaurs, and he represents the acquisition of knowledge from the Goddess. He taught many heroes their skills in music, medicine and hunting, all skills of the Goddess of the underworld. His story is remembered by the Christmas mummers, who portray Chiron as a hobbyhorse in their plays.

The Diamond marks this place as Slea Head, the tip of the spear, an augury of the symbols of power that the child will hold.

Year two
3. *Inheritance.* Leo
The Goddess can not endure the attempts by the guardians of the old
ways to eliminate her son. Despite the fact that she belongs to their
culture she argues strongly against harming her son. The Eluma Elish
again shows us this power of love:

> "As soon as Tiamat (the Goddess) heard this,
> She was wroth and called out to her husband.
> She cried out aggrieved, as she raged all alone,
> Injecting woe into her mood: "What? Should we destroy that which
> we have built?
> Their ways indeed are most troublesome, but let us attend kindly!"[4]

She contrives to protect the hero by hiding his light from the old
gods, that they might forget him and be quietened. The list of stories of
infants who have been hidden to protect them includes the fostering of
Lugh, the concealment of Arthur in the woods and of Moses in the
reeds, Rhea's harbouring of Zeus and the Holy Family's flight into
Egypt to save Jesus.

Brought up in seclusion by the old Goddess, the grandmother or
guardian, the story line now ignores the maelstrom of the struggle outside the protected sanctity of the wood or cave. As the child grows to
adulthood he discovers his true nature. In many legends he finds out
that one of his parents is divine whilst the other is mortal and his true
rank is that of king. This quisling feature is the mark of synthesis in
these two opposing natures. He is given the icons of his office, often in
the form of a buried legacy or a ring.

Such an initiation of rank is a common part of the story. In Celtic
tradition, each sun king has his own symbol of power, like a trademark.
Lugh gains his spear, Moses has his staff, the young Arthur pulls a
sword from the stone, Enkidu receives an amulet and Zeus has his
thunderbolt.

We probably evolved with the social ability to defer or submit to the
will of another species but the soul of humanity, unlike the animal
kingdom, has the potential to rebel against this shackle. The symbol of
this power is the spear, developed in the struggle, and with it comes the
gift of choice. For the Lion Warrior, it was against the time-honoured

traditions of nature that he rebelled, and his spear was quite literally the means by which he could accomplish this. It is a powerful reference to our past, one that deep down, we recognise.

The path of the labyrinth circles anti-clockwise, or 'widdershins', around the festival of *Lughnasa*, the sun king's destiny which occurs in the constellation of Leo. The Lion of the Goddess is his badge of office and he has to tame and master its destructive powers without being destroyed by them. This is a test of his ability to command the hearts and minds of the people. He also has the spear of Lugh, a symbol of this dual power. If a knight kept his spear point forward when entering a foreign land, it was considered a declaration of war; if he carried it on his shoulder with the point reversed, he came in peace. Ossian asks if Fingal, the young warrior, comes in peace, and Morannal, the king's steward replies, "In peace he comes not, King of Erin, I have seen his forward spear."

Having made the choice to accept his inheritance, the new king, son of the Goddess, is invested with his power and climbs to the peak of Brandon Mountain to swear allegiance to the forces of light.

4. *Pride and Wisdom* Scorpio

As the hero comes of age he receives the knowledge of his legacy and as he does so the nature of the forces that created him become apparent. But this knowledge is dangerous and the earth Goddess, the guardian of the sun king, will not part with it willingly. The hero is frustrated by her actions for he believes that it is his destiny to wield great power. So, impetuously, the sun king takes the knowledge, often secretly or sometimes unwittingly.

We can see here the Celtic picture of the youth as he tends the caul-dron of Cessair, the same as the one that the Tuatha Dé Danaan brought from their city of Murias. The brew has to be kept simmering for a year and a day and, season-by-season, Cessair adds magical herbs in their correct planetary hours. In the Welsh myth, Gwion, the young sun king, tends the pot, but three drops of the scalding liquid fly out and burn his thumb, which he puts in his mouth. In doing so he obtains the *awen*, the knowledge of all that is, and is to be. With the coming of the *awen* came arrogance and a dangerous desire to rule, even over the Goddess The Sumerian story of hero Ninurta (the divine child) and the Turtle tells us that:

"He contemplated great deeds and inwardly he was rebellious. He uttered a word which has no (meaning). The hero Ninurta set his sights on the whole world. He told no one and inwardly did not…"[5]

His insolence invokes the anger of the Goddess, who pursues him, forcing him further into the maze and the story. She is in her wrathful aspect of the black hag, the correct guise for this station of the year, but the future sun king refuses to succumb to his fear and give up his inheritance.

Returning to the world, the path circles clockwise, or 'deisal', around the witches' festival of *Samhain*. The path of the labyrinth passes around the sign of Scorpio, the mythological agent of the Goddess whose venom is symbolic of the *awen*, or knowledge. Gwion was transformed by this but the sting of the scorpion could also kill, as was the case with Orion, the Greek hero and sun king who refused to give up his throne at the end of his term. Its venom brings death for those whose loyalties fail the Goddess, or resurrection to those whose heart is true.

The Dingle Diamond places this struggle at the women's cemetery on Leataoibh Hill.

Year three
5. *The Defeat and Betrayal* Virgo
Pretentious and alone in the fastness of the old god's stronghold the hero meets a new aspect of the Goddess. This aspect is often represented by a young woman, the daughter of the old Goddess or the granddaughter of the old god. The youth falls under her spell, though their love is forbidden. In perusing his love the hero gets into trouble, often killing a trusted servant of the old god or trying, unsuccessfully to elope with his Goddess. The mission of restoring the forces of light against the power of darkness is compromised by this love, for the hero is exiled from the safe haven of his old life and is forced to go against the desires of his guardian, the old Goddess. Once outside her protecttion and being inexperienced in the ways of the world, he is vulnerable to the forces of the dark king. The old Goddess is petitioned by the old gods and agrees to set out against the hero. The Eluma Elish reports thus:

"Rouse up, our Mother! Pay them back and make them empty like the wind.'

Tiamat approved it, she said, 'I approve this advice: we will make monsters, and monsters and gods against gods will march into battle together."[6]

When the hero first laid claim to his throne, he was under the protection of the Goddess, and the physical response of dying for a cause was summoned within us. But now the solar hero has to face his enemy on his own, armed only with the secret knowledge that he has stolen from the Goddess. Betrayed because of his love for the Goddess in her aspect of spring maiden, this ill-fated challenge to the dark God tells us that idealism is a stronger force than our individual safety, going beyond even death. We are cast out on our own, the guiding hand withdrawn, Eden left behind us.

The Irish myth of the wooing of Étaín, or the Welsh legend of the Lion of the Steady Hand, Llew Llaw Gryffes, represent this betrayal as an act of the Goddess. In these myths and many others, she reverts to subterfuge to entrap the sun king. Samson's hair, the source of his strength, is cut; Enkidu, the earth twin of Gilgamesh, is led into captivity by the love of a young woman; even Jesus faces a dilemma with Mary Magdalene, who is represented as a whore.

With the first set of convolutions completed, the path returns to the autumn equinox for the second time. By now it has passed through the constellation of Virgo, the Virgin, and this is the aspect of the Goddess that the sun king has to fight for. It is here at this meeting that he encounters her in this form. But the meeting does not bode well for the young king. The sign of Virgo is thus a warning, showing us that the powers of the Goddess cannot be taken lightly. The dark God challenges the young sun king and the unequal battle commences. With the dark God's vast forces arrayed before him, the fate of the world is in his grasp. The solar hero knows that he can not win, but still chooses to join the struggle rather than turn away. Like Astrea or Cephalus in the Greek legends, he is destroyed by it. Torn apart by the Goddess and defeated by the dark God, the sun king is taken captive and subjugated.

Year four

6. *The Agents of the Enemy* Cancer

Often the myths represent this part of the theme as a term of imprisonment or service under the dark God. It is here that he encounters the agents of the dark God sent to destroy him. The old Goddess reveals to the old gods, a weakness, a flaw in his power that can be used to capture him: the heel of his foot. In the tale of Inurta and the Turtle, the turtle represents the power of the dark God, a power that the hero, alone, is unable to fight against:

"Against Ninurta, Enki fashioned a turtle from the clay of the abzu. Against him he stationed the turtle at an opening, at the gate of the abzu. Enki talked to him near the place of the ambush and brought him to the place where the turtle was. The turtle was able to grab Ninurta's tendon from behind. The hero Ninurta managed to turn back its feet. Enki, as if perplexed, said, "What is this!" He had the turtle scrape the ground with its claws, had it dig an evil pit. The hero Ninurta fell into it with the turtle. The hero did not know how to get out from .... The turtle kept on gnawing his feet with its claws".[7]

If he is to defeat these, the sun king must humble his pride and seek the help of the Goddess in her guise of the protective mother. As the weakness of the sacred king, this vulnerability is almost universal. The Irish myths record that Dermot's heel is pierced by a bristle from Benn Gulban, the terrifying boar of Celtic myth. In the Greek myth, Paris shoots Achilles, who gives his name to the tendon in this part of the foot. In the Indian epic, the Mahabharata, Krishna is pierced in the heel by an arrow shot by his brother, Jara, the hunter. A magic snake sent by Isis stings the heel of Ra in the Egyptian story. In the Nordic saga, the heel of Balder is pierced by mistletoe thrown by the god Holder at the insistence of Loki. A scorpion in the Greek legend stings the heel of Hippocrates.

It is in the sign of Cancer, the crab, that this vulnerability is exploited. Traditionally the crab is an agent of the dark power, sent to destroy the sun king by biting his one place of weakness.

The twisting turns of the labyrinth have now reached the summer solstice when the Entity is at his strongest. This is the most difficult and dangerous part of the journey for the sun king, and it presents us with what is probably the most complex part of the archetypal theme. Yet, on another level it is also the most simple, showing us that by knowing our weaknesses we can overcome them, and that to know our weakness we have to submit to a power that can hold us in captivity. But this conscious submission harbours the spark of rebellion, and for this the human spirit was hobbled, literally by cutting the Achilles tendon. This imprisonment evokes both our spirit of liberation and our fears.

The struggle with the agents of the dark God occurs on the solstice peak of Ballydavid Head at the apex of the Diamond, and is a precursor of the final battle that will take place on this same territory.

7. *The Help of the Goddess* Capricorn

Once the solar hero is held within the grasp of the dark God, in the underworld, the young Goddess weeps to see that he is held fast and tortured. As she weeps spring is taken from the world and an eternal winter reigns. The hero is held by the Old Goddess deep under the Earth. Never-the-less she decides to go and rescue him. The theme now subtly shifts to tell of the adventures of the Goddess as she faces the perils of the lower kingdom. The descent of the Goddess Ishtar into the underworld to rescue the hero from the clutches of the old Goddess Irkalla is told in the Babylonian tale of the Descent of Ishtar:

"To the land of no return, the land of darkness,
Ishtar, the daughter of Sin directed her thought,
Directed her thought, Ishtar, the daughter of Sin,
To the house of shadows, the dwelling of Irkalla."⁸

The theme now changes again as the balance of power alters; now it brings the hero help in the form of the Goddess. As he gains strength and maturity this alliance of love takes him through another initiation.

We are often told that knowledge is power. The complex mastery of the material world, for example the ability to split the atom, creates these feelings. This passage of the labyrinth takes us through all this and we mentally prepare ourselves for the coming conflict.

The path now travels around the cross of the year, inverting the pattern and re-entering the Diamond at the winter solstice. The route of the labyrinth has now reached its nadir and another change in the energies takes place. The strength of the Entity, although still at its height, is beginning to wane. The sun king travels with the help of the Goddess into the realm of the underworld. Here he receives the aid of Pan, or Bacchus, and the old wise Goddess. Capricorn is the influence on the sun king's path during this time. Now he is taught the old ways of magic and is sent on a series of trials to master them.

Year five
8. *Rebirth* Pisces
The mission to the lower world is successful and the Goddess and hero return together into the world of light. The Goddess and the hero declare their loyalties to each other, and it is this union that creates a greater power than the world has ever seen. Together they can alter the destiny of the world. The Babylonian tale of the hero, Tammuz, describes the joy of this event:

"As for Tammuz, the lover of her youth,
Wash him with pure water, anoint him with sweet oil:
Clothe him with a red garment,
let him play on a flute of lapis.
Let the courtesans turn his mood."[9]

Amid the hills of The Three Sisters — the aspects of the triple-goddess — the solar king emerges from the underworld with the Goddess at his side. At this time of the spring equinox, the balance between light and dark is again open to question. Now the year is moving away from the dark and towards the light of new hopes and possibilities. Pisces is the star sign of this part of his travail. The fish is a sign of the promise of resurrection and a new immortality. This is one of the reasons that the early Christians used it to represent Christ. The sun king, having surmounted all trials and battles, now emerges reborn to face the final challenge. But first he has to acquire his icons of office.

9. *The Icons of Office* Taurus
The hero now has to take his rightful place at the side of the Goddess. To do this he must pass through an initiation, or marriage, based on the icons of power held by the Goddess. His acceptance speech to the Goddess can be read in the Sumerian epic the return of Ninurta (the

hero). Although much of the test is missing the essence of the speech can still be perceived, Ninlil is the name of the Goddess:

"Lord Ninurta answered her: "My mother, I alone cannot ... with you .... Ninlil, I alone cannot ... with you, for me alone ... Battle arrayed like heaven; no one can rival me."[10]

The first of these is represented by the stone, the foundation of the new order and symbol of the power of the earth, the Goddess. Upon this stone their marriage is celebrated.

His task is to obtain the stone of destiny, the 'rock of the tanist'. This publicly declares him as the inheritor of the throne and allows him to be crowned as the new solar God of light. He does this in the sign of Taurus, the bull. In Old Europe, Ireland and India, the bull was a special symbol of the Goddess, often portrayed on the walls of temples and pottery. It represents the ancient power of the Goddess and the sun king combined, and the earth force of the old ways of the Goddess. Implacably opposed to the Temple of the dark power, the bull maintains the duality and conflict that the Diamond was constructed to alleviate. For this reason the Minotaur was held in the labyrinth at Knossos, and Gilgamesh has to overcome the bull of heaven to come into his inheritance. It is a source of power that the sun king has to master if he is to continue.

Here on the western edge of the world, the sun king is married to the Goddess creating a permanent and powerful union. The earth power of the stone of destiny and of the bull is consummated at the festival of *Beltane*, around which winds the labyrinthine path. The Diamond marks this as the spot where the young king Dermot was chased and bedded by the Goddess in the guise of Gráinne, in the hills of The Three Sisters. The Goddess and the new God are united in the bull.

Year six

10. *The Authority* Aquarius

This part of the theme describes a reconciliation of the Goddess and the power of the Lion Warrior, represented by the hero. Free from the clutches of the dark God, and united with the Earth Goddess, the army of the lion can be deployed to defend the forces of light.

The sun god's task is to acquire the sword of ruler-ship, and finally gain access to the source of his power. This power is the power of love and when the sword is wielded in the cause of love, as opposed to the law of domination, it is capable of freeing the hearts and minds of people. Once free from the influence of the Temple, it allows them to stand with the solar king in the coming battle. Not for nothing does it occur in the sign of Aquarius, the bearer of the waters of the spirit. He does this at *Imbolc*, with the help of the Goddess, and also celebrates and consecrates his relationship at this time. The story swoops into the present, into every war and conflict that afflicts us. It is about the ability to take life in the cause of another. Power and submission lie side by side in our souls and this invokes forgiveness. The Dingle Diamond marks the place sacred to the Goddess at this time on Sybil Head, at the place of the sacred fires. But even this brief period of joy and peace is brought to an end by the gathering of war clouds in the East. The Sumerian legend of Ninurta describes the ending of the festivities by a messenger telling them about war.

"Inspiring great numinous power, he had taken his place on the throne, the august dais, and was sitting gladly at his ease at the festival celebrated in his honour, rivalling An and Enlil in drinking his fill, while Bau was pleading petitions in a prayer for the king, and he, Ninurta, Enlil's son, was handing down decisions. At that moment the lord's battle-mace looked towards the mountains, the Šar-ur cried out aloud to its maste "The lord arose, touching the sky; Ninurta went to battle, with one step."[11]

11. *The Last Battle* Gemini

This is the final conflict bringing to an end the established order. Despite the epic drama that unfolds during the course of the war, the ending of an old way and the lament for it tinges the struggle with pathos. We feel this incongruity in the death throes of the monster, dark lord or dragon. Yet the prophecy is complete and a sense of closure is evoked.

Penultimately, in the sign of the twins, Gemini, the young God and Goddess take on the power of the dark God. The sign of the rival twins represents two sides of the same power. Both are now equal, one on the side of darkness and the other on the side of light. The sun king and the dark God are born of the same divine source, and this star sign represents their conflict. The battle occurs at Ballydavid Head, the site of the midsummer challenge. The Tuatha Dé Danaan took on this conflict in physical form when they defeated the Fomorians under their captain, Balor. The battle is a difficult and destructive affair, and in it the sun king must wield the deadly power of the Lion, as does the dark god (in this legend called the Asag).

"Ninurta's splendour covered the Land, he pounded the Asag like roasted barley, he ...... its genitals (?), he piled it up like a heap of broken bricks, he heaped it up like flour, as a potter does with coals; he piled it up like stamped earth whose mud has been dredged. The hero had achieved his heart's desire. Ninurta, the lord, the son of Enlil, ... began to calm down."[12]

The dark God is overcome in this battle. The victory is completed by a sacrifice, for the death of the dark king unravels the old order and for this to be accomplished, the old king of light, the father of the new heir to the throne, has to die, too. In older myths, the king of light is killed on the field of battle. But in more recent legends, such as those of King Arthur, or the New Testament, the old king of light and the new sun king become one and the same. These composite kings of light are the sacrifice to achieve victory, but we are expressly told that they do not die. Instead, often after a period of three days (a mark of the moon Goddess) they are reborn. Jesus, the Lamb of God, whose death and resurrection occurs during the Christian festival of Easter, or King Arthur, who was taken to the mythical Avalon, are two such examples.

Year seven
12. *The Victory* Aries
Lastly is the scene of celebration when the Goddess returns from the underworld at the side of her lover, and the old dark God is banished. This is in the sign of Aries, and the Dingle Diamond places it on the hills of The Three Sisters looking out to the west and the islands of the other world. Aries, the ram, is a symbol of the moon Goddess and, as the Greek myth of Athamas at Phrixous records, it is the time of the annual sacrifice of the old king and the birth of the new. There are many legends detailing the emergence of the God and Goddess from the underworld. The ram represents the cloak of the moon Goddess,

and the wearing of a fleece by a chosen 'king' during Easter is a living tradition in parts of Greece, to this day. The legend of Jason and the Golden Fleece is about fulfilling this quest. The Sumerian mythology describes the homecoming of the hero Ninurta after his defeat of the Old powers:

"The hero had conquered the mountains. As he moved across the desert, he ... Through the crowd, he came forth among their acclamations, majestically he ... Ninurta joyfully went to his beloved barge, the lord set foot in the boat Ma-kar-nunta-ea. The boatmen sang a pleasant song, for the lord they sang his praise. They addressed an eternal greeting to Ninurta son of Enlil."[13]

In these twelve stations of the maze, we see not only the story of the year but also a way to challenge the power that the Entity appears to hold over our will. In completing the journey, the sun king is raised once again to the side of the Goddess as an immortal, capable of defeating the dark God and transforming the powers of the sun into a beneficial role. If successful, it becomes a way whereby the message of the Temple can be transformed. No longer is it one of domination and might, but instead a message of love and harmony. In the place of oppression we are offered freedom. The unity of the Goddess and the duality of the Temple are brought together, healing the old rift and heralding a golden age.

This is not the end of the story of the Dingle Diamond. Its theme emerges later in history in the creed of the early Christian faith and its consequences reverberate down the centuries.

Danger is an integral part of this ancient formula, a danger affecting every person on the planet today for it invokes the very power that for over a hundred thousand years had been held by the neanderthals. It is a compulsion that can take over the mind of man and slip into our thoughts as easily as taking pleasure from a beautiful sunset. This cuckoo mentality can be used for creation or destruction.

The Tuatha Dé Danaan may have put an end to the conflict between the earth Goddess and the God of the Temple, the duality that we talked of in chapter three, but their methods are still a part of the 'shadow of the hawk'. If a book or a film that follows this protocol can invoke such powerful emotional responses, then how much more can a politician, whether from a democracy or a dictatorship, use it to 'spin' a myth, to engage us emotionally for their own gain? The book or film is, at the end of the day, merely fiction; however, the 'fiction' that is used to justify the real and physical acts of war, as well as the exploitation and destruction of our ecosystem, has very real consequences affecting our relationship with the earth and, if we choose to call it such, with the Goddess.

In this story we see the essence of the creed of Christianity, a guide to just how powerful the message of the Dingle Diamond is, for it has survived and instructed the minds of humans for over two thousand years. From it, and from the need to keep its liberating message out of the minds of the masses, have arisen Masonic secret societies with their occult lore, the agencies of the Pentagon, and just about every group connected with civil or military control. To control the myth of the maze is to control the mind. In this way, contemplation of the labyrinth engages the vacuum left by the neanderthals, and enters the human mind to alter the destiny of the world.

History records that what happened to the Tuatha Dé Danaan and their mission is an almost exact re-telling of this story. Their legacy is woven into our consciousness. The journey of the sun king through the labyrinth reminds us that whenever the forces of the dark temple are invoked we can support or defy their actions, we have a free choice. Understanding that the story of the labyrinth is a universal poetic theme is the first step in remembering who we are, for in knowing this our minds might not be so easily manipulated.

Is this thought your own?

Chapter Eleven
The Last House in the West

On Thursday, the Kalends of May, on the 17th of the Moon, the fleet
of the sons of Milidh occupied Erinn at Inbher Sgene.
Cronicum Scotorum.

L egends say that the Tuatha Dé Danaan became a part of the
land, and certainly their buildings, tombs, mounds and temples
cover the Irish landscape, subtly affecting the generations that have
lived with them. Many are of such impressive size that their construction must have entailed a considerable degree of technical expertise,
not to mention logistical organisation. Brown Hill Dolmen in County
Carlow, in the south-east of Ireland, for example, is the largest dolmen
in Europe. Its capstone, weighing in excess of one hundred tons, was
brought twelve miles through dense forest. Though the stones are silent, this is not the case with the peat bogs of Ireland. The artefacts that
they have preserved make it possible to trace the evolution of the Irish
population. The growth of the bogs continued apace throughout the
Neolithic period, and five-thousand years of history lies mostly undis-
covered in this unbroken blanket of dark turf.

The picture that emerges shows that the Tuatha Dé Danaan continued to use copper and started working with bronze. This was an Industry of considerable importance, for in the Belderg Valley in County
Mayo, an area of very poor land, a ten-metres-long house has been
excavated. Dated around 1400 BC, hence well into the Bronze Age, the
building shows evidence of a mining community. In nearby Ballyglass
a court tomb has been erected over the remains of a wooden house
from around 3160 BC, showing almost two-thousand years of continuous habitation during which time the artefacts, and therefore the culture, do not appear to evolve. Gold, for torcs and collars, was panned in
the streambeds of County Wicklow, and tin for bronze was imported

Diagram 11.1

from Cornwall. This extensive and durable history suddenly comes to an end: by about 1400 BC, many of these mines were abandoned.

A similar change in the quality of artefacts can also be traced to this time. Compared to the degraded quality of pottery in Europe between 3000 BC and 1400 BC, the same period in Ireland marks a flowering of decorative pottery. The style of items unearthed recalls the more ancient Old European, central Balkan culture. Many of the graves in Ireland that have been excavated contain complete vases, urns and bowls, all decorated with the meanders, chevrons and triangles similar to those of the older European style. This Irish renaissance in pottery style suddenly ceases around 1400 BC and is replaced by roughly finished, undecorated pieces. Coincidentally, the number of hidden caches or hoards of treasure increase dramatically indicating that the changes that society went through were of degradation, for the need to hide valuable objects only occurs at times of struggle and war.

During the time that the Tuatha Dé Danaan occupied Ireland, a

The Last House in the West

period of nearly two-thousand years, the use of stone and flint as the basic material for tools continued and the skills needed to make beautiful objects, such as the ceremonial stone axes unearthed all over Ireland, developed. This in itself is a pointer to the establishment and maintenance of a stable society, one that did not need to make the technological advances that the warlike peoples of Europe and the East were undergoing during this time.

The discovery of iron [1] was one such development that changed the course of history forever. The sword was delivered from the stone and iron appeared in Europe for the first time around 2000 BC, from Egypt and the East. At first it was a rarity and only the most privileged warriors could make use of this very costly material. Although the beginning of the Iron Age in Ireland is dated around 800 BC, it would be easy to imagine that some artefacts would have travelled long distances as trade objects. It is quite possible that iron swords came to Ireland around 1400 BC, but they were a rarity and, since they quickly rust, would leave behind no definite evidence.

These were the last years of the Tuatha Dé Danaan. For nearly two-thousand years their civilisation had flourished in Ireland and had not only kept alive the traditions of the Goddess and her culture, but had integrated them into their Temple, displaying their remarkable knowledge of the earth, the heavens and other cultures.

Europe and the East had evolved into a multitude of warring civilisations and empires based on the order of law, the lion of war and the rule of the priest and king. The list is familiar to everyone as a canon of cultural advancement: Egypt, Mesopotamia, Greece, Scythia, the Hittites, Babylon, the Harappan of the Indus Valley, all in constant struggle where the slightest weakness brought ruin. Yet, left out of the history books and classified as barbarians by the literature, the Tuatha Dé Danaan had found a way to make one of the most remarkable and enduring contributions to our world today.

The Dé Danaan were conquered in the last of the five fabled invasions of Ireland by a tribe from Spain, known as the Milesians, or the 'Sons of Gaedhuil' (Green Gael). They were Scythians, 'the people of the horse' from the Balkans, still fresh from the plunder of Old Europe. Moving by way of Egypt, they dominated Spain and from there, set their sights on Ireland.

The secrets of the Tuatha Dé Danaan and the Temple were nearly

227

Diagram 11.2
Brandon Mountain, over which the sun appears on Midsummer's Day.

swept away by an invading force that disrupted and destroyed the earlier culture. Yet not everything was lost, for we read in the Irish histories that several of the noble families of the Dé Danaan were saved
from the destruction and their daughters given in marriage to the kings
of Miled. Some of the survivors were banished to the south-west of
Ireland, whither they carried the spark of their tradition, but they were
constantly persecuted and harassed. Their achievements in transforming the Entity of the Temple into the Lord of Light, consort of the Goddess, was a source of such strength that the Milesians were forced to
make use of it in establishing and building their subsequent rulership
over the land and its people.

The Sons of Miled were not the noble Celts of popular mythology,
nor were they a more sophisticated or advanced people that would fit
the paradigm of a world continually bettering itself. They were a task
force intent on destroying the Temple of the Goddess and her people
who had, in the majority, lived a peaceful existence. In short, they were

barbaric destroyers who plunged Ireland into a dark age that was to last for nearly six generations. That the onslaught must have been remorseless can be seen in the complete reversal of the archaeological record in Ireland, except in the far west, where only an echo of the older culture was left.

The story of the downfall of the Tuatha Dé Danaan is recorded in detail in The Book of Invasions and contains a wealth of information about the invaders themselves. It starts with an exploratory mission to assess the strength of the people of the Goddess.

Íth and a party of scouts arrive in Ireland and parley with the Dé Danaan. Their mission is to find any weak points of defence and to gauge the wealth of the land. They also become engaged in politics, according to the legend. The Dé Danaan are convinced that Íth intends to return with an army and, to put a stop to this, they try to kill his party. They succeed in mortally wounding Íth, but his scouts escape home. This is the excuse needed to invade. The Milesians draw together an army and sail from Spain, arriving in due course in the southwest of Ireland.

The coming of Íth gives us an insight into the designs of the Milesians, for to send a druid to discover the secrets of a tribe is a common theme in all later Celtic wars. Julius Caesar himself used it on several occasions, and sometimes even won his opponents' surrender without a fight because he could expose the secrets of their Temple, their methods of worship and the names of their gods. This mystical rivalry is rather difficult for us to understand today, yet we still apply similar methods. Propaganda, the war of words that nations use today, is a key part of any conflict. The side that loses this battle of words loses the support of its population and will lose the war. The conflicts of the last century — the First and Second World Wars and the Vietnam War — show this in its most basic form. It is probable that this power was the same three-thousand years ago although manifested differently, more suited to the epoch and its people.

To miss this point is to misunderstand the conflict of ideologies and the subtle way the Tuatha Dé Danaan lost the physical war but won the ideological one despite the best efforts of the Milesians' chief druid, Amergin. If we listen closely to our customary use of language, we find that the terms we use to define our enemies come, in fact, from the mouths of those who have won the war of words.

The Discovery of the Dingle Diamond

The boats of the Milesians approach the Irish shore, the Tuatha Dé Danaan are ready and use their enchantments to foil the invasion.

"But when the Tuatha Dé Danaan saw the ships coming, they flocked to the shore, and by their enchantments they cast such a cloud over the whole island that the Sons of Miled were confused, and all they could see was some large thing that had the appearance of a pig." (This is a reference to the 'white sow', a common manifestation of the omnipotent triple-goddess.) "When they were hindered from landing there by enchantments, they went sailing along the coast till at last they were able to make a landing at Inver Scéine in the west of Munster."

Here they meet with Banba, wife of Mac Cuill, the hazel god. She asks them what they want and requests that they name Ireland after her. A few days later they meet Fódhla, wife of Mac Cécht, god of the plough, who makes the same request. Lastly, they are introduced to Ériu, wife of Mac Gréine, the sun god, who also asks that Ireland be named in her honour. Amergin, the druid and poet of the Milesians, replies that he will do so.

This meeting of the druid and these aspects of the Goddess tells much about the different cultures. She speaks not with the king or commander but with the druid, who holds the real power. This is a reference to the emerging druidic, or bardic, class of the Celtic peoples, a class that was to wield power for the next thousand years across Europe, and who were only defeated when the Romans conquered Europe. The question that the Goddess asks is a very serious one: will the druid's people undertake to keep the Temple of the triple-goddess alive in Ireland? What she offers in return is a bloodless conquest. Cybele, the heir to the lore of the ancient Goddess, also resorted to this tactic; fifteen-hundred years later in Rome she would plead in the same way with Tarquinius, the Etruscan king.

The Sons of the Gael arrive at the court of the Dé Danaan at Teamhair, though this was not its name then. Here they find the three sons of Cermait, he of the Honey-Mouth, son of the Dagda, fighting over the possessions of their father. Amergin informs them that he is surprised to see this quarrel but that he will, at any rate, be taking their country from them and enquires whether they want to surrender or fight? He makes them this offer: he and his army will withdraw their boats and if the Dé Danaan can, by means of their enchantment, hinder his landing, he will turn around and return to Spain; if they cannot prevent him setting foot on the land, then they must surrender all claim to Ireland. The Dé Danaan take stock. They do not have an army, or even enough weapons, so they agree to his conditions. The Milesians, convinced by Amergin, withdraw for nine days.

This quarrel is a reference to the differences between the Temples of the dark and the light, for in creating or transforming the dark God there is willing betrayal and, as we saw in the previous chapter, this struggle with the dark force creates the necessary conditions to free the God to unite with the Goddess. What the legends recall is told through Amergin's eyes, the eyes of the victor. It is unlikely that Amergin would have committed the grave tactical error of withdrawing, thus allowing his enemy to regroup. To be powerful themselves, the Milesians had to be seen to have had an epic struggle, and so this was written into the tale. Firstly, therefore, there is a battle of the poets, a battle between the power of each side's magic and, in its most basic form, the first ideological challenge to the Goddess by a priest of the Temple of the dark lord. For this reason, the Slieve Mis Mountains, the home of the Goddess and location of the Dingle Diamond, is chosen for the conflict.

The legend says that Amergin and the Milesian fleet retired to a distance of nine waves from the shore. The Tuatha Dé Danaan promptly conjured a great storm that almost finished them off, wrecking boat after boat on the rocky coast. Finally, Amergin calms the waves with his famous song:

I am the wind on the sea
I am the wave of the sea
I am the bull of seven battles
I am the eagle on the rock
I am a flash from the sun
I am the most beautiful of plants
I am a strong wild boar
I am a salmon in the water

The Discovery of the Dingle Diamond

I am a lake in the plain
I am the word of knowledge
I am the head of the spear in battle
I am the god that puts fire in the head
Who spreads light in the gathering on the hills?
Who can tell the ages of the moon?
Who but I knows the secrets of the unhewn stone?

This is no idle boast or beautiful embellishment. It is an invocation, a paean of victory. The twelve signs of the Celtic zodiac are invoked. The last three lines are addressed to the midsummer arrival of the sun god and the three phases of the Goddess as they come together in the temple. This invocation informs us that Amergin knows the story of the maze, which when invoked in any tale or myth causes an instant response in the minds of humans, and also that he wants to control it for his own ends. The winds of the enraged Goddess of Ireland are thus

Diagram 11.3
Gallarus Oratory, the strange Dark Ages church of the earliest Christians.

calmed by a magician who states that he knows the rites and secrets of her Temple and will continue to perform them and keep her law. The waves subside, and the knell of doom has sounded for the Dé Danaan.

In an act that typifies the theme of sacrifice, the three goddesses of Ireland are killed in the ensuing struggle. The battle is fierce and desperate. No quarter is given. The *Annals of the Four Masters* records:

"Their three queens were also slain: Éire by Suirghe, Fódhla by Edan, and Banba by Caicher."

As this is foretold, it becomes the required act of voluntary sacrifice that ensures their immortality. The battle is at length gained against the Tuatha Dé Danaan, and they are "slaughtered wherever they were overtaken."

There are, in fact, three fierce battles, one for each of the goddesses, and in each, the heroes of the Dé Danaan compete but lose the struggle. Finally, they have to surrender. Just as the sacred king has to surrender to his dark tanist in order to achieve immortality, so the people have to suffer the same. Their defeat and surrender meant that their message of love would never die. The power of Amergin and the Milesians resulted from taking over the Goddess in her triple form and using this structure to maintain their rule over the population of Ireland, which by 1400 BC was relatively large. To do this, they had to use the only power available to them: the power of the Temple, a unique tool for the Milesians, for by taking over rather than destroying it, they ensured that forever there would be a voice of harmony in its rule. But it was also a tool for social control and, used in this way, it set a precedent for the next three-thousand years, influencing the building of every temple in Europe. It was only in the new world of South America that the old Temple of the Entity was free to flourish without this healing principle. There it created a microcosm of hell.[2]

The remnant of the People of Dana were given land in the west where the Goddess still thrives today. The Milesians, meanwhile, took over the rule of Ireland, a position they were to hold for the next thousand years. The seed that the Tuatha Dé Danaan planted was a powerful psychological weapon, the power of which was recognised by the Christians. Jesus made this plain when he said that "the Kingdom of Heaven is like a grain of mustard seed which a man took and sowed in his field; it is the smallest of all seeds, but when it has grown, it

Diagram 11.4
The remains of a rath, or fortified home, of the Celtic people.

becomes the greatest of all shrubs and becomes a tree."

The Tuatha Dé Danaan still tread the labyrinth of our temples, and in the fairy mounds and castles of their myths, maintain their influence on Irish history, just as Irish history has maintained its influence over all of Europe. During the three-thousand years following their epoch, not a single event has been left uninformed by their rituals, first introduced into the temple in the hills of Kerry. The Dé Danaan's sway over our religions and their ability to transmit thoughts and desires into the far future, is a direct result of the systematic labour they put into building the Dingle Diamond.

Chapter Twelve
After-word

"There might come once more some kind of Renaissance out of the hopelessly condemned and trampled past, when certain ideas come to life again, and we should not deprive our grandchildren of a last chance at the heritage of the highest and farthest-off times."[1]

There is little similarity between religion and spirituality, for religion is a practical matter and is concerned with the collective, whereas spirituality is a personal affair and is focused on the individual. Yet the former evolved out of the latter and its first appearance, 33,000 years ago,[2] was in the form of the Great Goddess. Her parents were our evolutionary condition and our social relationship with another species and as a true deity she was incorporeal, authoritative and omnipotent. Before her advent there was no godhead and no concept of one. This is not to say there was no spirituality; grave goods and even etched designs recovered prior to this watershed show us that humans and neanderthals were spiritual beings. They paid tribute to their dead and observed customs in the styles of burial that they undertook. But it would be a serious error to confuse this practice with religion, for there are no recorded cases of a religion without a deity accompanied by its icons and, as far as we know, there are no icons older than thirty-three thousand years.

In the parts of the world where humans mixed with neanderthals, the pace and direction of human society was altered by the neanderthal world. The inventions, thoughts and legends were set by an agenda that was not entirely human and held in place by the social glue of tradition. Only with the creation, or discovery, of the Goddess came the signature of the rise of religion, the figurines. It was an event so powerful that it was recorded in stone. With the advent of religion as a social force came the institutions that religion always carries with it empowered by the committed foot soldiers of its will, the Lion Warriors. For the first time, human society was organised around collective needs that were defined by the nature of the Goddess; this is the key to her effect on human society. She is a strange chimera constructed, and clearly displaying, the three aspects of human life that would have been most prominent in Palaeolithic society.[3]

One part of her is tradition. She certainly did not arrive fully formed; she had a past. That past was based on the neanderthals, the goddess being created in their image, with their habits and mannerisms probably attributed to her. In this way the new religion would be effective, for it tugged at the same neurological pathways as the neanderthals did in their evolutionary role, effectively invoking the same responses in our minds. There is no escaping the fact that religion is a very powerful method of 'rousing the masses', its role and effectiveness today being no different than in the time of the ancient Goddess. Another part of the Goddess is communal. She was born out of a necessity to act as a common collective. Very probably this was based around evolutionary skills of survival, such as hunting, but in this case the focus of the hunt was not an animal but an intellectual ideal. The last part of her makeup is spiritual. A route to this spiritual landscape appears to be hard-wired into our brains[4] and probably evolved with us. It exists because each one of us has the capacity to experience it – a tangible verification of the existence of non-physical realms. When these three aspects were combined in the ideal of the Goddess, human society and human religions assumed their present form. The balance of these three ingredients, it seems, dictates the nature and effectiveness of the religion. Nature abhors a vacuum; with the neanderthals gone there was a huge vacuum, into which poured the Goddess. Without her there could have been no recognisable society.

Twenty thousand years ago the balance was dominated by spiritual and traditional guidelines. The deity was female. The result was a rapid development in farming, literacy, and husbandry skills and little in the way of war or greed. A cataclysmic shift occurred in this balance in the region of Persia, about six thousand years ago. The power of a God, made manifest in the institutional religious complexes of the ziggurat, became dominant. The fear of the 'shadow of the neanderthal' was amplified, and the expression of spirituality was confined to a small and privileged class who denied the masses access to it. The result was a rapid development of war skills, the control of society by an elite, and the establishment of money. This deity was male.

This male form of society, based on nations, is so familiar to us that we tend to think of it as normal. Nevertheless, the arrival of money, soldiers, kings, laws, priests and gods some six thousand years ago was a novel event. It marked a dialectic, or polarisation, in belief between male and female, good and evil, heaven and earth, and it marked, too, the subordination of our spirituality to a collective elite in the name of an institution.

The Dingle Diamond was one of a number of attempts to reintroduce a sense of proportion into the world of religion.[5] The architects deliberately created an experiential spiritual religion, reclaiming the energy of the Goddess, thereby redressing the polarisation of male and female.

When the Tuatha Dé Danaan built their monuments, they secreted, in their lore, the means and the method by which they sought to introduce and reconcile the Goddess with the power of the male God. They were well aware of human history and the powerful evolutionary forces that speak in our minds. They knew as well that, unfettered, the male God would lead them to a sterile and dismal future. It was this, more than the rough barbarism of the Kurgan, that they were determined to avoid. And they were committed to ensuring that their traditions and wisdom would not be forgotten. This call to awaken and remember is their heritage. Their undertaking was so successful that it echoed down the centuries, creating the branches of occult, arcane and Gnostic knowledge that eventually pierced and illuminated the veils of the medieval churches, bringing beauty and harmony. Every tributary of Gnostic wisdom and every word written in the light of Sophia are based upon the Dé Danaan's single-minded drive to protect their worldview. The Cistercian cathedrals sprinkled across Europe perfected this movement. Directly related to the knowledge of the Goddess and with a lineage that led back to the Tuatha Dé Danaan, they created spiritual oases in a desert of contemporary, authoritarian religious dogma.

The Dingle Diamond is not unique in facilitating this form of religion — stone circles and alignments dot the globe. If their religious nature is intriguing, the clues they hold to spirituality are more so. Those who built the Diamond did so to engender genuine spiritual experience. They were not concerned with empty ritual, but with creating a spiritual environment that would provide experiential understanding and nourishment, not in the form of mass rallies and ecstatic religious gatherings where control of the spiritual encounter is collective, but a definitive personal contact with another dimension of human consciousness. They clearly demonstrate that the experience is affected by the seasons and by the earth. Only in certain places and at certain times of the year would the spiritual aspect of religion be strengthened, and its total effect as a religion be a powerful enough tool to affect the human will. It seems that the path in our brain that allows us to experience the spiritual realm is, in fact, amplified or reduced according to the time of year and the particular place within the earth's magnetic field.

In the epochs following the age of the Great Goddess, it is almost as if a powerful struggle was taking place in the hearts and minds of people, polarised as light and dark. Both elements — the personal and the communal — are equally capable of conjuring a religion leading to a particular form of society but the outcome of each is very different. One of the paradoxes of this struggle is that the stronger the influence of the institutions of the state, the more intense is the influence of its religions. Today's world of apparent increasing religious hostility, of fundamentalism, superpowers and corporations, makes it difficult to strip away the whorl of technological wizardry and uncover the true relationship between religion and state. Surprisingly, there is no official explanation that adequately describes this link, nor has anyone made a convincing model, so far. The simple question of what makes a human being willing to die for a cause that has nothing to do with family, health or food has, until now, had no realistic answer. When millions marched away from their countryside life to end up on the killing-fields of the Somme, what force possessed them to die horribly for a king and a God? The bravest arguments simply state that the God they died for was merely a spectre, while the true driving forces behind it were the blind mechanics of evolution or economics. It is not a double helix of chemicals that creates, for instance, the invasion of Iraq, nor is it money that motivated the attack on New York on September 11th, 2001. Individual humans carry out these actions and each has the capacity to choose whether or not to act. This deified spectre has the potential to cause the deaths of millions. Allied to a king or queen, the three tiers of religion — tradition, group action and spirituality — operate at every level, in every society. God and king are thus inseparable, for there have been no known kings without their gods, and while the existence of God can be debated, kings certainly exist. Our modern way of life still depends upon their influence.

Far from fading in the glare of the modern age of enlightenment, religion has re-doubled its strength and, with it, the institutional control of the state has become more prominent. Unless this relationship is recognised, we cannot see the mechanism by which these two powerful social forces gain control of our actions.

Possibly by understanding the physical evolution of our culture in the light of the extinction of the neanderthals and our relationship with them, we can begin to accept that spiritual experience is a very real and important part of our welfare. Our judgement of good and evil, right or wrong, or even who is a friend or an enemy, is illuminated and guided by this inner awareness. Conceivably, we can begin to see that a philosophy that does not allow for the reality of the spiritual experience is truly stagnant. It is, in fact, worse than stagnant, for by denying this vital part of our humanity we relinquish our control of it and, without it, we are no longer free to make moral choices. When that happens, we allow other authorities to monopolise this realm and thereby leave ourselves vulnerable to domination and even enslavement. We may also give up our control of the dailiness of spirituality; already, many of us are quite content to allow our expression of love, our sexuality, our beliefs, our clothes, even our social interactions, to be dictated by outside forces, more often than not the dictates of an institutional church, a Temple.

The message of the Dingle Diamond is clear: for twenty thousand years, human culture existed without the need for war, gold or a God. In comparison, the relatively short and blood-soaked years that humans have existed in the shadow of the Temple are not a fair standard by which to judge human potential, nor are they a useful template for so-called 'human nature'.

The final disclosure of the labyrinth contained in the Dingle Diamond highlights the importance of the spiritual in the realm of the physical. Through its story we can see the process of, and the antidote to, surrendering our birthright as humans. It is unlikely that we could have a recognisable society without a religious institution of some form, but those that predominate today are taking us to the brink of self-destruction. It is, as the Gnostics have always said, through experiential knowledge that we can begin to remember that we all have this capacity to take control of our spirituality, and by empowering our spirituality we can draw into balance the polarity of religion and so change our world, politically and socially. Perhaps through the knowledge of our past, we can reconstruct our future as humans.

Notes and References

Chapter One
The Dingle Diamond

[1] William Stuckeley, for example, in the 18th century surveyed and charted the avenues of stones that connected circles at Avebury in England.

[2] Hills often have 'ley' names as do streams and roads. The word has had many different meanings: the Saxons defined a ley as a clearing in a forest, but it can also be recognised in the Irish word lugh, meaning 'the shining one'. Further, a ley can mean a field or meadow.

[3] Alfred Watkins, living in the prosaic era of the 1930s, chose to describe leylines as ancient paths. However, he attributes his discovery of them to a vision he had on a hill near Wales as a network of silver lines traced in the countryside.

[4] True north differs from magnetic north in that it points towards the spinning axis of the earth and can be measured by observing the sun or stars. Magnetic north is found using a compass needle. This was something that we presume was discovered in 1090 AD by the Chinese.

[5] Cruach Mhárthain can be loosely translated as 'the peak of existence'.

[6] Leataoibh is pronounced 'Leative'.

[7] Saint Bridget was a contemporary of Saint Patrick and was involved in recording the pagan Irish mythology.

[8] The *fleur-de-lis* the symbol of Mary, but the lily traces its roots to the royal insignia of the Sumerian Kings. The set square is a tool of trade, used by masons. Both can be found in Rosslyn Chapel near Edinburgh.

[9] This is in the place of the more traditional Saint Jude, who also holds a ship.

[10] *Navigatio Sancti Brendani Abbatis*

[11] St Brendan of Kerry, the Navigator: his life and voyages. Gearóid Ó Donnchadha. Four Courts Print Ltd. 2004.

The Discovery of the Dingle Diamond

¹² The Tuatha Dé Danaan, or 'folk of the goddess Dana', were an early race of settlers in Ireland. They were known as the 'children of light' and one of their chief gods was Lugh, the sun god.

¹³ The site is now registered as such with An Chomhairle Oidhreachta, the Heritage Council of Ireland.

¹⁴ The 'black stone of Mecca' is said to have been a gift from God to Adam. It was a symbol of forgiveness to absolve Adam of the original sin, committed by eating the forbidden apple from the tree of knowledge. For this reason pilgrims travel to Mecca to visit it.

¹⁵ There is an intriguing legend concerning the Sibyl's gift of prophecy and Rome. The priestess of the Cumea Sibillia sold three books of prophecy to Tarquinius Superbus, the Etruscan king of Rome in 510 BC. They were written in Greek hexameters and, as recorded by the Roman historian Livy, were consulted by the Roman government on every important decision concerning the empire. The story of these books and their author is entwined with the earliest histories Ireland.

¹⁶ 'For when the world was deluged with a flood of waters, and one man of good repute alone was left and in a wooden house sailed o'er the waters with the beasts and birds, in order that the world might be refilled, I was his son's bride and was of his race'. The Sibylline Oracles, translated from Greek into English blank verse by Milton S. Terry (1899).

Chapter Two
The Tuatha Dé Danaan

¹ Fir Ó'l nEchmacht, the province of the Fir Bolg, can be translated as the 'fifth province of the men' and is in Connacht in the lands around Sligo.

² This is the usual translation of Knocknarea, a sacred mountain near Sligo.

³ The Fir Bolg, or 'men of the bags', were the mythical people who held Ireland before the arrival of the Tuatha Dé Danaan.

⁴ King Eochaid, son of Eric, was the king of the Fir Bolg at this time.

⁵ The Grey Ridge, Laithdruim, or Drum Cain, or Druim na Descan were all names for Teamhair, the hall of the High King of Ireland.

⁶ Adapted from several ancient legends concerning the arrival of the Tuatha Dé Danaan in Ireland. The earliest is recorded in *Lebor Gabála*

Érenn, The Book of Invasions.

[7] That such works had an ancient lineage can be seen in the ninth century King of Munster's *Glossary* compiled to explain the use of obsolete words recorded in these works.

[8] Tales such as that of Scotia, an Egyptian princess who arrived in Ireland with the sons of Miled, are backed up by archaeological evidence dating from a time before Christianity.

[9] Mahon O'Heffernan, Who will buy a poem?, translated by O.J. Bergin, *The Irish Review*, Vol. III (1913).

[10] Julius Caesar, *The Conquest of Gaul*, translated by S.A. Handford, Penguin Classics (1951).

[11] *Tales of the Elders of Ireland*, translated by A. Dooley and Harry Roe, Oxford World Classics (1999).

[12] Ibid.

[13] Around the time that St. Patrick was taken to Ireland as a slave, Columcille was born in County Donegal. He was a close heir to the throne of Ireland and came from a line of kings who had ruled in Ireland for six centuries.

[14] A detailed record of the lifestyle of these people can be found in the artefacts and remains at Mount Sandel on the lower reaches of the Bann River in the north-east of Ireland. They were a people who either had no knowledge of farming or chose not to use it and, as such, were in step with the many nomadic hunting and fishing populations of Europe at that time.

[15] Banbha is a reference to the tribe of Ban, or Van. The name translates as 'the place of the good Bans'. This is a reference to the matrilineal peoples of Europe who arrived in Ireland. The nature of Cessair and her peoples fits perfectly with the main cultural milieu of Europe at the time and it would be strange if the new arrivals in Ireland did not follow the same conduct as their parents. If this were so, it would place their arrival around 6000 BC as part of the expanding civilisations of matrilineal peoples of the Old European Starceva cultures.

[16] A legend recounts what happened to this closely watched boiling pot. The male hero, a representative of the sun called Gwion, in Welsh, inadvertently receives three drops of the brew. Instantly he undergoes enlightenment and is released from his position. The cauldron becomes poison and Gwion, who is renamed Taliesin of the Shining Brow, is chased by the Goddess. Once he is caught she cannot kill him, for he is

her own son so he is allowed to live. The power of the Lion is thus released to run amok in society bringing about the downfall of the Goddess and the paradigm of the matrilineal world. The three drops that escape the cauldron become the *Awen* or the divine inspiration of the prophet. The *awen* - literally the 'flowing spirit' - is the divine guidance on which the word of the solar God is carried. It is in this flowing of the spirit that can be found Ireland's greatest gift of the Goddess: the healing of the rift between heaven and earth.

[17] The meaning of the word 'Nemed' is 'sacred or privileged person'.

[18] The Scythians were a nomadic people who flourished from the eighth century BC. They held sway over lands that stretched from Europe to China and the height of their empire included Southern Russia and India. They ruled by terror and were famed for their gold, their fierce warriors and their cavalry. Although the Scythian culture is rooted in the Kurgan, it is likely that the later Mongols also had the same roots.

[19] The bogs also show evidence of a series of Icelandic volcanic eruptions on a scale not seen since. This takes the form of tiny glass beads called *tephra*, which are found in the bogs of Ireland and correspond with dramatic displacements in weather patterns. Tree-ring analysis shows that the oaks experienced several years of very low growth during this time; both the tree rings and *tephra* point to 4370 BC as the date of this occurrence. This was the herald of change for the woodlands.

[20] Dated around 4000 BC, the remains of a square wooden house have been found in the north-east of Ireland. This sturdy type of hut is typical of the urn-burying Kurgan peoples as is pottery found near the hearth. The dimensions of the house were about six by seven metres and it was built on an east-west axis. In Kerry, the earliest evidence of farming is in a layer of charcoal dated around 3800 BC, which has wheat, barley and ribwort pollen in it. From this time on there are many examples of burning and planting and the permanent houses of new peoples as they occupied the land. What is clear is that these people had their own culture, distinct from that which pertained before.

[21] A similar sequence of events can be seen in the old henges of Britain such as Stonehenge, which were built around 6000 BC using large tree trunks and only much later converted to stone. Just why this very distinct culture still used old sites for their sacred activities is open to

conjecture. It seems likely that, like the Roman Catholic Church's use of earlier sites for its own religious buildings, it was a mixture of need, continuity and a stamping of legitimacy on the new beliefs. The result was an upgrading of the old religious sites creating not only a place to worship but also a temple that emphasised the use of stone, which allowed the kings and priests to have a base from which to evoke the new ruling spirit in their society: the Entity.

[22] Nemed built two royal forts: Rath Chimbaith in Semne and Rath Chindeich in Ui Niallain.

[23] These three goddesses are the Tuatha Dé Danaan's trinity of war; they are often considered to be aspects of one triple-faced goddess taking on a name of each one in different ages. Morrigu, for instance, is the Arthurian and mediaeval name.

[24] Here is a hint that though the Tuatha Dé Danaan were matriarchal, the Fir Bolg were patriarchal.

[25] This fits with many such legends concerning the war of the Goddess and the God. The Goddess arrives in spring and fights the evil God at midsummer.

[26] Adapted from several legends of the battle of the Fir Bolg and the death of their king.

[27] Keating wrote in the 1600s.

[28] The quicken-tree, or mountain ash as it is sometimes called, is the rowan tree brought to Ireland by the Tuatha Dé Danaan. Its red berries were the food of the gods, capable of restoring life and health and the druids burnt its twigs to summon the spirits before battle. Irish legends say that a rowan-stake, hammered through the heart of a corpse, prevents the soul from leaving the body.

[29] This was the mythical undersea home of the Fomorian pirates of the eighth and ninth centuries who were the Norsemen, or Vikings. In untangling this it seems entirely possible that the Dana and Dane were one theme, the earlier part of the myth having no reference to Denmark. It is far more likely that they travelled to Darcia in the central Balkans and got their name on the banks of the river Danube.

[30] These daughters were the light side of the sisters. The dark side, as we have seen, were the triple-goddesses of war.

[31] Mac Cuill, or Sethor, the hazel god. The hazel was the Tree of Life on which grew the seven hazelnuts of knowledge. 'The whole matter in a nut shell' shows the hazel's link to the earth dream, also seen in its

use as a divining rod. Mac Cuill, or Coll, is the bardic symbol for the number nine, sacred to The Muses. He married Banba, the earth goddess.

Chapter Three
Mother

[1] Some of which, such as *The Cin of Drom Snechta*, referred to in many other manuscripts, is purported to give details about the first peoples to arrive in Ireland.

[2] Mycenae at this time was a flourishing city on the mainland of Greece, one of a number of influential trading ports that were part of a more general civilisation, called by archaeologists 'the Minoan sphere of influence'. A few hours sailing to the south was the centre and power-house of these peoples, the Minoan state of Crete.

[3] Dorothy Garrod in Palestine first challenged this view. Her work was published in the radical period of the 1920s but was later ignored.

[4] Sir Arthur Evans did the same thing for Crete some twenty years later, giving us access to a vital bridge between an old and a new Europe. Robert Graves, with the Celtic alphabet, Marija Gimbutas and Joseph Campbell are other notable examples of those who have married myth and archaeology to produce a living understanding of the past.

[5] A mark of how far archaeomythology has come since then can be seen in a new study proving that even the Homeric descriptions of battles were very accurate.

[6] The Cucuteni peoples of Moldavia, the site at Catal Huyuk in Anatolia and the Starcevo excavations of the central Balkans are just a few examples where similar very long periods of habitation have occurred in Old Europe.

[7] The ceramic shape of a seated being was discovered in the earliest levels of a tell left by the Vinca in the central Balkans over eight thousand years ago. The seat, or stool, is about the only recognisable form in the sculpture. The figurine has large buttocks and feet resting on a cushion. However, her head is simply a cylinder upon which lines have been incised to represent hair. This form of symbolic representation of the Goddess with large buttocks but no body or head is not uncommon.

[8] Persephone, Aphrodite and Gaia are the Greek goddesses of spring

who rise from the earth.

⁹ The triangle and the diamond (two triangles back to back) are motifs that occur in the cultures of many peoples around the globe. For instance, they are commonly found engraved on thin half-moons of gold plate from Ireland dated from the time of the Tuatha Dé Danaan. They identify a people as having their roots in the Danube region of Europe.

¹⁰ The list of occurrences in Old Europe for this most disturbing goddess is extensive: Belgrade 5000 BC, Yugoslavia 4000 BC, central Balkans 6000 BC, Bulgaria 4500 BC, Hungary 5000 BC and Macedonia, circa 4500 BC.

¹¹ Some time after 5000 BC, cemeteries begin to appear outside the enclosures and villages, some quite large.

¹² In a study of blood groups by the archaeologist Zalai-Gaal using molecular techniques in the Lengyel cemetery in Hungary, the adult females and children were shown to have related blood groups, whilst those of the males in the same cemetery were unrelated.

¹³ One, possibly the priestess, is depicted as larger than the others and is decorated with chevrons and tri-lines.

¹⁴ In an open fifth millennium shrine of the Cucuteni, there are twenty-one clay figurines performing a ritual. These figures are some twelve centimetres high. With them are fifteen chairs on which the larger figures can be enthroned. The three largest figures are covered in whorls, triangles and red ochre. This portrayal of the Three Muses, guardians of the temple, recalls the much later Cretan, Greek and Roman temples and their vestal virgins. There are too many ancient ceremonies from across Europe involving women in this way to recount here.

¹⁵ In Catal Huyuk, each house has a rectangular room in which five raised plaster platforms provide the furniture.

¹⁶ Also Ancient Greece, the Chinese and Roman Empires and even the medieval European states and the nation states of today.

¹⁷ In the five thousand years of Old European civilisation a remarkably homogeneous spiritual and sociological norm existed. Yet different societies were culturally distinct. Some were based on agriculture, such as the Lengyel sites of Hungary and eastern Austria spanning two thousand years where, although people lived in small villages, the population density was quite high. Others, such as the Cucuteni, seem to have had a leaning towards hunting and to have occupied larger townships of up to twenty thousand people. In the northern regions, a semi-settled

'slash and burn' lifestyle is evident.

[18] Carved mammoth ivory attests to the antiquity of this symbol found on abstract figurines and ornaments from Mezin in the western Ukraine, dating from over eighteen thousand years ago.

[19] The *kathados* and *anodos* (the going up and the coming down) are rites associated with the Greek mysteries of Eleusis. Two images depicting them in the museum at Herakleion are at least four thousand years old.

[20] The first roundel builders were from the Lengyel culture on the banks of the Danube in the heartland of Old Europe. These temples spread into Bohemia in southern Germany and the Middle East, across the Levant and into Anatolia. They also appeared in northern Europe and Britain.

[21] As late as 2500 BC, the British were covering the countryside with stone circles and standing stones that presented an even more complete set of alignments than the earlier wooden structures. Some twenty-five thousand stone circles remain. This was also the case in some other parts of Europe such as Corsica, the Basque country, Ireland and Brittany. In the Near East and central Europe the emphasis had switched to temples and other large buildings connected with cities and city states. Similar structures also appear in Malta but the building of Cyclopean stone structures was abandoned around 3000 BC.

[22] Solitary and ritual burials, large quantities of vases, axes, flints and figurines feature with the animal remains of sacrifice and feasting. In Slovakia on the Danube is a roundel eighty metres in diameter and seven thousand five hundred years old. A circle of wooden posts and two concentric ditches surround it and a magnificent feasting hall fifteen metres long had been built in one of the quadrants marked out by the four cardinal gates.

Chapter Four
Goddess

[1] We exist on the boundary between the future and the past and although the future is unfathomable, the past can be analysed allowing the mechanism that drives us through history to be revealed. We find that the nature of this mechanism is to maintain the status-quo for long periods before catastrophically breaking the paradigm. It is as if we

stand on the edge of a sea-cliff. The ground around us seems solid enough but the force of the waves gradually eating away at its base is remorseless until one day the whole cliff falls into the sea. History is full of such cataclysmic changes and their pattern governs the events of today, for the past is always with us. Archaeology — the study of the past — becomes not just the science of uncovering this story but the skill of finding these crucial moments which hold the clues to the preceding and following epochs, for it is from such crisis points that we can begin to understand the phenomenon of our development. The arrival of art into the world of humans is one such vital moment.

[2] The commonly accepted nomenclature is that humans are Homo sapiens, or humans. Neanderthals are Homo neanderthal, or Neanderthal. This capitalisation of Neanderthal presents an unequal picture of the two species, as 'human' has no capitalisation. In the interests of species equality, we have used the somewhat unorthodox 'neanderthal' format, without capitals.

[3] The 250,000-year-old hand held stone axes found near the skull of a young woman in Swanscombe, England, are typical of the Mousterian toolkit.

[4] One of the clues that suggests this part of the myth came from a very ancient lineage is hidden in the way that the description was written. As a tale from an older time, it was adopted by a people who lived in the comfort of a sophisticated city. To them, a nomadic hunter-gatherer lifestyle would have seemed primitive, and they said as much.

[5] Adapted from The Marriage of Martu, The Electronic Text Corpus of Sumerian Literature, http://etcsl.orinst.ox.ac.uk

[6] Recent re-constructions of facial muscle and skin, based on neanderthal skulls, have shown us a portrait of beauty — a low head, large eyes and a small chin.

[7] The original Sumerian and its translations can be read at The Electronic Text Corpus of Sumerian Literature, http://etcsl.orinst.ox.ac.uk

[8] The feudal world of mediaeval times, the Egyptian style of semi-enslavement of whole tribes, as well as the city to pastoral relationships of the city-states of the earliest civilisations, are a few examples.

[9] Even if it were a case of having to carry baskets, the human carriers of those baskets would have been under pressure to find more efficient ways of fulfilling their task. A comparative study of neanderthal and human bones by Chris Ruff of John Hopkins University shows that

humans did travel large distances and, with their lighter bodies, were better suited to crossing mountains and rough terrain than the neanderthals.

[10] An example can be seen in the aboriginal societies of Australia. Here, there had been little change in over forty thousand years until they came into contact with outsiders.

[11] The sociological skills that we take for granted today such as leadership, personal sacrifice and reliance on others, combined with a faith that actions are sanctified by a 'greater power', would have required the creation of a structure of myth to contain them.

[12] The skill of following the earth energy to discover these centres of power is known as the practice of geomancy. The best known surviving practitioners of this art are the *feng shui* masters of China. This obscure art appears in the earliest written records as a fully-fledged system combining science, astrology and intuition to discover unseen forces which produce harmony. Explained as 'that which can not be seen and can not be grasped' by experts, it also extends into the *chi*, the life force of the body, giving rise to a holistic form of medicine that includes acupuncture and the esoteric practice of enlightenment. The mystery of the occurrence of such complex systems, and the evidence that points to them once being widespread, suggests that they were once part of our common heritage.

Chapter Five
Lion

[1] In modern times, two of the more far reaching of these writings include *The White Goddess*, a seminal work by Robert Graves in which he followed the meaning of myth backwards from a Celtic poem to arrive at its quintessential form, and *The Myth of the Goddess* by Anne Baring and Jules Cashford, tracing the story of the Goddess and her consort down through the ages.

[2] Herodotus, the fifth century BC Greek historian has this to say about the mysteries: "All the details are known to me but I will say no more. Similarly, I propose to hold my tongue about the mysterious rites of Demeter."

[3] It seems likely that the intricate Chinese medical methods were based on this knowledge.

Notes

[4] James Frazer's epic historical and ethnological thesis *The Golden Bough* has seven hundred pages detailing sacrifice in thousands of different cultures, as well as their folkloric, mythic, legendary, religious and contemporary relationships to this practice.

[5] The Gospel of Thomas, translated by Thomas O. Lambdin

[6] Why this was so is open to speculation. It may have had something to do with the accumulation of materials or the availability of natural resources in this area.

[7] Bus Mordeh existed from 7100 to 6600 BC. Ali Kosh, which archaeologists think existed from 6600 to 6000 BC, was the second largest of the many cities in Khuzistan province: Mohammad Jaffar (6100 to 5800 BC), Sefid (5800 to 5700 BC), Surkh (5700 to 5600 BC), and many others.

[8] Perhaps the most famous of these underworld myths is that of the Greek goddess Persephone, Demeter's daughter.

[9] Slowly, this eastern culture replaced the prominence of the Goddess with the role of the male. J.G. Frazer in *The Golden Bough* describes how, time after time, the ancient kings wriggled out of their role as sacrifice of the year and re-enacted the ritual of the killing of the god with a surrogate, sometimes even giving up the life of a son.

**Chapter Six
Flood**

[1] The Sibylline Oracles, translated from Greek into English blank verse by Milton S. Terry (1899).

[2] The only recent global change in sea levels was as a result of melting ice from the last Ice Age, fifteen thousand years ago. Large areas of what is now continental shelf and lowlands by the shores were submerged. People would have been driven towards high ground, leaving behind the way of life that they had known. It could be that this physical catastrophe gives tangible reality to the tale of the flood but such an explanation ignores the dating of the emergence of the legend and the type of changes it is reported to have brought to society.

[3] The Building of Ningirsu's Temple, translated from the original clay tablet.

[4] Enuma Elish, translated by E. A. Speiser, with additions by A. K. Grayson, *Ancient Near Eastern Texts relating to the Old Testament*,

251

third edition, edited by James Pritchard (Princeton, 1969), pp. 60-72; 501-503, with minor modifications.

[5] The Hymns of Zarathustra, translated by J.Duchesne-Guillemin, the Wisdom of the East Series.

[6] Enuma Elish, translated by E. A. Speiser (1969).

[7] Across Europe, 5,500 to 6,000 years ago, highly evolved arts and cultures disappeared to be replaced by radically more culturally impoverished ones, as evidence of war and killings appear more frequently.

[8] It is not until Hammurabi's reign in 1795 BC in the city of Babylon that we find a translatable copy of a set of laws carved in stone. These laws were given by a new god as Hammurabi, the greatest ruler of the much later empire of Babylon states: "Hammurabi the Prince called 'Bel' am I, who…made great the name of Babylon…who recognises the right, who rules by law." These later codified laws were backed by the power of a strong state and army in order to punish transgressors, but the earlier codes were more like an agreement between populations.

[9] The Kurgans were not a single tribe but were made up of many different peoples, loosely related by family ties. Their early culture shows a remarkable degree of homogeneity. It is only later, after settling in the areas that they had invaded, that we begin to see a diversification in the archaeological record leading to the establishment of local cultures that embraced the character of the peoples that they had replaced.

[10] A more ancient historical account of this process can be seen in 500 BC. The Greek historian Herodotus describes the invasion of Araxes in north-eastern Turkey by the Scythians in the eighth century BC. The Cimmerians, a semi-nomadic warrior people, then populated the land.

"The Cimmerians could not agree upon what line to take when they saw hordes of Scythians flooding into their country, but split into two sharply opposed opinions, that of the princes and that of the people…. It is clear that the Cimmerians entered Asia Minor to escape the Scythians and built settlements on the peninsula where the Greek town of Sinope now stands."

[11] Some places were lucky enough to be isolated by the sea or other geographical features from the onslaught. Crete, with its Mycenaean civilisation, was such a place. Here, people had time to accommodate and realign the holistic belief in the Goddess, and without losing the unity of the trinity, they managed to defend themselves against enemies who tore the mainland apart. It is one of the ironies of history that a

volcanic eruption and earthquake destroyed their civilisation.

[12] 'Havoc!' was a battle cry sounded to mark victory and to signify the onset of pillaging — not at the start of a battle. It was a British battle cry and did not belong on the lips of Julius Caesar. It means 'to destroy or disrupt the orderly run of events'. After a captured castle or town had been ransacked and looted and its people slaughtered, buildings were often razed to the ground. The training of dogs for war was a very effective weapon. On a mythological level, the statement contains a contradiction that displays the mark of the solar God. Dogs guard the entrance to the underworld where the dead slain in war pass over. The dog is also the consort of the Goddess of death and only those who have died can pass this fierce guardian. The dogs of war are the dogs of the goddess Hecate, the plunderers of mens' souls. When the lions of war are no longer kept in thrall by the laws of nations, and the glue that holds society together begins to come apart, the Goddess is loosed and all things become possible.

Chapter Seven
Temple

[1] The Hymns of Zarathustra, J. Duchesne-Guillemin, The Wisdom of the East Series (1952), John Murray Books.

[2] 'Temple', capitalised, refers to a priesthood and the society that stems from it. Whether it be Sumerian priests, ecclesiastical dignitaries or Masonic Lodges, the structure of this society is identical. Both contemporary and ancient sources refer to this plan and the people who attempt to create it as the 'Temple'.

[3] From the Enuma Elish, the Babylonian creation myth, translated by N. K. Sandars.

[4] The methods of the Christian missions of the last three centuries bear testimony to the fundamental importance and longevity of this blueprint.

[5] The Electronic Text Corpus of Sumerian Literature, (2003), The King Lists.

[6] First found in the nineteenth century, it was not until after extensive excavations in the 1920s and 30s that a translation could be made.

[7] The Electronic Text Corpus of Sumerian Literature, www.etcs.orient.ox.ac.uk (2003), The building of Ningirsu's Temple.

[8] Ibid.

[9] Ibid.

[10] Ibid.

[11] Ibid.

[12] Inside the temple is the royal bedchamber surrounded by power objects, hidden from all eyes. This 'holy of holies' is the inner power base, a reflection of the outer temple's imposing size and lavish decoration. The detailed instructions regarding the construction of the Temple of Solomon are an example of the importance placed on the correct way of building such a structure.

[13] This is a fine example of the way geometry was described in these times. 'Seven hundred and twenty sons in pairs' is a reference to two interlocking circles of three hundred and sixty degrees each.

[14] Early examples of the wheel can be seen in the iconology of a number of civilisations and their religions; for example, the Hindu 'wheel of life', the Wiccan 'wheel of the earth' and the 'wheel of the sun' sacred to Mithra. Every Irish king wore a broach in the shape of a wheel, referred to as the 'king's wheel'. This represented the idea that the king must die in order to allow the wheel to turn full circle and was a reminder of the earlier destiny of kings. Even peoples of the New World, who rarely used the wheel in everyday life, represented the cosmic to social interaction in this way.

[15] Hymns of the Atharva-Veda, translated by Maurice Bloomfield, *Sacred Books of the East*, Vol. 42 (1897).

[16] The Book of Exodus, Ch.20.

[17] The Code of Hammurabi (2500 BC), translated by L. W. King.

[18] Exodus Jewish Publication Society's English translation of the Jewish Bible, the Tanach (1917).

[19] The Hymns of Zarathustra, J. Duchesne-Guillemin, The Wisdom of the East Series (1952), John Murray Books.

[20] The Electronic Text Corpus of Sumerian Literature, www.etcs.orient.ox.ac.uk (2003), The building of Ningirsu´s Temple.

Chapter Eight
The Gift

[1] The 'stone of destiny', Fal, also known as the 'stone of knowledge', is the most enigmatic of the surviving relics of the Tuatha Dé Danaan,

for on it kings were crowned. It was a stone of power that cried out when the true king sat on it. The stone was installed at Tara where the Tuatha were to establish their political headquarters. It is said that it was later taken to Scotland around 500 AD by King Fergus to establish his kingship there, and it is further alleged that this was the stone carried away by King Edward I in 1296, who installed it under the coronation throne in Westminster Abbey. Here it remained as the stone on which all monarchs were crowned until it was returned to Scotland in 1996. However, it is unlikely that this is the same Stone of Fal that the Tuatha brought to Ireland, for it is said that it arrived in Ireland with a druid some five hundred and fifty years before Christ, and was the pillow on which Jacob rested his head. Other legends allege that it was the stone rejected by the builders of Solomon's Temple. The stone that the Dé Danaan brought three thousand years earlier is said to have been hidden somewhere in Ireland. Whatever the true story, it is enough to note that throughout history great importance has been placed on its origin.

[2] Mac Cuill, also known as Sethor, the hazel god. The hazel was the Tree of Life on which grew the seven hazelnuts of knowledge. 'The whole matter in a nut shell' is a common phrase articulating the hazel's link to the earth dream, further reinforced by its use as a divining rod. Mac Cuill, or Coll, is the bardic symbol for the number nine, sacred to The Muses. He married Banba, goddess of the earth.

[3] A good account of the scale of such battles can be read in *Cath Maige Tuired*, the Second Battle of Mag Tuired, translated by Elizabeth A. Gray.

[4] Enuma Elish, the epic of creation, translated by L.W. King. *The Seven Tablets of Creation* (1902), published in London.

[5] A collection of Welsh Celtic tales recorded in 1325 AD, in the codex called *The White Book of Rhydderch*, contains many Arthurian legends, as well as myth, folklore and history. Known as the *Mabinogion*, the collection shows a clear evolution from early Celtic lore to later medieval romantic tales.

[6] *Lebor Gabála Érenn*, The Book of Invasions

[7] *Gods and Fighting Men*, arranged and put into English by Lady Gregory with a preface by W. B. Yeats, (1904).

[8] The Holy Bible, Mathew 16:21

Chapter Nine
Seasons

[1] Tír na nÓg, the Celtic 'land of eternal youth', is often spoken of as being beneath the waves, and is said to be found in the waters of Dingle Bay. Other writers record stories of a sea fairy, or 'marrow', who came from a city beneath the waves. John M. Synge, in his book *In Wicklow and West Kerry* (1912), tells of an old man recounting the legend of such a place under the waters of Smerwick Harbour.

[2] Nineteen, the number of years it takes for the new moon to coincide with the sun's winter solstice, is her sacred number; hence, there was a priestess for every year. This tradition is still maintained by *Ord Brighideach* , the Order of Brigidine Nuns,.

[3] Traditionally, the festival of *Imbolc* occurs on February 2nd, the same day as the Christian celebration of Candlemas representing the purification of the Virgin; this is also, significantly, St Bridget's Day, a date that has been adopted by Wiccan covens and modern 'new age-ists' alike. However, these festivals have occurred at other times in different places. The Eastern Orthodox Church, for instance, celebrates the same idea on January 14th while the Romans celebrated it as the festival of *Lupercalia* dedicated to Pan, their god of sexual love and fertility, which probably fell on February 4th. It has also been confused with the Feast of St Valentine.

Chapter Ten
The Secret

[1] St Apollinaire is the Christianised representation of the Greek sun god Apollo, a fact that the builders of Chartres Cathedral were obviously acquainted with.

[2] In the story of the Apocalypse, there are seven candlesticks, seven seals, seven stars, seven trumpets, seven plagues and the lamb with seven eyes. There are seven deadly sins and seven gifts of the spirit, seven heavens and seven levels of hell. Sailors sail the seven seas and there are seven senses: animation, feeling, speech, taste, sight, hearing and smell. There are the seven sisters of the Pleiades, the Seven Wonders of the World and seven notes in the musical scale.

Notes

³ Enuma Elish translation of E. A. Speiser, with the additions by A. K. Grayson, Ancient Near Eastern Texts Relating to the Old Testament, third edition, edited by James Pritchard (Princeton, 1969), pp. 60-72; 501-503, with minor modifications.
⁴ Ibid
⁵ Ninurta and the turtle, ETCSL translation : t.1.6.3, The ETCSL project, Oriental Institute, University of Oxford.
⁶ Enuma Elish translation of E. A. Speiser, with the additions by A. K. Grayson, Ancient Near Eastern Texts Relating to the Old Testament, third edition, edited by James Pritchard (Princeton, 1969), pp. 60-72; 501-503, with minor modifications.
⁷ Ninurta and the turtle, ETCSL translation : t.1.6.3, The ETCSL project, Oriental Institute, University of Oxford.
⁸ Descent of the goddess Ishtar into the lower world, From The Civilization of Babylonia and Assyria, M. Jastrow, 1915.
⁹ Ibid
¹⁰ The return of Ninurta to Nibru, ETCSLtranslation : t.1.6.1, The ETCSL project, Oriental Institute, University of Oxford.
¹¹ The Exploits of Ninurta, The ETCSL project, Oriental Institute, University of Oxford.
¹² Ibid
¹³ Ibid

Chapter Eleven
The Last House in the West

¹ As in the medieval romantic legend of King Arthur.
² There is evidence that the Sumerians visited South America and established there the first temple to a god. In doing this, they were able to circumnavigate the calming influence of the Goddess and deny her a place in the new religion. See Fonta Magna.

Chapter Twelve
After-Word

¹ Hamlets Mill, Giorgio de Santillana and Hertha Von Dechand
² Hohlenstein-Stade figurine of the Lion Warrior and the Galgenburg Goddess figurine.

[3] These definitions equate with the three faces of the Goddess described in chapter 4.

[4] *Inside the Neolithic Mind*, David Lewis-Williams and David Pearce, Thames and Hudson (2005).

[5] In relatively recent times, there have been a number of studies done on ancient sacred sites that show a remarkable similarity to the Dingle Diamond.

Appendix

A brief time-line for the events in this book.

Years ago	Event
40,000	Start of the decline of the neanderthal
33,000	First icons of a religion appear
30,000	Start of the Age of the Great Goddess
26,500	First semi-permanent settlements
26,000	First evidence of fired clay figurines
24,000	Last known neanderthal dies
23,000	Height of cave art
20,000	Climax of the Ice Age
14,000	First settled communities
12,000	End of the Ice Age
11,000	First evidence of agriculture
10,000	First towns and cities established
9,000	The flowering of the Old European civilisation
8,000	First known pottery and woollen textiles
7,500	True writing first appears in Old Europe
6,200	Bronze first appears
6,000	The Kurgan invasions
5,750	Tuatha Dé Danaan arrive in Ireland
5,700	Construction of Irish Megalithic monuments
5,600	End of the Age of the Great Goddess
5,500	First Temples in the walled city states
5,200	Earliest readable documents in Mesopotamia
4000	Minoan civilisation in Crete
4590	Cheops builds the Great Pyramid in Egypt (Minoans)
3728	Babylonian Empire
3628	Egypt unified under Menes
1500	Tuatha Dé Danaan defeated by the Milesians
800	Greek city-states
753	Rome is established
0	Christ is born

Selected Reading

A Different View — C. P. R. May
Banton Press — *2002*
A History of the English Church and its People — Bede trans. L. Sherley-Price
Penguin Clasics — *1983*
A Journey Through Wales — Gerald of Wales trans. Lewis Thorpe
Penguin Classics — *1978*
A Picture for Harold's Room — Crockett Johnson
Scholastic Book Services — *1960*
Alice in Wonderland — Lewis Carroll
Wordsworth Classics — *1992*
An Illustrated History of Ireland — Mary Frances Cusack
Senate — *1995*
Ancient Ireland — Laurence Flanagan
Gill and Macmillan — *2000*
Beowulf and its Analogues — G. N. Garmonsway, et al
J.M.Dent and Sons — *1980*
Catalogue of Illuminated Manuscripts — British Library
http://prodigi.bl.uk/illcat/welcome.htm
Celtic Fairy Tales — Ed. Joseph Jacobs
Senate — *1892*
Celtic Studies — University College Dublin
http://www.ucd.ie/celtic/
Chronicles of the Crusades — Joinville & Villehardouin trans. M. R. B. Shaw
Penguin Classics
Complete Irish Mythology — Lady Gregory
The Slaney Press — *1994*
Corca Dhuibhne Archaeological Survey — Judith Cuppage
Oidhreacht Chorca Dhuibhne — *1986*
Count Belisarius — Robert Graves
Penguin Books — *1989*
Earth Mysteries — Paul Devereux
Piatkus — *1999*
Elizabeth Daynes — Artist and model maker for reconstruction
http://www.daynes.com
Finger Print of the Gods — Graham Hancock
Mandarin — *1995*
Folklore & Ethnology — University College Cork
http://www.ucc.ie/folklore/
Folklore and Customs of Rural England — Margaret Baker
David and Charles Publishers

Goddess
Thames and Hudson
Heavens Mirror
Penguin Group
How the Irish Saved Civilization
Anchor Books
I Ching
Unwin Paperbacks
Iliad
Wordsworth Classics
Inside the Neolithic Mind
Thames and Hudson
Irish Folk and Fairy Tales Omnibus
Warner Books
Irish Folktales
Penguin
Islamic Patterns
Thames and Hudson
John Dee
Banton Press
Le Morte D'Arthur
Wordsworth Classics
Living Water
Gateway Books
Lost Civilisations of the Stone Age
Arrow
Maps of the Ancient Sea Kings
Unlimited Press
Meglithomania
http://www.megalithomania.com/
Nero and the Burning of Rome
Penguin Books
Odyssey
Wordsworth Classics
People of the Black Mountains (2 Vols)
Paladin
Project Gutenburg
http://www.gutenberg.org/
Qabalah, A Primer
Skoob Books
Reading the Irish Landscape
TownHouse Dublin
Resurrection and the Hereafter
Sozler Puplications
Shelley Poetical Works
Oxford University Press
Stonehenge Decoded
Book Club Associates

Adele Getty

Graham Hancock & Santha Faiia
1998
Thomas Cahill
1995
Trans. John Blofeld
1976
Homer trans. T. E. Lawrence
1994
David Lewis-Williams & David Pearce
2005
Michael Scott
1989
Ed. Henry Glassie
1987
Keith Critchlow
1989
Charlotte Fell Smith
1993
Sir Thomas Malory
1996
Olaf Alexandersson
1990
Richard Rudgley
1998
Charles H. Hapgood
1996

Tacitus trans. M. Grant
1995
Homer trans. T.E. Lawrence
1994
Raymond Williams
1989

John Bonner
1995
Frank Mitchell and Michael Ryan
2001
Bediuzzaman Said Nursi
1985
Ed. Thomas Hutchinson
1970
Gerald S. Hawkins
1973

Selected Reading

Tao Te Ching	Lao Tzu
Penguin Classics	*1963*
The Aeneid	Virgil trans. C. Day Lewis
Oxford University Press	*1986*
The Age of Bede	Trans. J. F. Webb & D. H. Farmer
Penguin Classics	*1983*
The Ages of Gaia	James Lovelock
Oxford University Press	*1989*
The Anglo-Saxon Chronicle	Trans. G. N. Garmonsway
Everymans Library	*1953*
The Basque History of the World	Mark Kurlansky
Vintage	*2000*
The Book of Fairy and Folk tales of Ireland	Compiled by W. B. Yeats
Chancellor Press	*2000*
The Book of the Dead	Trans. E. A. Wallis Budge
Routledge & Kegan Paul	*1977*
The Celts	T. G. E. Powell
Thames and Hudson	*1980*
The Conquest of Gaul	Julius Caesar trans. S. A. Handford
Penguin Classics	*1951*
The Death Of King Arthur	Trans. James Cable
Penguin Classics	*1971*
The Description of Wales	Gerald of Wales trans. Lewis Thorpe
Penguin Classics	*1978*
The Dingle Peninsula	Steve MacDonogh
Brandon Press	*2000*
The Divine Comedy (3 Vols)	Dante Alighieri trans. Allen Mandelbaum
A Bantam Classic	*1982*
Electronic Text Corpus of Sumerian Literature	Oriental Institute, University of Oxford
http://etcsl.orinst.ox.ac.uk/index.html	
The Epic of Gilgamesh	Trans. N. K. Sandars
Penguin Classics	*1972*
The First Civilisations	Glyn Daniel
Pelican Books	*1968*
The Fourth Dimension	Rudolf Steiner
Anthroposophic Press	*2001*
The Goddesses and Gods of Old Europe	Marija Gimbutas
University of California Press	
The Golden Bough	J.G.Frazier
Chaucer Press	*1976*
The Great Goddess	Jean Markale
Inner Traditions	*1999*
The Greek Myths (Vols 1 and 2)	Robert Graves
Penguin Books	*1960*
The Hero with a Thousand Faces	Joseph Campbell
Fontana Press	*1993*
The Histories	Herodotus trans. Aubrey De Selincourt
Penguin Classics	

The Discovery of the Dingle Diamond

The History of the Church
Penguin Classics
The Hymns of Zarathustra
John Murray London
The Internet Sacred Text Archive
www.sacred-texts.com
The Irish Fairy Book
Senate
The Jewish War
Penguin Classics
The Key of Solomon the King
Samuel Weiser, inc.
The Key of the Mysteries
Rider
The Key to the Temple
Judy Piatkus
The Key
Turnstone Books
The Kingdom of the Arc
Simon and Schuster UK
The Koran
Oxford University Press
The Living Goddesses
University of California Press
The Mabinogion
Penguin Classics
The Masks of God (3 vols)
Penguin Books
The Measure of Albion
Bluestone Press
The Method of Zen
Routledge & Kegan Paul
The Mysteries of Chartes Cathedral
Thorsons Publishers
The Mystic Spiral
Thames and Hudson
The Myth of the Goddess
Arkana Penguin Books
The Nature of the Gods
Penguin Classics
The Neandertal Enigma
William Morrow
The New View Over Atlantis
Thames and Hudson
The Old Straight Track
Abacus
The Online Resource for Irish history
http://www.ucc.ie/celt/

Eusebius trans. G. A. Williamson
1965
Trans. Jacque Duchesne-Guillemin
1952 (1st)
J. B. Hare

Alfred Perceval Graves
1994
Josephus trans. G. A. Williamson
1980
Trans. S.Lddell MacGregor Mathers

Eliphas Levi trans. A. Crowley
1986
David Furlong
1997
John Philip Cohane
1973
Lorraine Evans
2000
Trans. A. J. Arberry
1985
Marija Gimbutas

Trans. Jeffrey Gantz
1976
Joseph Campbell
1976
Robin Heath & John Michell
2004
Eugen Herrigel
1979
Louis Charpentier trans. Sir R. Fraser
1972 (1st)
Jill Purce
1992
Anne Baring and Jules Cashford
1993
Cicero trans. H. C. P. McGregor
1972
James Shreeve
1996
John Michell
1995
Alfred Watkins
1995
University College Cork

Selected Reading

The Origin Of Humankind	Richard Leakey
Wedienfeld and Nicolson	*1994*
The Pattern of the Past	Guy Underwood
Abacus	*1969*
The Phoenician Origin of the Britons	L.A Waddell
Banton Press	*1990*
The Politics	Aristotle trans. T. A. Sinclair
Penguin Classics	*1992*
The Rig Veda	Trans. Wendy Flaherty
Penguin Classics	*1981*
The Stars and the Stones	Martin Brennan
Thames and Hudson	*1983*
The Stone Circles of the British Isles	Aubrey Burl
Yale University Press	*1979*
The Tain	Trans. Thomas Kinsella
Oxford University Press	*1970*
The Tibetan Book of the Dead	Ed. W. Y. Evans-Wentz
Oxford University Press	*1957*
The Triple Gem	Gerald Roscoe
Silkworm Books	*1994*
The Two Lives of Charlemagne	Einard & Notker the Stammerer trans. L. Thorpe
Penguin Classics	
The Upanishads	Trans. Juan Mascaro
Penguin Classics	*1965*
The Voyage of the Argo	Apollonius of Rhodes trans. E. V. Rieu
Penguin Classics	*1959*
The White Goddess	Robert Graves
Faber and Faber	*1977*